Elements of Literature®

Fourth Course

Resources for Teaching Advanced Students

- Pre-AP*
- Honors
- College Prep

GENERAL EDITOR

Carol Jago
Santa Monica High School
Santa Monica, California

CONSULTANT

Rosa Fonseca
Franklin High School
El Paso, Texas

HOLT, RINEHART AND WINSTON

A Harcourt Education Company

Orlando • **Austin** • New York • San Diego • Toronto • London

ISBN 0-03-043448-3

4 5 6 912 09 08 07

Contents in Brief

Table of Contents

Introduction

I. Tips and Tools

II. Collection Resources

Collection 1

Collection 2

III. Handbooks

Introduction

Foreword

by Carol Jago

Outstanding student work doesn't just happen. It requires support and thrives in particular classroom climates. Though it may appear effortless, first-rate student achievement is, in truth, the product of focused instruction, clear expectations, extensive reading, and challenging curricula that help students develop their learning skills.

> "Outstanding student work doesn't just happen."

A 2005 survey by Achieve, Inc., found that "as many as 40 percent of the nation's high school graduates say they are inadequately prepared to deal with the demands of employment and postsecondary education." The research indicates that preparation gaps cut across a range of core skill and knowledge areas—most notably "work habits, ability to read and understand complicated materials, and writing skills." Nearly 65 percent of college students report that they wish they had applied themselves more in middle and high school. And more than 80 percent of recent high school graduates say they would have worked harder if their school experience had demanded more of them.

I never tell my advanced students that learning will be proof against bad times or troubles. Too often we make false promises to students about the benefits of a good education, lining up any number of goodies that await them at the finish line: entrance to prestigious colleges, high-paying jobs, financial security. In fact, the race only begins at graduation. The truth is that students who have had an excellent education have acquired the most important skill there is: a well-developed ability to learn. Of course, a teacher often needs wizardlike skills to teach students how to learn.

Anyone who works with teenagers knows that convincing students to work hard in middle and high school is a tremendous challenge. Competing demands for student time often interfere with teachers' desire to assign complex works of literature and long papers. Students should be working in what Lev Vygotsky calls the Zone of Proximal Development, in which instruction is conducted on the level at which students can learn with the aid of a teacher or more knowledgeable peers; the texts chosen for classroom study by advanced students should be ones those students are unable to read and understand without help from the teacher. In too many cases middle and high school instruction is not operating in this Zone of Proximal Development (ZPD) but rather in what I call a ZME, or Zone of Minimal Effort. In this instructional zone, the texts are as short as possible, every day's lesson stands alone to eliminate reliance on students' doing homework reading, and basic skills are retaught *ad nauseam*. While I understand the reasons teachers find themselves working in this Zone of Minimal Effort, such conditions dangerously shortchange advanced students.

We can take heart from Achieve's findings to reaffirm our own commitment to offering advanced students a rich curriculum full of classic and contemporary texts that push students outside the Zone of Minimal Effort. Vygotsky writes, "the only good kind of instruction is that which marches ahead of development and leads it" (104). Instead of looking for ways to get through the day without student complaints about the texts being too hard, good teachers scaffold student reading and thereby open up to their advanced students the glorious worlds of Shakespeare and Sophocles, Kafka and Kincaid.

One mistake I used to make was confusing pleasure reading with the study of literature. With so many students reading hardly anything at all, it seemed preferable to have them read something rather than nothing. While there is some reason to this argument, I believe challenging literature possesses qualities that popular fiction does not. Students' reading lives should include two very different kinds of literature. One kind acts as a mirror—reflecting students' own experiences with peers, parents, and popular culture. Young people need stories in which someone who looks and thinks much as they do has handled these problems, for better and for worse. Apart from a lively book talk, advanced students shouldn't need a teacher's help with "mirror" stories. In fact, discussions about foreshadowing, symbolism, and themes sometimes ruin such stories for students.

Students also need literature that acts as a window. These stories offer advanced students access to other worlds, other times, other cultures. Few young people think they have much in common with Odysseus until an artful teacher helps them see how we are all on a journey toward self-discovery. Few relate to Pip until they walk for a while in Dickens's fictional world and begin to understand their own great expectations. Students need both kinds of stories. Of course, students need help to see through the windows of most classical texts. Left on their own, even advanced students can see through it only darkly. These texts seem opaque, full of incomprehensible references and unfamiliar language. It is the teacher's job and the purpose of instruction to clear that window so that students can peer through—to challenge students to emerge from the Zone of Minimal Effort and enter the Zone of Proximal Development.

> "Students also need literature that acts as a window."

Reading is not a vaccine for small-mindedness, but it does make it difficult to think only of oneself. If one purpose of education is to prepare students for the complex responsibilities of citizenship, there is no better preparation for these responsibilities than reading the works of writers like Frederick Douglass, Stephen Crane, John Steinbeck, and Alice Walker. The more my students tell me that they don't need these "depressing stories"—thinking to themselves of their bright futures as lawyers, CEOs, or scientists—the more I tell them to read. Literature creates empathy, and without empathy there can be little hope of a civilized society. Our advanced students may someday be voting in the U.S. Senate. They need to have experienced the harshness of battle alongside Norman Mailer and Tim O'Brien. They may someday sit on a jury in a murder trial. They need to know what it is like to be Bigger Thomas.

In her book *Poetic Justice,* Martha Nussbaum writes about her experience as a visiting professor in law and literature at the University of Chicago Law School. The university had determined that for these future attorneys and future judges to be fully prepared for the work that lay ahead, they needed to educate their imaginations. Nussbaum argues, "If we do not cultivate the imagination in this way, we lose, I believe, an essential bridge to social justice. If we give up on 'fancy,' we give up on ourselves" (xviii).

The classroom texts we choose for advanced students should pose intellectual challenges. That students, even advanced students, should struggle is a good thing. With guided practice through middle and high school, students will build the reading muscles they need to approach difficult texts with confidence. As Walt Whitman wrote, "The process of reading is not a half-sleep; but in the highest sense an exercise, a gymnastic struggle; that the reader is to do something for himself."

This book, *Resources for Teaching Advanced Students,* will support you in your work to provide students with a rich, challenging curriculum. The guidance in the Tips and Tools section, the Lesson Plans and Test Practices for advanced students in Collection Resources, and the additional resources available in the Handbook have all been created to help you support your students' development as readers and thinkers. (For additional help getting started with this book, please see To the Teacher on page xiv.)

Works Cited

Peter D. Hart Research Associates / Public Opinion Strategies. *Rising to the Challenge: Are High School Graduates Prepared for College and Work?* Washington, D.C.: Achieve, Inc., 2005.

Nussbaum, Martha C. *Poetic Justice: The Literary Imagination and Public Life.* Boston: Beacon Press, 1995.

Vygotsky, Lev S. *Thought and Language.* ed. and trans. Eugenia Hanfmann and Gertrude Vakar. Cambridge, MA: MIT Press, 1962.

To the Teacher

This book, **Resources for Teaching Advanced Students,** provides support for teachers of advanced students, including AP, pre-AP, honors, and college-prep students. It contains three major sections: Tips and Tools, Collection Resources, and the Handbook.

Tips and Tools

This section of the book provides a wealth of advice and information about teaching advanced students. It includes three articles by Carol Jago: "Reading Instruction for the Advanced Classroom," "Guidelines for Teaching Novels," and "Moving from Concrete to Abstract Thinking." Other topics covered in Tips and Tools include metacognitive strategies, discussion methods, and annotating passages. *For a complete list of features in Tips and Tools, see the Table of Contents on page 1.*

Collection Resources: Lesson Plans and Test Practices

Lesson Plans provide instructional strategies for teaching key reading selections and Writing Workshops found in the Student Edition of *Elements of Literature.*

Lesson Plans for reading selections cover poetry and prose selections, fiction and nonfiction. The selections chosen for inclusion in *Resources for Teaching Advanced Students* are rich, challenging texts particularly appropriate for close reading, analysis and discussion, and advanced writing assignments.

Each Lesson Plan includes

- Instruction in **literary skills**—one skill that builds on instruction in the Student Edition, and an additional, advanced skill that extends and enriches the curriculum.

- An **Author Focus:** information about the author that goes beyond the information offered in the Student Edition.

- **Close-Reading Activities:** a **Metacognitive Strategy** to help build students' awareness of their own reading processes and a **Close-Reading Practice** on a particular passage from the selection. Both close-reading activities are designed to engage students in high-level textual analysis and to prepare them for demanding writing tasks like those found on AP exams.

- **Vocabulary instruction** on words from the selection. This feature helps to build higher-level lexical skills and to develop students' ability to see the interplay among word choice, tone, characterization, and theme.

- **Postreading,** including **Discussion Methods** for engaging students in oral textual analysis and a **Writing Activity** with a prompt of the kind found on AP tests.

Lesson Plans for reading selections also note **Related Works** in the Student Edition. These related works offer teachers additional opportunities for teaching the literary skills covered in the Lesson Plan.

Lesson Plans for Writing Workshops build on instruction in the Writing Workshops in the Student Edition. They offer more sophisticated strategies for completing the writing assignment in the Student Edition.

Test Practice black-line masters provide practice with the kinds of tasks common on AP exams and other literature, language, and composition tests. There are three kinds of Test Practices, all of which use passages of recognized literary merit:

- **Literature and Composition** test practices provide rich, challenging literary reading passages, including poems, short stories, and excerpts from longer stories, dramas, or other imaginative literature.

- **Language and Composition** test practices include exemplary nonfiction passages from essays, articles, and longer texts.

- **Language and Composition: Synthesis** essay practices provide three or more thematically linked reading passages and at least one related graphic.

Every Test Practice includes

- **Reading Passages:** One or more authentic, high-level texts, chosen to complement and extend the curriculum in the Student Edition. Test passages are by canonical and contemporary authors appropriate for advanced students.

- **Multiple-Choice Questions:** Ten questions testing students' ability to analyze the passages. The questions use standardized formats like those on AP exams and will help prepare students for those and other literature and language arts tests. An **Answer Key** provides correct answers for the multiple-choice questions. The answer key for each Test Practice also provides explanations for two questions that students may find especially difficult.

- A **Writing Prompt** for an on-demand writing assignment like those on AP exams and other tests. The prompts are designed to elicit essays demonstrating analytical skills and advanced writing ability. Questions on Synthesis exams require students to use multiple sources to formulate an expository or persuasive response.

- **Scoring Guidelines** for responses to the Writing Prompt. These use a nine-point scale similar to the AP exam's scoring guidelines.

- A **Sample Response:** Each prompt is accompanied by a model essay that represents a high-scoring response to the Writing Prompt.

Handbook

This handbook, which you may wish to share with students, includes definitions of **literary, rhetorical,** and **grammatical concepts** common on AP exams and in advanced literature study. It also contains **Word Banks** of terms useful in discussing **tone, style, mood,** and **character.**

Sample Letter to Parents

The following is a letter you may wish to send to the parents or guardians of pre-AP students.

Dear Parent or Guardian:

Congratulations on your child's enrollment in pre-AP English. As you are probably already aware, both the demands and the rewards of participating in a pre-AP class are significant. During this school year, expect that this class will require your child to

- complete a large amount of out-of-class reading and writing
- conduct in-depth research
- develop focused, long-term projects

This out-of-class work is crucial in preparing your child for the level of discussion and analysis that will take place in class on a daily basis. As a result of this deep involvement in pre-AP English subject matter and skills, you can expect that your child will develop or enhance important personal qualities, such as

- intellectual curiosity and courage
- perseverance
- self-confidence and reliance on reason
- the ability to analyze and synthesize information (critical thinking)
- the ability to consider all sides of an issue

These qualities will help your child succeed not only in school but in adult life. Of course, pre-AP English will also prepare your child for Advanced Placement classes and exams, which in turn can reduce the number and expense of required college courses.

I look forward to working with your child in class and working with you to help your child maximize his or her potential. Please get in touch with me if you have any questions or concerns about your child's pre-AP work during this school year.

Sincerely,

Tips and Tools

Reading Instruction for the Advanced Classroom

by Carol Jago

A successful curriculum for advanced students combines rich, challenging texts with focused instruction and careful test preparation. Yet even the best books, best teaching, and best exams won't matter if students don't read with care. In order to immerse themselves fully in literature, students must develop a rich vocabulary, practice and master the art of close reading, and understand the significance of reading rate.

Building Vocabulary

Why are many advanced students' vocabularies so limited? Why don't kids know more words? The answer is that bright as these students are, they don't read enough. Children who are avid readers build huge vocabularies from immersion in the world of language. They aren't consciously trying to learn new words—it just happens. Students who read only for school assignments learn far fewer words per day, per week, and per year than their avid reading peers.

It would be so tidy if there were a magic word list we could have students memorize, thereby immunizing them against meeting unfamiliar words forevermore. Alas, learning language doesn't work that way. What teachers *can* do is help students develop habits of mind for approaching unfamiliar vocabulary. As Stahl and Shiel have reminded us, for vocabulary instruction to make a difference, it must be productive. That is, it must involve teaching a target set of words that generates knowledge of a much larger set of words. Stahl and Shiel recommend

- teaching prefixes, suffixes, and roots
- teaching students to derive meaning from context
- teaching words as part of semantic groupings

Your students were doubtless exposed to these vocabulary skills years ago, but the skills need to become second nature. Help your students see that learning new words is a natural act. Once they get into the habit of using affixes, roots, and context clues every time they meet an unfamiliar word, the vocabulary load in challenging texts won't seem nearly as onerous. The chart on the next page lists some basic do's and don'ts of effective vocabulary instruction of which we should all be mindful.

Vocabulary Instruction	
Do	**Don't**
• Do choose literature for your curriculum that is rich in vocabulary.	• Don't have students copy out dictionary definitions.
• Do make word study an integral part of every day's lesson.	• Don't ask students to use these defined words in meaning-laden sentences without classroom discussion of the word's multiple meanings and use.
• Do use personalized examples when defining new words: "I wonder if Wendy's *doleful* expression is a result of not having her homework completed."	
	• Don't administer vocabulary quizzes that punish students who may be learning many new words yet earn a D or F because all the words on the list began as complete unknowns.
• Do keep lists of new words posted around your classroom for constant reference. Try to use these words as you teach.	
• Do create tasks for students that make them pay attention to words they don't know.	• Don't hand out word searches or other word games and puzzles that eat up valuable time that is needed for reading, talking, and writing.
• Do model how you use prefixes, suffixes, and roots to help you figure out a word's meaning.	• Don't give students a full period to illustrate one word; you aren't teaching an art class. Fifty-five minutes to learn one word isn't a good enough return.
• Do model how you use context to help you figure out a word's meaning.	
• Do encourage students to try out the new words they are learning in their writing. Reward their efforts.	
• Do celebrate questions about words. Never be afraid to say, "I don't know. Let's check the dictionary." The best vocabulary teacher is a person who loves learning new words.	

Reclaiming the Benefits of Close Reading

Careless interpretations of Louise Rosenblatt's theory of reader response have led some teachers to abandon the practice of close reading. Unfortunately, even the most heartfelt student responses are often based on an inaccurate reading of the text, leading the student to confusion rather than understanding. Teachers need to take time in class to show students how to examine a text in minute detail: word by word and sentence by sentence. Ann E. Berthoff, in her essay "Reclaiming the Active Mind," claims that the chief means of teaching critical reading and writing is to "offer students assisted invitations to look and look again at words, sentences, paragraphs" (676). Only then will they develop the skills they need to be powerful readers. Berthoff goes on to explain:

The disappearance of close reading is not to be confronted with the calm resignation (or secret jubilation?) evinced by those redrawing the boundaries. Without it, as the chief instrument of Practical Criticism, "reader response" is merely personal, merely psychological, merely opinion. The chief value of Practical Criticism is that it is—practical: it is pragmatic. Close reading teaches that the transactions with the text are always tentative and subject to the pragmatic maxim: "If we take it—metaphor, syntax, word, line—this way, what difference would it make to the way we read the rest of the poem? the opus? the age?" Close reading is entailed in critical reading. It is not an elitist, nose-to-the-text, words-on-the-page pedantry but the way of attending to the interplay of saying and meaning. (677)

The kind of close reading that Berthoff describes does not come naturally to teenagers, even advanced students. Most prefer a broad brushstroke when explaining what they think about what they have read. The challenge for the teacher is to help students refine how they examine a piece of literature without destroying their confidence as readers. It helps to start with students' responses, then ask prodding questions that encourage them to return to the text for answers. You can almost hear the pages turning as students dig to unearth the truths behind questions like these:

> "You say you hate the way Odysseus lies to everyone he meets when he returns to Ithaca. Let's look at that scene with Penelope again. What is Odysseus trying to find out with his lies?"

> "The scene where Odysseus's dog dies of a broken heart upon seeing his master is one of my favorite scenes, too. What does this moment tell you about Odysseus? Read those lines again. What does the state the dog is in hint about the state of Odysseus's kingdom?"

> "It is indeed gross when all the unfaithful serving maids are hanged. Look at the epic simile Homer uses to describes this scene: 'As when either thrushes with their long wings or doves / Rush into a net that has been set in a thicket, / As they come in to roost, and a dreadful bed takes them in; / So they held their heads in a row, and about the necks / Of all there were nooses, that they might die most piteously. / They struggled a little with their feet, but not very long.' Why do you think Homer compares the serving women to birds?"

We need to go beyond encouraging responses from student readers and push them to understand exactly what the author has done with words, sentences, syntax, and diction to elicit such a response in them as readers. Berthoff concludes her essay with these words:

> I have been suggesting that close reading and close observation soften and sharpen hard, dull wits (and bright, confident wits) because they offer occasions to enjoy a pleasure in the exercise of the mind. To practice Practical Criticism by rehabilitating looking and looking again and reading slowly—and again—would thus be to reclaim the Imagination, the agency of the active mind. (680)

Understanding the Significance of Reading Rate

Advanced students are not immune to the common phobia of long books. However, bowing to this fear can result in a curriculum that uses page count as the primary consideration for choosing books. Many students have no idea how long it will take to read twenty or thirty assigned pages, and they make no distinction between reading a simple text and a complex text. Their eyes move across a line of print and down the page at much the same rate and with much the same level of attention, whether the text at hand is *Walden* or *People* magazine.

To help students become more aware of their reading rate, have them make these simple calculations. The informal methods used here are designed to give students ballpark estimates only. Remind students that differences in the number of words on a page will make a big difference in their reading rate.

1. Record your starting page number.
2. Read for twenty minutes as quickly as you can while understanding what you read.
3. Record your ending page number.
4. Determine how many pages you have read.
5. Multiply the number of pages by three to estimate the number of pages you are able to read in an hour.
6. Divide by sixty to estimate the number of pages you read per minute.

From this estimate, students can calculate how long it will take them to complete a homework assignment. For many students this is an epiphany. They never imagined they could actually figure out how much time they need to set aside to read a particular number of pages. Finally, have students calculate how many hours it will take them to read a whole book. Rapid readers typically cover close to a page a minute, and two minutes per page for a difficult book is about average. When students require over four minutes a page, they are probably getting so bogged down negotiating sentences that they are losing the drift of the story.

Having a sense of the rate at which they read gives advanced students greater control over their academic lives. If a student knows it is going to take forty-five minutes to read Chapter 17, he or she can be more strategic about planning after-school hours. If the student has soccer practice until 7 P.M. and fifteen problems due in math, he or she may see that there won't be much time for talking on the phone that night. Even if the student doesn't see that at all, you will at least have given the student a way to determine how much time will be needed to prepare for success in an advanced classroom.

Works Cited

Berthoff, Ann E. "Reclaiming the Active Mind." *College English* 61.6 (July 1999): 671–80.

Stahl, S. A., & T. R. Shiel. "Teaching Meaning Vocabulary: Productive Approaches for Poor Readers." In *Read All About It! Readings to Inform the Profession.* Sacramento, CA: California State Board of Education, 1999: 291–321.

Handling the Paper Load

Frequent writing opportunities are crucial to helping students develop key advanced skills. Do not shy away from assigning writing for fear of creating an unwieldy load of papers to grade each night. Instead, use the following hierarchy to determine how and which writing assignments to evaluate.

Level 1 Assignments (Daily)

Purpose and Types of Writing: Level 1 writing tasks give students practice with a particular concept. These pieces are short, frequent, and not meant for revision. Examples include but are not limited to

- imitation of professional models for grammar or style
- practice providing elaboration for vague sentences or paragraphs
- responses to news photos, editorial cartoons, or other simple images
- practice connecting random concepts (for example, three words or objects pulled from a hat)
- journal entries or quickwrites

Assessment Method: Ask student volunteers to share their responses in class, and invite other students to comment on what the student did well. You might walk around the class skimming student responses and marking a completion grade. Do not collect these papers, but invite students to keep favorites in their writing portfolios as fodder for future creative writing assignments.

Level 2 Assignments (Once per Week)

Purpose and Types of Writing: Level 2 writing tasks provide structured practice for literary analysis—in particular, timed writing practice. These pieces are not meant for revision but will give you a snapshot of your students' analytical skills to guide further instruction. The time you allot for a writing task may vary; you might start with ten or fifteen minutes early in the year and work up to forty minutes—the time allotted for an AP exam response. You may ask students to respond to

- a fine art image
- a poem, essay, very short story, or nonfiction or novel excerpt
- a slide show of photographs on the same topic or theme
- a provocative quotation or question

Assessment Method: When planning the task, create a 4-point rubric for evaluating student responses (4 points = A, 3 = B, 2 = C, 1 = F). In most cases, you will collect the papers, read them once, and highlight the applicable rubric points; you may also highlight particularly insightful parts of responses or deft use of language, but do not edit for correctness or spend more than a minute or so per paper. Papers and marked rubrics should be returned to students the next class day. Alternatively, you might give students the rubric and have them work in groups of three or four to evaluate each other's papers. Each group member should highlight in a different color, and scores should be averaged for a grade.

Level 3 Assignments (Once per Month or Grading Period)

Purpose and Types of Writing: Level 3 writing tasks require students to use the writing process to craft a polished piece. These pieces require multiple revisions and teacher feedback throughout the process. They may also require students to complete research. At various points in the process, you might share professional models of the assigned type of writing with students or have the class discuss and contribute to certain types of revisions on an overhead or in small groups. Level 3 tasks include but are not limited to

- research reports
- reflective or autobiographical essays
- literary criticism
- persuasive or editorial writing
- expository writing, including comparison-contrast, cause and effect, definition, and explanation of a process

Assessment Method: Give students a rubric (or ask them to contribute to one) when making a Level 3 assignment. To keep students on track and to assess their use of the writing process, give a completion grade at each stage of the process. You will discuss drafts with students and may mark line edits and comments on finished papers. To assess improvement in drafts, mark the characteristics of each draft (dated or in a different color for each draft) on a single copy of the rubric. You may wish to have students use this marked rubric and a self-evaluation essay to determine their own grades; then, you can discuss with students any adjustments you feel are necessary to this grade before finalizing it.

Guidelines for Teaching Novels

by Carol Jago

It is not easy to teach the rich, complex novels of Robert Louis Stevenson, Mary Shelley, Ralph Ellison, Fyodor Dostoevsky, Mark Twain, Toni Morrison, F. Scott Fitzgerald, or Gabriel García Márquez. Guiding students, even advanced students, through these books takes dedication and perseverance. For a teacher to persist—sometimes coaxing, sometimes driving—requires an act of will. Of course, kids will complain. The reading is difficult, and there are many pages to go before they sleep. Therefore, simply assigning books is not enough; teachers need to have an instructional plan that makes difficult texts accessible.

Criteria for Choosing Books

There is an art to choosing books for students. First, look for literary merit. Without this, the novel will not stand up to close scrutiny or be worth the investment of classroom time. Many good books that students love to read and should read do not belong on a course syllabus. Texts that work best for class study

- are written in language that is perfectly suited to the author's purpose
- expose readers to complex human dilemmas
- include compelling, disconcerting characters
- explore universal themes across different periods and cultures
- challenge readers to re-examine their assumptions
- tell a good story with places for laughing and places for crying

Great literature deepens our experience, heightens our sensibilities, and matures our judgment. Teenagers want to have these experiences but have not realized that reading books can provide them. Warner Berthoff explains that literature "bears witness to significant human action, and to the possibility of such action, by re-creating concentrated versions of it within some discernible field of occurrence; to bear witness, that is, to what in specific acts of thought and feeling men and women . . . actually do and undergo in life" (7–8). Teachers should select novels that invite students to explore big ideas and develop their critical reading skills.

Support Materials

In order to make literature accessible to students, teachers need to possess a deep knowledge of the text, understanding the historical setting, the author's background, the impact the text had on readers in its own time, the peculiarities of the author's style, and the work's structure. When preparing to teach a novel for the first time, take advantage of online materials, reader's guides, and other study aids. Not all of this information belongs in an introductory lecture, but the more fully the teacher knows the work, the more likely students will be to have their questions answered. At the same time, never be afraid to say to a student, "I don't know. Let me find out and get back to you tomorrow."

Approaching the Novel

Complex novels pose challenges for all readers. Instead of pretending that obstacles don't exist, address potential stumbling blocks directly. Forewarned is forearmed.

- **Structure and length:** Take students on a budget tour of the novel they are about to read. Point out the various sections of the book. Show them where the narrator changes or scenes shift. Use a calendar to plot out the reading assignments with students.

- **Vocabulary:** Encourage students to keep a list of the new words that they learn as they read. Developing a strong vocabulary not only will help students do well on Advanced Placement, ACT, and SAT exams but also will help them write about literature with greater clarity and authority.

- **Syntax:** Particularly in the opening chapters of a novel, the author's sentences may seem hard to understand. They are likely to be longer than the ones students are used to reading in newspapers and magazines. Slow readers may find that by the time they get to the end of a sentence, they have forgotten what happened at the beginning. Help students learn to pick up the pace. If the first pages really aren't making sense to students, read a few paragraphs out loud to them. This will help the class hear the rhythm of the author's sentences.

- **Unfamiliar settings and time periods:** Every novel invites readers to enter a fictional world. Finding our way in that world is always easiest when the fictional world is like the world we know. The more foreign the world is to our own, the harder the book is to "get into." Urge students not to give up. One of the greatest joys of reading is traveling to places they will never see. Help students visualize landscapes that they can't quite picture. Readers may also come across allusions to political figures or historical events that are unfamiliar. Have students put a sticky note next to each allusion and ask about it in class.

- **Unfamiliar character names:** Often students have trouble at the beginning of a novel when several characters' names begin with the same letter or when they are difficult for English speakers to pronounce. Encourage students to pronounce the names out loud. This seems to embed the names in a reader's brain more firmly. In a novel with many characters, students can keep an annotated list of names on a sticky note and keep this inside the front cover. Some novels include a family tree. Create one for the class if you find students are getting confused.

Pacing

While the length of a book should not be an important criterion for selecting a novel, it is interesting to note that many of the novels most commonly taught fall in the two-hundred-page range: *Of Mice and Men, 1984, Animal Farm, The Pearl, The Old Man and the Sea, The Red Badge of Courage.* Instead of eliminating longer works from the curriculum, teachers need to figure out ways to help students persist and prevail. Be forthright with students about the fact that they are going to have to give up some of their TV and telephone time in order to complete their reading. Students have the time for longer books. They just need to be persuaded to reallocate minutes from other pleasures.

At the beginning of a novel, assign only fifteen to twenty pages per night. Students need to read the first chapters slowly, figuring out characters and character relationships, getting familiar with the setting of the fictional world, becoming comfortable with the author's style. As these preliminary textual challenges are met, increase the reading load. For particularly long books, take advantage of long weekends or school holidays to assign fifty to sixty pages so that the novel unit does not drag on for so long that students become bored with the book.

Holding students accountable for their homework reading is a constant challenge. Quizzes always seem like a game of "Gotcha!" inadvertently sending students the implicit message that it's the plot details that matter rather than the big ideas. It is particularly frustrating when a student who has done the reading does poorly simply for having forgotten a detail. An easy way to see if students have done the reading is to take a few lines from the end of the reading assignment and ask students to write for three to five minutes on how this relates to what has gone before. Tell students who have not completed the reading not to make up a fairy story but instead to copy the following sentence onto their papers: "I promise with all my heart to make up the reading tonight and come to class prepared tomorrow."

Assessment

The challenge for teachers is to devise ways of assessing students' reading that actually teach them more about what they have read and stretch their understanding. You might ask students to write about a character in the novel who was most like them and to explain the similarity using examples from their own and the character's lives. In addition to achieving the primary assessment goal of checking for understanding, the prompt offers students an opportunity for further learning by inviting them to see the heroic dimensions of their own lives. This does not happen when students match names with quotations or identify true-or-false statements. What you are likely to discover as you read these essays is the relationship students have developed with the text—for some a passing acquaintance, for others a bond. This is the information teachers need to assess the appropriateness of a particular book as well as the quality of their instruction.

Keeping Track of Student Reading

Having advanced students keep a record of their reading helps teachers monitor students' development as readers. It also provides a resource for students who are preparing for the open-ended question of the Advanced Placement Literature and Composition exam. The student's form can be as simple as a log that includes the book's title, author, and date completed, or it can be more fully developed, such as the form on the next page. Students may find it helpful to complete the form for each unassigned book they read.

Works Cited

Berthoff, Warner. *Literature and the Continuances of Virtue.* Princeton, NJ: Princeton University Press, 1986.

Reading Log

Name:_____ Date:_____

Title:_____

Author:_____ Genre:_____

Characters: List the important characters.

_____

_____

Setting: Give the time and place in which this story unfolds.

_____

Plot: Write a one-sentence plot summary.

_____

_____

_____

Tone: What is the author's attitude toward the subject, characters, and story?

_____

_____

Style: What is unique about this author's way of writing or constructing a story?

_____

_____

_____

Themes: What message(s) about life does the author convey? What are the book's "big ideas"?

_____

_____

_____

Moving from Concrete to Abstract Thinking

by Carol Jago

Most students entering advanced classes in high school are adept at summarizing what they have read. They can answer *who, what, where* questions and even make a stab at *why*. However, they often need help moving from concrete to abstract thinking. In order to develop this skill, students need to acquire the language of literature. In many ways the limits of students' thinking are defined by the limits of their language.

The Language of Literature

Often students consider the formal study of literary devices the epitome of school for school's sake. What they don't see is that understanding how literary devices work gives them power over literature. The more clearly students understand how a writer works his or her magic in a line of poetry or prose, the better able they will be to analyze that line. In *Literature as Exploration,* Louise Rosenblatt asserts, "The problem that the teacher faces first of all, then, is the creation of a situation favorable to a vital experience of literature. Unfortunately, many of the practices and much of the tone of literature teaching have precisely the opposite effect" (61). Remembering how we had been taught literature in high school, with heavy emphasis on form and background over any kind of authentic reader response, many of us embraced Rosenblatt's theories with open arms. We stopped teaching students about literary devices and focused on eliciting authentic readers' responses. We banished any reference to literary terminology from our lessons. In retrospect, I think this was a mistake. I also don't think for a minute that this was what Louise Rosenblatt intended.

The language of literature helps readers express what we see in what we read. Terms like "personification," "allusion," and "metaphor" give us words to describe what we see and feel as we read. Knowing these terms makes students more articulate. None of this is to suggest that we turn our conversations about literature into games of literary trivial pursuit: find the simile, identify the alliteration, spot the allusion. I teach the specialized vocabulary of literature study in order to facilitate richer discussion.

Teaching Students to Think Abstractly

The World Is Too Much with Us
By William Wordsworth

The world is too much with us; late and soon,
Getting and spending, we lay waste our powers:
Little we see in Nature that is ours;
We have given our hearts away, a sordid boon!
This Sea that bares her bosom to the moon;
The winds that will be howling at all hours,
And are up-gathered now like sleeping flowers;
For this, for everything, we are out of tune;
It moves us not.—Great God! I'd rather be
A Pagan suckled in a creed outworn;
So might I, standing on this pleasant lea,
Have glimpses that would make me less forlorn;
Have sight of Proteus rising from the sea;
Or hear old Triton blow his wreathèd horn.

You could take an entire class period offering students background information on this poem. You might talk about the Romantic period and the genesis of *Lyrical Ballads*. You could also tell students about Wordsworth's love of the Lake District and the criticism he received from reviewers who called him an enemy of progress. The problem is that young readers, even advanced students, don't have a place to store this information until they have made some sense of the text for themselves. I almost always start with the poem.

I tell students that in order to make sense of a poem, they have to do more than simply say "I don't get it" and wait for a teacher to explain. "Thinking aloud" is one strategy that helps.

Thinking Aloud

The goal is to make visible the thinking that goes on inside a good reader's head during a first reading. I model the first few lines for students and then have them work with a partner, taking turns reading a selection and thinking aloud about it.

Good readers commonly

- pose questions
- identify unfamiliar vocabulary or allusions
- make connections to their own experience
- rephrase inverted lines
- comment on the poem

My modeled lines are set in italics below. Since you have read the Wordsworth poem many times before, you are of course re-creating an imagined first read. You might want to have students bring in a contemporary poem to stump you (advanced students love this game) and use a think-aloud strategy in front of them cold. You want to demonstrate that on a first read you always have more questions than answers, but that comprehension emerges as you work through your questions thoughtfully, carefully, with the help of a dictionary, and sometimes with the help of other readers.

The World Is Too Much with Us
William Wordsworth

The world is too much with us; late and soon,
I like the sound of this. Reminds me of my cell phone going off when I'm trying to think. I wonder why he says "late and soon" instead of sooner or later. Maybe it's for rhyme.
Getting and spending, we lay waste our powers:
Can't spend money unless you get it. I guess laying waste our powers means something like using up all your energy.

After pairs wrestle with the poem for 10 minutes or so, I bring the class together and ask if there are unresolved questions. It is always more effective to respond to student questions—after checking that no one else in the classroom has answers—than to simply tell them this information unbidden. This think-aloud strategy has other benefits as well.

- It gets everyone in the class talking. Discourse can easily become dominated by a few students. This activity requires everyone to speak.

- Students discover that they are not the only ones with questions or who find a line difficult to unpack.

- Students often express insights that surprise their partners, opening up the poem to richer interpretations.

- The intimacy of pairs invites personal reflection of a sort that might feel inappropriate or uncomfortable within the larger forum.

I always invite students to consider why Wordsworth would choose the traditional structure of a sonnet for a poem advocating a return to more primitive times. Here are some more questions that trigger stimulating discussion:

- Do you find that electronic devices like cell phones cause the world to be too much with you?

- Is a return to more primitive ways a practical solution?

- Do you think it is possible to remain in tune with nature and yet "get and spend"?

Poetry is a vehicle for abstract thinking. It will serve your students well not only on AP, ACT, and SAT exams but throughout their lives.

Works Cited

Rosenblatt, Louise M. *Literature As Exploration.* New York: The Modern Language Association, 1983.

Metacognitive Strategies

For many advanced students, reading has long been an effortless activity. These students generally focus on *what* they are reading without much thought as to *how* they are reading. In fact, many of these students will not have received explicit reading instruction since elementary school. Some of the texts on your class's syllabus may present a real challenge to these advanced students, who are not accustomed to dealing with obstacles to comprehension. For these students (or for anyone who struggles with a text), metacognitive strategies can help. Metacognitive strategies enable students to expose and refine the often unconscious processes of reading. The metacognitive strategies below form the essential components of any reader's toolbox.

Annotating Texts

Making notes while reading helps students' comprehension. When it comes to gaining a basic understanding of the text, it doesn't particularly matter whether students' annotations consist of questions, predictions, or critiques. The simple act of annotating, of engaging in a conversation with the text, is what is important.

When students have a particular purpose in reading a passage, however, their annotations should reflect that purpose. For close readings of the type assigned in this book's Lesson Plans, for example, students' annotations should focus on the literary element identified in the close-reading activity.

If students have the ability to annotate directly on the page, they may use any number of annotation techniques, including

- circling or boxing unfamiliar words
- underlining key words, phrases, or sentences
- bracketing key passages
- jotting notes in the margin
- using an asterisk to identify a particular recurring element

If the student does not own the text, he or she may be able to use a pencil to make light annotations, which can be erased later, or use sticky notes.

For specific examples of annotations, see **Annotating a Passage,** *page 30.*

Thinking Notes

Thinking notes are a specific set of annotations that students can use to record very basic responses. Thinking notes may be particularly appropriate when (1) students have just been introduced to the idea of making annotations and they need a simple predetermined list to practice with, or (2) the whole class is reading the same text and you want them to share the same language of annotation. Below are examples of thinking notes; you or your students can add to or modify this list as needed.

☺ I agree with this. / I like this passage.

X   I disagree with this.

?   This is confusing.

!   This is surprising.

*   This is important.

✔   This is an example of [specific literary element].

☹   This is disturbing.

Think-Aloud

As originally conceived, the think-aloud is a strategy in which the teacher reads a passage aloud, pausing intermittently to model the thinking processes involved in comprehension. During a think-aloud, you might

- ask questions about what is happening in the text or about the author's choices
- make predictions and speculations
- make connections to your life or your prior knowledge
- review or summarize meaning
- interpret meaning
- reflect on the meaning
- evaluate characters, message, or language
- figure out the meaning of unfamiliar words
- monitor your comprehension and correct your mistakes

Teachers can ask students to conduct think-alouds to assess their reading processes. Students can also be instructed to conduct think-alouds with partners when working through difficult passages. A pre-AP or AP teacher may want to adapt think-alouds to focus on analysis of particular literary concepts in a given selection.

Reading Aloud

Reading aloud requires a heightened level of reading awareness. Rather than passively observe the text, the student must inhabit it, as an actor inhabits a character. Students have to make conscious decisions about, among other things,

- the tone of the narrator or speaker
- the tone of other characters whose words appear in quotations
- the rhythm of the individual lines, phrases, and sentences

- the emphasis to place on individual words
- the volume and pacing of lines and passages

All of these decisions require understanding on the literal level, including the meaning and pronunciation of individual words. But in addition, the reader needs to analyze

- the individual literary elements that compose the narrator's or speaker's tone
- the elements of characterization that provide clues about a character's tone
- a clear understanding of the piece's overall structure to provide guidance on pacing

Give students opportunities to read aloud in a variety of genres: prose, poetry, drama, fiction, and nonfiction.

Tips and Tools

Ladders of Questions

This strategy is initially teacher-directed, although eventually students learn to use the strategy on their own. The strategy—which can be applied to any complex reading selection, literary or informational—involves generating and classifying three levels of questions:

- **literal:** answer resides in the immediate text
- **interpretive:** answer must be inferred by considering information from throughout the text
- **experiential:** answer generated from students' applying own experience, prior knowledge, or other texts to text at hand

Below, the strategy is applied to the poem "'Arcturus' is his other name." You might use this excerpt and accompanying questions for a whole-class activity or select your own reading passage and generate questions for that passage. Before students discuss the questions, have them work as a class or in groups to paraphrase the selection. This first paraphrase will likely be a literal prose translation of the poem.

Arcturus is his other name,— I'd rather call him star! It's so unkind of science To go and interfere! I pull a flower from the woods,— A monster with a glass Computes the stamens in a breath, And has her in a class.	Literal Questions: 1. What is the meaning of *stamens* in the second stanza? 2. Describe what becomes of the butterfly in the third stanza. 3. What does the speaker say about heaven in the fourth stanza? Interpretive Questions: 1. What is the effect on the speaker of science's interference?

Whereas I took the butterfly

Aforetime in my hat,

He sits erect in cabinets,

The clover-bells forgot.

What once was heaven, is zenith now.

Where I proposed to go

When time's brief masquerade was
 done,

Is mapped, and charted too!

—Emily Dickinson

2. How does the speaker feel about the flower's and the butterfly's fate?

3. Why does the speaker use the past tense in the second line of the fourth stanza?

Experiential Questions:

1. Is the speaker like anyone you know? Explain.

2. What impact has the acquisition of scientific knowledge had on your imagination?

3. What information can you find about Emily Dickinson? What light does that information shed on your interpretation of this poem?

After answering the last set of questions, have students work in groups to paraphrase the poem again. By the time students have discussed the experiential questions, the second paraphrase will likely be richer, more insightful, and filled with connections. Be sure to have students compare the two paraphrases and reflect on the differences.

After leading students through the strategy, have students work individually or in small groups to create and respond to ladders of questions on a new selection.

Reading Journals

Reading journals provide students with an excellent way to maintain a dialogue with longer texts and to build their close-reading skills. The method is simple.

- Students draw a line down the middle of a page in their reader's log.
- In the left-hand column, students copy a brief passage that is significant to them.
- In the right-hand column, students write their response to the passage.

Students' responses may begin with an explanation of why they chose the passage. Was it puzzling? Did it resonate? What does it mean to the student? In answering these questions, students should be encouraged to analyze the specific language in the text that drew them to it. In briefly reviewing students' journals, you can assess students' understanding of and engagement with texts. You can also respond to journal entries, and you can give students the option of marking some entries as private.

Discussion Methods

You can use the discussion methods explained in this section to further students' analytical skills and foster a cooperative atmosphere in your classroom. You may find that you can closely guide each type of discussion the first few times and then gradually allow your students more control over the discussion logistics and topics.

Fishbowl Discussion

This method is also known as the "inner-outer circle method." It allows all students, even usually reticent ones, to contribute ideas about literature and have those ideas carefully considered by others.

Steps

1. First, plan a discussion question or prompt, which may be suggested either by the teacher or by a student. You may wish to have all students respond to a single prompt, or you might prepare a second prompt for use in step 3.

2. Seat students in two concentric circles facing each other (an inner circle and an outer circle). Read aloud the question or prompt. Students in the inner circle should consider the prompt and explain their responses to it to their partners—the students sitting directly across in the outer circle. Students in the outer circle should listen to and make notes on their partners' responses.

3. Students should change seats with their partners so that those formerly seated in the outer circle are now in the inner circle. Students now seated in the inner circle may do one of three things:
   - respond to the comments made by the partner in step 2
   - provide their own response to the same question asked in step 2
   - respond to a new question provided by the teacher or another student

Follow-up: The follow-up to a fishbowl discussion may take a variety of forms. The teacher may provide a brief assessment of students' overall understanding based on their comments, students may share striking insights they heard, or the teacher may request that students expand on their ideas in writing. In some cases, the teacher may feel that no follow-up is needed.

Timed Discussion

In a timed discussion, students are required to speak on topic for a certain amount of time. This method can help students learn to think on their feet, refer to the text for support, and avoid rambling. It can also help reserved students freely share their ideas and have those ideas considered by classmates.

Steps

1. The teacher may choose to organize the class into groups of about five students each or use this method for a targeted whole-class discussion. If the latter approach is chosen, the teacher may wish to identify ahead of time students whose participation would most benefit both themselves and their classmates.

2. Depending on the class, the teacher may begin the discussion with a broad question about a text or allow the first student to begin by talking about a point of interest or confusion in the text. The teacher or a student in each group should monitor the time and say "stop" when the speaker reaches the time limit. The student speaking may then take a little more time to finish a thought in progress. Early in the school year, try a minimum speaking time of about thirty seconds per student; as students' skills improve, increase the time, working up to two minutes or more.

3. After the first student has finished speaking, choose the next speaker (or let students volunteer). This student and each subsequent speaker should respond and add to the comments of the previous speaker and have the same time limit.

Follow-up: To follow up on a timed discussion, the teacher may choose one of the following options.

- Allow the first student who spoke to respond to the comments of the other speakers.

- Ask students to write notes summarizing the path the discussion took and insightful ideas they heard. If students worked in small groups, have them name in their notes students who made especially strong contributions to the discussion.

- Provide an overview of the ideas and threads students discussed, and add comments if necessary. If students worked in small groups, this overview—based on what the teacher heard—will help the entire class share in the insights of a particular group.

Reading Conference

The teacher can focus a reading conference on a particular close-reading skill. Before meeting in small groups, students should prepare by making notes about a chosen section of the work to be discussed. This method requires direct teacher involvement in the small groups and thus may be best used while other students are performing other tasks or participating in other activities.

Steps

1. The teacher first asks a broad question about the themes, significance, or effect of the passage or work. Students should discuss the question briefly, using evidence from the text or their notes.

2. Next, the teacher will ask individual students specific questions about the passage, based on points they made in their step 1 responses. These questions may concern techniques the writer uses, the tone of the passage, or other close-reading skills the teacher wishes to highlight.

3. Finally, students should generate and briefly discuss their own questions about the passage or work, with the teacher guiding the direction and depth of questions.

Follow-up: Because of the strong involvement of the teacher in this type of discussion, follow-up may be unnecessary.

Bulletin-Board or Threaded Discussion

These written forms of discussion provide a forum for students who lack confidence in their impromptu speaking skills to share ideas they have had time to formulate.

Steps
1. The teacher will first choose the basis for initial student writing—a quotation from the text, a teacher-provided question, or students' own individual questions about the text. Students should write from a paragraph to a page in response, supporting their ideas with evidence from the text. These initial responses may be posted on a class bulletin board or in an electronic forum.

2. Next, students will choose a particular posting to respond to in writing. To keep the discussion focused, the teacher should determine how many rounds of responses will take place.

Follow-up: The teacher may note which discussion threads inspired the most responses or highlight strong insights in posted responses.

Literature Circle

Participating in a literature circle requires students to take an active approach toward both reading and discussion. A student may take on a different role at each meeting to help the group function smoothly.

Steps
1. The teacher may provide students a choice of high-quality works, on related themes if possible. Groups form around titles chosen; if one title attracts a large number of students, the teacher may create two or more groups to facilitate discussion on that title.

2. For a group's first meeting, students should choose or be assigned roles:
   • The **leader** keeps the discussion on track and chooses questions when necessary.

- The **encourager** monitors participation of group members, directing questions to reticent group members as needed and reminding eager talkers to avoid dominating the conversation.
- The **note taker** jots down responses to questions and may add illustrations where appropriate. If the teacher wishes to monitor group dynamics, the note taker should also mark each comment with the initials of the member who shared it.
- All other members are **participants.** Participants should respond to questions, seek textual support for ideas, make connections between the text and their lives or other works they have read or seen, and suggest new questions or avenues of discussion.

These roles will rotate among group members for subsequent meetings.

3. Groups meet on an established schedule. The teacher may assign a particular section of the chosen work to be read before the next meeting and may also assign a few crucial questions for the group to discuss before moving on to questions generated by the members.

Follow-up: Once students in a literature circle have finished reading and discussing the work they have chosen, the teacher may follow up by asking students to

- provide a written assessment of the group's work and the understanding of the text they gained as a result of participating in the group
- create a project that exemplifies a key text idea or theme that arose in discussion
- present a panel discussion analyzing the text's themes, motifs, or ideas

Analyzing Tone

In a piece of writing, *tone* is the writer's attitude toward the subject. To determine the attitude of someone speaking, you listen to his or her words and tone of voice. Depending on the speaker's tone of voice, a single word or phrase can be a compliment or an insult, a statement of fact or a sarcastic comment. An affectionate tone of voice can turn insulting words into an endearment. In English, a rising intonation at the end of a sentence can turn that sentence into a question.

Just as tone of voice provides clues to the meaning of spoken words, the tone of a piece of writing provides clues to the meaning of the selection, whether it is a poem, a play, a story, a novel, or a nonfiction selection.

Tone is closely tied to the theme of a selection. A reader cannot accurately determine the theme and meaning of a selection without analyzing its tone.

How do you define tone? You can start by describing the emotions or feelings that the writer seems to be expressing. The following list of words provides a starting point for diagnosing the tone of a selection. Which words most closely match the attitude of the writer of the selection you are analyzing? If you are unsure of the meaning of a particular word, consult a dictionary.

angry	listless	bored
confused	elated	hypercritical
lofty	mealy	puny

You can add to this list by reading the stage directions for several plays. The way the dialogue of a play is spoken can significantly change the meaning of the play, so many playwrights give detailed stage directions specifying not only the physical actions of the actor speaking the lines but also the way in which the lines are to be spoken. Some playwrights leave it to the director or the actors to interpret the lines, so be sure to select plays that include detailed stage directions.

Shift in Tone

Tone does not always stay the same, even in a short selection. Just as a voice or a piece of music may use many tones, a piece of writing may include more than one tone. This is especially true for longer selections such as plays and novels. The writer may shift the tone to develop the theme, to carry the reader along as a main character learns lessons about life, or for many other reasons.

Some works of literature even present different accounts of the same events, to show how different characters view the same facts. What is emphasized, included, or omitted can reveal a shift in tone. To determine the tone of the entire selection, you need to consider the tone of each part of the selection and what each shift in tone reveals about the writer's theme.

As you become more comfortable with analyzing tone, watch for changes in tone. You can better understand the theme and meaning of the selection if you understand why the writer has shifted the tone.

You can determine the tone of a piece of writing by examining its diction, imagery, point of view, and syntax, as well as the details that are included or omitted.

Diction

The *diction* of a selection is the writer's choice of words. Words with the same *denotation,* or dictionary definition, can have very different *connotations,* suggested or associated meanings. Some words have a positive connotation, some have a negative connotation, and still others have a neutral connotation.

EXAMPLE

Connotations	
positive	slender, weighty, fleet
neutral	thin, strong, swift
negative	skinny, heavy, hasty

Word connotations change over time, so the historical context of the selection should be noted along with the context in which the words are used.

Diction also includes the writer's overall use of language. A scientific research article is likely to include many technical terms with which the general reader is unfamiliar. A newspaper article about the research will use a more general vocabulary or will define uncommon words. The dialogue in a short story about high school students will include teenage slang. Selections set in a particular region, country, or historical period will try to duplicate the speech of people in that region, country, or period.

In the following poem, note how the words describing the giant statue reveal the poet's attitude toward the king, whose statue lies broken on the ground.

> I met a traveler from an antique land
> Who said: Two vast and trunkless legs of stone
> Stand in the desert . . . Near them, on the sand,
> Half sunk, a shattered visage lies, whose frown,
> And wrinkled lip, and sneer of cold command,
> Tell that its sculptor well those passions read
> Which yet survive, stamped on these lifeless things,
> The hand that mocked them, and the heart that fed;
> And on the pedestal these words appear:
> "My name is Ozymandias, king of kings,
> Look on my works, ye Mighty, and despair!"
> Nothing beside remains. Round the decay
> Of that colossal wreck, boundless and bare
> The lone and level sands stretch far away.
> "Ozymandias" by Percy Bysshe Shelley

Highlight words describing the statue. The poet uses words such as "shattered," "lifeless," "decay," and "colossal wreck" to describe the legacy of Ozymandias. Shelley contrasts the damaged statue with the arrogance of Ozymandias. Words such as "frown," "wrinkled lip," "sneer of cold command," and the king's arrogant statement of his power reveal the poet's ironic view of the king's long-lost power.

Imagery

Imagery includes figurative language. Imagery can help make a piece more vivid, providing the reader with mental images and sensations. The writer's choice of images and figurative language also reveals his or her attitude toward the subject. Figurative language can help the reader hear, feel, and see what is being described.

What does this passage reveal about the author's view of writing a narrative?

> I had imagined that this Al-Asbah had made it possible for me to conclude his story the way it had ended in the previous chapter, and with this his role in the tapestry of the story had ended too. But here I am traveling along the road to Silwad holding on to the end of the thread he had spun and interwoven with the warp and woof of my life. Like a weaver I yank at that thread and find myself wondering about the opportunity that has presented itself to me as a result of the new turn of events, and before I have sufficiently considered my next steps, I comb out the unraveled thread and card it again, then turn to impart to it a completely different color and to weave it once more into the frayed tapestry, mending what had unraveled. What guarantee do I have that this act is not a proclamation of liberty on the part of that thread, once it had been unbound? All at once a story that had apparently come to its end is exposed to a capricious thread, which will draw it into unexpected regions in an adventure whose outcome we cannot foresee.

Notice how Shammas compares narrative writing to the weaving of a rug, a metaphor that is extended throughout the novel.

Imagery can also provide extra layers of meaning by alluding to, or referring to, other events or literary works. Many literary works include Biblical allusions that lead readers to make comparisons between the Biblical narratives or characters and those in the selection. Other works allude to political or historical figures or events, much as students allude to musicians, actors, and TV series in popular culture.

Point of View

Point of view also helps determine the tone and reveal the writer's attitude toward the theme or subject.

In informational selections, the point of view is often that of the writer. For example, an editorial expresses the views of the writer or the editorial board of a

From *Arabesques* by Anton Shammas, translated by Vivian Eden. Copyright © 1986 by Michaelmark Books Ltd. Am Oved Publishers Ltd.; English translation copyright © 1988 by Harper & Row, Publishers. Reproduced by permission of **HarperCollins Publishers, Inc.**

newspaper or magazine. The point of view of a strictly factual article, such as an article in an encyclopedia, is straightforward.

However, the point of view in a poem, story, novel, or other fictional selection is not always so straightforward. The following questions can help you determine the point of view of a selection or of a particular section of the selection.

■ Who is relating the events? Is he or she a character in the selection (first-person narrator) or someone who stands outside the action, relating events from an emotional distance (third-person narrator)?

■ What does he or she know? Does the narrator know everything that happens, including the thoughts and feelings of the characters (omniscient narrator)? Is the narrator's knowledge of events limited? How much information is provided to the reader? Does the reader learn information as the narrator learns it, or is some information withheld until later in the narrative?

■ Is the narrator reliable? Is he or she fully aware of what he or she is relating, or does the narrator describe events without understanding the implications? Does the narrator become more aware as the narrative progresses?

■ Why do you think the writer chose this narrator? What effect does this narrator have on how the reader responds to the selection?

Remember that a narrator using "I" and "me" pronouns to relate the events is a first-person narrator and one using "they," "he," and "she" is a third-person narrator.

Syntax

Syntax is the grammatical structure, including sentence structure, of a selection. How sentences are structured can affect the reader's response to the selection. This is particularly true for poetry. Whether sentences are short or long, simple or complex affects the rhythm of the selection. In conjunction with diction, syntax may be used to mimic the events or objects being described.

Note how the structure of the following sentence mimics the process that the author is describing.

> His stories were plaited into one another, embracing and parting, twisting and twining in the infinite arabesque of memory.

Shammas is comparing the construction of a narrative, whether spoken or written, to the work of someone weaving an elaborate carpet or rug, an important feature of traditional Arabic culture.

Details

Details included by the writer also contribute to the tone. For a reader familiar with the events described by the writer, details that are omitted also reveal the writer's theme. Details included are ones the writer considers important, for one reason or another. If details are omitted, either the writer considers them unimportant or he or she does not want the reader to notice those details.

In literary works that include accounts by more than one character, the omission of details from one account reveals something about that character.

When all these aspects of tone—diction, imagery, point of view, syntax, and details—are analyzed, the reader has a better understanding of the writer's theme and the meaning of the selection.

Sample Analysis of Tone

Now that you have had a chance to consider the various aspects of tone, practice analyzing tone by identifying and describing the diction, imagery, point of view, syntax, and details in the following passage. You might want to use a different color highlighter to mark the various aspects.

> LONDON. Michaelmas Term lately over, and the Lord Chancellor sitting in Lincoln's Inn Hall. Implacable November weather. As much mud in the streets as if the waters had but newly retired from the face of the earth, and it would not be wonderful to meet a Megalosaurus, forty feet long or so, waddling like an elephantine lizard up Holborn Hill. Smoke lowering down from chimney-pots, making a soft black drizzle, with flakes of soot in it as big as full-grown snow-flakes—gone into mourning, one might imagine, for the death of the sun. Dogs, undistinguishable in mire. Horses, scarcely better; splashed to their very blinkers. Foot passengers, jostling one another's umbrellas in a general infection of ill-temper, and losing their foot-hold at street-corners, where tens of thousands of other foot passengers have been slipping and sliding since the day broke (if the day ever broke), adding new deposits to the crust upon crust of mud, sticking at those points tenaciously to the pavement, and accumulating at compound interest.
>
> from *Bleak House* by Charles Dickens

Note that the **diction** emphasizes how cold and bleak the weather is, describing the effect of the mud on animals and humans alike. The smoke of human fires makes the weather even worse, creating large flakes of soot that join the mud in making outdoors unpleasant for dogs, horses, and humans.

The **imagery** connects the muddy streets to scenes you might imagine from prehistoric times when dinosaurs ruled the earth. Large flakes of soot are compared to snowflakes, creating an ironic tone. The bad weather has created an "infection of ill-temper" among people who have to walk in the muddy streets. The mud is "accumulating at compound interest," emphasizing the speed at which it is increasing.

The **point of view** is that of a third-person narrator, because the narrator is describing the scene as a spectator observing all that happens. This excerpt is not long enough to allow a reader to determine whether the narrator is omniscient, because the thoughts of the people being observed are not described, but there is enough information for a reader to predict that this narrator will prove to be omniscient.

The **syntax** of this passage is particularly interesting since the reader knows this is an excerpt from a novel by Charles Dickens, one of the greatest Victorian writers. Most of the "sentences" are not actually sentences. They seem to be jottings in someone's journal. Niceties of complete sentence structure are sacrificed to emphasize the description, providing a passage dense with detail. It is almost as though the reader were lured into the book and mired in the mud along with the inhabitants of the novel.

The **details** described emphasize the bleakness of the scene, letting the reader know that the theme hinted at in the title, *Bleak House,* will be extended through the novel. The unpleasant weather contributes to the bleak mood and helps set the physical scene, a street in London. Dickens uses references to the courts (Lincoln's Inn Hall) and financial terms (deposits, compound interest) to foreshadow the murkiness of the legal and financial issues that will dominate the novel.

The aspects of tone in this excerpt, the first paragraph in the novel, indicate that Dickens will treat legal and financial institutions ironically and perhaps caustically. His use of diction, imagery, point of view, syntax, and details reveals his attitude toward bureaucracies that can ensnare and damage the lives of individuals. For Dickens, the Megalosaurus is a metaphor for the entire structure of legal and financial bureaucracies during Victorian times.

Annotating a Passage

Annotating texts helps readers engage the text and plumb its depths. Sometimes it's difficult to judge what is important enough to take note of. The following guidelines can help.

The Three Levels of Reading

A close reading of a text is a careful, thoughtful, engaged reading. Close reading means looking for meaning on multiple levels. The search for meaning can take place in one slow read, but in most cases, the reader needs to return to the text, or to passages of text, to develop all the layers of meaning.

The goal of annotating texts, then, is to develop that deepest layer of meaning. Annotations can help readers make links from level 1 to level 2, and from level 2 to level 3.

Level 1: On the Lines

The first layer of meaning lies on the literal level. It's the *who, what, when, where* and *why* of the text. During the first reading of the selection, the careful reader also notes

- **vivid images:** language that appeals strongly to one or more of the senses
- **striking comparisons:** figurative language, including metaphors, similes, and personification
- **striking diction:** words that stand out because of their strangeness, beauty, or harshness

Level 2: Between the Lines

The next layer of meaning is formed at the inferential or interpretive level—what is understood from reading between the lines. This level requires the reader to draw conclusions about the more abstract meanings of words, implied or explicit comparisons or contrasts, symbols, and so on by gathering clues and applying background knowledge. Read at a deeper level, usually in a subsequent reading, Level 1 elements no longer appear isolated. Instead, the reader begins to notice

- **repetition:** repeated words, phrases, or ideas
- **contrasts:** sharp changes in descriptions or in mood or syntax, for example

Level 3: Beyond the Lines

The deepest layer of meaning is formed at a very abstract level. At this level of reading, the reader is asking not just "What?" but "So what?" Questions about the author's purpose and theme percolate up at this level. The reader makes connections to the text, evaluates the author's message, and even examines his or her own life in light of that message. To form a more abstract understanding of a passage (or a work as a whole), the reader looks for the following elements:

- **patterns:** repetition of a sequence of events, for example, or of a series of contrasts
- **tone:** the cumulative effect of imagery, figurative language, and diction and syntax in expressing the author's attitude
- **theme:** patterns of meaning, viewed through the lens of tone, revealing the work's theme

Annotating Prose

Students can annotate fiction or nonfiction for the writer's choice of words, images, sentence structure, and attitude or point of view. Below is an example of annotations to an excerpt from Henry James's novel *The Portrait of a Lady.*

LEVEL 1
(annotations are boxed)

Isabel is wealthy and sees herself as a strong person.

Is Isabel worried about being useless?

Ephemeral means "not long lasting."

Third-person-omniscient narrator allows readers to see into the characters' minds.

It was one of her theories that Isabel Archer was very fortunate in being independent, and that she ought to make some very enlightened use of that state. She never called it the state of solitude, much less of singleness; she thought such descriptions weak, and, besides, her sister Lily constantly urged her to come and abide. She had a friend whose acquaintance she had made shortly before her father's death, who offered so high an example of useful activity that Isabel always thought of her as a model. Henrietta Stackpole had the advantage of an admired ability; she was thoroughly launched in journalism, and her letters to the *Interviewer,* from Washington, Newport, the White Mountains and other places, were universally quoted. Isabel pronounced them with confidence "ephemeral," but she esteemed the courage, energy and good-humour of the writer, who, without parents and without property, had adopted three of the children of an infirm and widowed sister and was paying their school-bills out of the proceeds of her literary labour. Henrietta was in the van of progress and had clear-cut views on most subjects; her cherished desire had long been to come to Europe and write a series of letters to the *Interviewer* from the radical point of view—an enterprise the less difficult as she knew perfectly in advance what her opinions would be

LEVEL 2
(annotations are underscored)

Isabel is concerned about what kind of life she might lead.

Isabel believes that her life should serve a purpose and seems to slightly envy Henrietta's career.

Isabel is somewhat condescending to Henrietta. She doesn't seem to regard Henrietta as particularly "enlightened."

The narrator seems to think that Henrietta is narrow-minded and something of a phony (?)

and to how many objections most European institutions lay open. When she heard that Isabel was coming she wished to start at once; thinking, naturally, that it would be delightful the two should travel together. She had been obliged, however, to postpone this enterprise. She thought Isabel a glorious creature, and had spoken of her covertly in some of her letters, though she never mentioned the fact to her friend, who would not have taken pleasure in it and was not a regular student of the *Interviewer*. Henrietta, for Isabel, was chiefly a proof that a woman might suffice to herself and be happy. Her resources were of the obvious kind; but even if one had not the journalistic talent and a genius for guessing, as Henrietta said, what the public was going to want, one was not therefore to conclude that one had no vocation, no beneficent aptitude of any sort, and resign one's self to being frivolous and hollow. Isabel was stoutly determined not to be hollow.

Henrietta strongly admires Isabel.

A very strong word, hollow, is repeated twice.

Is Isabel somewhat embarrassed by Henrietta?

Isabel seems to be wary of marrying.

The repetition of the word reinforces Isabel's concern about the direction of her life.

LEVEL 3

One of the main concerns in this excerpt is the effect of class divisions in American society. The author suggests that people who work have very different views of the world from those who are leisured. Isabel seems to be both superficial and, at the same time, quite concerned about the direction of her life. Henrietta has a rather narrower view of the world, and her life—in contrast to Isabel's—seems to have definite purpose. James seems to be making a general observation that having wealth can result in living a hollow, trivial life. But, in his characterization of Henrietta, he shows an unwillingness to play down the possible negative effects of having to struggle to earn a wage.

Annotating a Poem

Annotating poetry is like annotating prose, but with an additional challenge: Students also need to expand on the sometimes compressed language of poetry and consider structural elements such as rhythm, rhyme, stanzas, and line breaks. Here is an example of annotation using W. H. Auden's poem "That Night When Joy Began."

LEVEL 1
(annotations are boxed)

Joy makes their hearts beat faster.

War imagery

Personification

The couple has become used to being happy.

The speaker looks toward the future.

The speaker may view himself as trespassing on love's territory.

That Night When Joy Began

That night when joy began
Our narrowest veins to flush,
We waited for the flash
Of morning's levelled gun.

But morning let us pass,
And day by day relief
Outgrows his nervous laugh,
Grown credulous of peace,

As mile by mile is seen
No trespasser's reproach,
And love's best glasses reach
No fields but are his own.

LEVEL 2
(annotations are under-scored)

The war imagery makes love seem like a struggle.

Both people had bad experiences with love before and expected things to end badly.

The speaker doesn't seem to be sure that he deserves love.

"That Night When Joy Began" from *Collected Poems* by W.H. Auden. Copyright © 1937 and renewed © 1965 by W.H. Auden. Reproduced by permission of **Random House, Inc.,** and electronic format by permission of **Curtis Brown, Ltd.**

LEVEL 3

The speaker in this poem has had bad experiences in love. The excitement that he expresses in line 2 of the poem is a mixture of elation and the fear—expressed by the revelation in line 4—of having love taken away or destroyed. The use of personification highlights the speaker's belief that, in matters of love, events are mainly out of his direct control. The phrase "morning let us pass" suggests that the two people simply got lucky. By describing himself as a trespasser, the speaker suggests that his love is in some way a "crime" that deserves punishment. In the end, though, the speaker and the person to whom this poem is addressed are safe from harm on "love's" territory.

Allusion Sources and Tips

An **allusion** is a reference to a well-known person, place, event, or idea from such sources as religion, mythology, literature, history, science, or popular culture. Writers use allusions to reinforce ideas, intensify emotion, or compress meaning.

Steps to Understanding Allusions

Understanding allusions takes three steps:

1. **Notice an allusion.** Often, an unusual proper noun ("He's a regular Romeo") or adjective ("You can park this Lilliputian car anywhere") can signal an allusion. Sometimes the allusion will refer to something familiar to you—a fairy tale or a recent pop-culture event, for example. To notice allusions that aren't immediately obvious, though, you'll need to learn not to skip over unfamiliar ideas. If a reference seems surprising or you can't rephrase it in your own words, think, "What is this really saying? Could it refer to something else from literature, mythology, or history?"

2. **Identify the source and meaning of the allusion.** Especially if it's crucial to understanding the passage, take the time to identify the allusion. Think about what you already know—could this allusion relate to a familiar story or idea? If not, ask someone knowledgeable or consult a reference source. You can often find brief explanations of common allusions in a good dictionary. Specialized references include *The Oxford Dictionary of Allusions* and other sources, such as those listed in the Common Allusion Sources section on the following pages.

3. **Connect the allusion to the text.** A writer can say a great deal about a topic, character, or situation through an apt allusion. Think about how the allusion applies to the text and why the author chose it. Often an allusion may build a particular tone or point toward the theme of the passage.

Try applying the steps above to this passage from an editorial about a local political issue.

> Councilperson Ford, with the careless fervor of Icarus, continues to tempt fate by proposing too much downtown development without regard to citizen concerns about traffic congestion and lack of investors. City planners have made it plain that such development is unrealistic and unsustainable, but, as with Daedalus, their entirely reasonable warnings fall on deaf ears.

1. Allusion cues: Icarus, Daedalus

2. This allusion refers to the Greek myth in which Daedalus carefully crafts wings so he and his son Icarus can escape imprisonment. Though Daedalus warns Icarus against flying too close to the sun or the sea, Icarus ignores his father. He flies too close to the sun, and the wax holding his wings together melts. Icarus falls into the sea and drowns.

3. This allusion points out how foolish the writer thinks Councilperson Ford is being. In refusing to listen to warnings from those who, like Daedalus, know best, Ford, like Icarus, is taking serious risks. Through this allusion, the writer presents himself or herself as farseeing and wise.

Common Allusion Sources

Though an allusion can come from nearly any source, the most common sources are the Bible, classical literature and mythology, the works of William Shakespeare and other well-known classics, and momentous events in science and history.

The Bible

Writers have been using the Bible as a source for allusions for hundreds of years. For instance, the anonymous eighth-century author of *Beowulf* calls the monster Grendel a descendant of Cain—an allusion to Adam and Eve's son who murdered his brother Abel. The contemporary writer Sandra Cisneros alludes to the episode of the three wise men who bring gifts to the baby Jesus in her story "Three Wise Guys: Un Cuento de Navidad / A Christmas Story." Some key Bible stories to know for allusions include

- the birth, life, death, and resurrection of Jesus
- the creation of the world
- Adam and Eve in the Garden of Eden
- Moses leading the Israelites out of Egypt
- Job, whose endurance and faith were sorely tested
- David slaying the giant Goliath
- Jonah being swallowed by the "great fish" or whale
- Samson, whose great strength came from his hair, and Delilah, who betrayed him by cutting it off as he slept
- the wise Solomon devising a test to discover to whom a baby belonged
- the parable of the prodigal son, whose father celebrated his return more than his brother's unfailing loyalty

Classical Literature and Mythology

Mythology, folklore, and ancient literature such as the works of Aesop and Homer overflow with archetypal characters and situations and are therefore the source of many powerful allusions. You can refer to general sources such as *Bulfinch's Mythology*, *Mythology* by Edith Hamilton, the *Larousse Encyclopedia of Mythology*,

Grimm's Fairy Tales, and Jack Zipes's *Beauties, Beasts, and Enchantment.* Some of the ancient tales most frequently alluded to are

- Homer's *Iliad* and *Odyssey,* detailing the Trojan War and Odysseus's ten-year journey home
- Virgil's *Aeneid,* which recounts the adventures of the Trojan leader Aeneas after the fall of Troy
- King Midas and his golden touch
- Phaëthon and the chariot of the sun
- Narcissus, who falls in love with his own reflection
- Sophocles' *Oedipus Rex,* about a king who unknowingly kills his father and marries his mother
- Euripides' *Medea,* in which the abandoned wife of Jason (who is known for stealing the Golden Fleece) murders their children and Jason's new wife
- fairy tales, including "Cinderella," "Snow White," "Rumpelstiltskin," "The Three Little Pigs," and "Jack and the Beanstalk"
- Aesop's fables, including the stories "The Ant and the Grasshopper," "The Fox and the Grapes," and "The Tortoise and the Hare"

Shakespeare and Other Classics

Ben Jonson said that Shakespeare "was not of an age, but for all time." Allusions to Shakespeare's works are so commonplace that it's easy to be unaware of their source. Allusions to Shakespeare often occur in titles: The title of Aldous Huxley's novel *Brave New World* ironically alludes to these lines in *The Tempest:* "How beauteous mankind is! O brave new world, / That has such people in't" (V.1.183–84). The title of William Faulkner's novel *The Sound and the Fury* alludes to these lines in which Macbeth bemoans the pointlessness of life: "It is a tale / Told by an idiot, full of sound and fury, / Signifying nothing" (V.5.26–28). While you might miss allusions to specific lines in Shakespeare's plays that you have not yet read, you can prepare yourself for Shakespearean allusions by becoming familiar with the basic plots of his most famous plays:

- *Romeo and Juliet,* about doomed lovers from feuding families
- *Hamlet,* about the efforts of a prince to prove that his uncle murdered his father
- *King Lear,* in which a king attempts to divide his kingdom among his three daughters, two of whom are deceptive schemers while one is loyal and honest
- *Macbeth,* concerning a Scottish lord and his wife, who will stop at nothing to win power
- *Julius Caesar,* about the assassination of the Roman ruler
- *Othello,* in which Iago sows jealousy to destroy the marriage of Othello and Desdemona
- *A Midsummer Night's Dream,* in which a fairy called Puck orchestrates a night of enchantment, confusion, and love

Other classic works of literature commonly alluded to include *Beowulf,* Chaucer's *The Canterbury Tales,* Milton's *Paradise Lost,* Dante's *Divine Comedy,* and Swift's *Gulliver's Travels.*

History, Science, and Popular Culture

While you can't expect to recognize every allusion relating to history, science, or popular culture, you can prepare yourself for those most likely to crop up. Be aware that popular-culture allusions will include not only recent trends and events but also outdated fads, long-gone figures from politics and sports, and events from decades before your time. Older relatives and friends can often explain these less-familiar allusions. Some useful resources include *The Timetables of American History; Asimov's Chronology of Science & Discovery; Dictionary of Twentieth Century Culture; Visual Arts in the Twentieth Century; Panati's Parade of Fads, Follies, and Manias; Who Was Who in America;* and the *Dictionary of American Biography.*

Common allusions from history include

- World War II events and people, including the Holocaust, the first atomic bomb, Hitler and the Nazis, Rosie the Riveter, kamikaze pilots, and D-day
- the American Revolution, through which the United States won independence from Great Britain
- Napoleon's defeat at Waterloo
- the rise and fall of the Roman Empire

Common allusions from science include

- the invention of the light bulb and telephone
- the first moon landing ("The *Eagle* has landed.")
- the development of the first antibiotics and vaccines ("the magic bullet")
- the cloning of animals, including a cloned sheep named Dolly

Remember that in addition to the tips and sources listed above, the best way to prepare yourself for allusions you might encounter is to read, read, read. Wide reading is the best preparation for recognizing and understanding allusions.

Analyzing Multiple-Choice Questions

General Tips

The multiple-choice questions that appear on many standardized tests range in difficulty from simple recall of information to complex analysis. Here are some tips for doing your best on literature and language arts tests.

1. Do not expect that only certain kinds of questions will appear with a selection or that questions will be arranged in order of difficulty. With any passage, whether literary or nonfiction, be prepared to answer questions about
   - literary techniques, including figurative language and imagery
   - tone, or the author's attitude
   - vocabulary used in the passage
   - the writer's style
   - persuasive techniques, including evidence and point of view
   - the effect of grammatical choices and the functions of words
   - contrasts or shifts within the passage
   - inferences and predictions based on the passage

2. Read everything carefully; do not skip anything in the passage or the questions. At the same time, try to avoid using personal knowledge that goes beyond what is in the passage. Objective test questions are designed to assess what you understand from reading the selection only; questions may include distracters on concepts related to the passage topic. If you use personal knowledge that goes beyond the selection, you may choose one of the distracters over the answer that best fits the passage.

3. After reading the question stem, try to think of an answer before you read the choices. Then, read all the choices carefully. If more than one choice seems right, remember that you need to choose the *best* answer. If you can't eliminate any choices, you should skip the question and return to it later; many tests deduct points for wrong answers to discourage random guessing.

4. If you skip a difficult question, be careful not to lose your place on the answer sheet.

Analyzing an Item

Be sure you understand both the question stem and the answer choices that follow it. Consider this question about the story of Little Red Riding Hood:

> 16. The protagonist's experience supports the key theme that
>   (A) it is the duty of children to take care of their older relatives
>   (B) talking to strangers who seem friendly can be dangerous
>   (C) people have a surprising capacity for self-preservation
>   (D) a child should always be accompanied by an adult

To answer this kind of question, you need to take several steps.

1. Be sure you understand the passage well enough to tell someone else about it.

2. Identify the question stem's subject and verb. Here, you can boil down the stem to its essentials: "The theme is . . ." Always pick out the basic question, watching for negatives such as *NOT* and *EXCEPT*. Modifiers in the stem may help you decide between two strong choices.

3. Paraphrase each answer choice to be sure you understand it. Then, try each choice as a response to the stem. Do not be distracted by
   - choices related to the story but not to the question
   - choices contradicted by the story
   - high-level wording that makes an off-base choice sound "smart"
   - the length of choices; a short choice is not necessarily wrong, and a long choice is worth taking the time to understand

4. You may need to skim parts of the passage provided to choose the better of two strong options.

With these guidelines, you can eliminate choice C, which is not supported by story events. You can also eliminate choice A, which relates to the story but is far from a key theme. To choose between B and D, you might skim the version of the story on the test to see whether it emphasizes that Little Red Riding Hood is traveling alone. If not, B is the best choice because it is a central idea supported by story events.

Sample Scoring Guidelines and Rangefinders

After each writing prompt in the Test Practice in this book, you will find Scoring Guidelines specific to the prompt and a sample high-scoring response to the prompt. The following section can help you pinpoint the subtle distinctions among acceptable essays—which range in score from 5 to 9. It provides more detailed Scoring Guidelines and a range of sample responses to the writing prompt that appears below and on page 161. This prompt and the following responses are based on "Heaven and Earth in Jest," an excerpt from *Pilgrim at Tinker Creek* by Annie Dillard, on pages 158–159.

Writing Prompt

> In "Heaven and Earth in Jest," Annie Dillard considers the beauty and horror of the natural world as she observes and interprets a gruesome yet fascinating event in nature. As you re-read the essay, notice the author's use of rhetorical strategies, including repetition, rhetorical questions, figurative language, parallelism, and restatement. Also, think about the essay's theme. Then, write an essay in which you analyze three of Dillard's rhetorical strategies and explain how they support her theme.

Scoring Guidelines

9 Papers earning a score of 9 meet the criteria for score 8 papers and, in addition, are especially full or apt in their analysis or demonstrate particularly impressive control of language. They may demonstrate profound or surprising insight into Dillard's use of rhetorical strategies and what they reveal about the theme.

8 Papers earning a score of 8 effectively analyze Dillard's use of three rhetorical strategies such as repetition, rhetorical questions, figurative language, parallelism, and restatement to support the theme. These essays use textual evidence and quotations appropriately, effectively, and accurately to establish points. The prose demonstrates an ability to control a wide range of the elements of effective writing but is not necessarily flawless.

7 Papers earning a score of 7 fit the description of score 6 papers and provide a more complete analysis or demonstrate a more mature prose style. They demonstrate the ability to analyze the use of language in a literary work.

6 Papers earning a score of 6 adequately analyze Dillard's use of rhetorical strategies to develop the theme. The textual evidence and quotations are appropriate, and the interpretations are sound. The writing may contain errors in the conventions of written English, but generally the prose is clear.

5 Papers earning a score of 5 analyze Dillard's use of rhetorical strategies to develop the theme but do so unevenly or superficially. The textual evidence and quotations are thin or inadequate. The writing may contain errors in the conventions of written English, but it usually conveys the student's ideas.

4 Papers earning a score of 4 respond to the prompt inadequately. They may incorrectly evaluate the use of rhetorical strategies, misstate the theme, or offer little analysis. Textual evidence may be inadequate, lacking entirely, or inappropriate. The prose generally conveys the student's ideas but may suggest immature control of writing.

3 Papers earning a score of 3 generally meet the criteria for a score of 4 but are less perceptive in analyzing Dillard's use of rhetorical strategies to develop the theme. These papers may be inconsistent in their control of the elements of writing.

2 Papers earning a score of 2 do not successfully analyze Dillard's use of language. These papers may demonstrate misunderstanding of the prompt, offer vague generalizations, or substitute simpler tasks such as summarizing the essay. The prose demonstrates consistent weaknesses in writing.

1 Papers earning a score of 1 generally meet the criteria for a score of 2 but are less developed, especially simplistic in their analysis, or weaker in their control of language.

0 A score of 0 indicates an on-topic response that receives no credit, such as one that merely repeats the prompt.

— This score indicates a blank response or one that is completely off topic.

Sample Responses

All of the following responses would meet the criteria for an adequate essay. You might want to give copies to students and point out the differences between exemplary (9), solid (7), and adequate (5) responses.

Score Point 9

In the essay "Heaven and Earth in Jest," writer Annie Dillard explains how she witnesses the sudden but completely natural death of a frog and how that death leads her to raise age-old questions about our place in the universe. Dillard's writing style reflects her theme—that the world is at once a dangerous, mystifying, and beautiful place that we humans may never fully comprehend. Her use of figurative language (similes and metaphor) and rhetorical questions reflects her struggle to make connections, question assumptions, and search for answers, and her rhetorical strategies invite readers to join in the same struggle.

By associating the unfamiliar experience of the frog's death with everyday objects, Dillard uses figurative language to reflect her struggle to understand an extraordinary event. Most of her similes appear in the second paragraph, where Dillard describes the appearance of the frog as it dies. For example, "The spirit vanished from his eyes as if snuffed," "his very skull seemed to collapse and settle like a kicked tent," and "He was shrinking before my eyes like a deflating football" indicate that Dillard seeks to understand the frog's death in terms of the familiar. Similarly, she describes the frog's skin as "formless as a pricked balloon" and says that it lies "in floating folds like bright scum." Later in the essay, she associates a runaway God with another easily understood image, "a wolf who disappears round the edge of the house with the Thanksgiving turkey." This use of figurative language provides readers with vivid imagery and helps Dillard make sense of what she has just witnessed. By drawing connections between a confusing new experience and ordinary objects such as tents, balloons, and footballs, Dillard tries to make the experience familiar and more comprehensible, indicating that she is struggling to understand the meaning of the frog's death.

Likewise, the rhetorical devices Dillard uses in the last paragraph of the essay—rhetorical questioning and repetition—indicate that she is trying to understand the meaning of life and the place of living things in the universe. In this paragraph, she asks seven rhetorical questions, all of which address the meaning of life. Ironically, those questions will not prompt realistic answers: Why was the universe formed? Was the universe created by a kind or a cruel creator? Will we ever be able to figure out the meaning of the universe? The repetition does not clarify Dillard's position; instead, the rhetoric points to her confusion. Answers are not her goal. Her questions are intended to challenge readers to begin "working" the problem. Dillard's devices are designed to bring readers into the same confusing realm that she has entered—a philosophical and religious world that inspires inhabitants to join the struggle to make sense of a universe that sometimes does not make sense.

In her essay, Dillard recalls a small creature's death and then uses figurative language and rhetorical questions to share her confusion with readers. These devices are meant to prompt readers to consider the greater questions of existence. As a writer, Dillard appears quite disturbed by the scene she has witnessed, and she is clearly uncertain about its meaning for the rest of us. Her use of rhetorical strategies—figurative language, questions, and repetition—reflect this struggle to make meaning of a world that we all share.

Commentary. This paper earns a top score by answering the prompt thoroughly and insightfully. It effectively analyzes Dillard's use of figurative language, rhetorical questions, and repetition to support the theme and delves further into the text to connect the rhetorical strategies to Dillard's own struggle with the universal questions. The paper uses apt examples and quotations to support ideas and shows mastery of clear, effective prose.

Score Point 7

Annie Dillard uses a frog's death to discuss questions about life and death and the role of humans. In "Heaven and Earth in Jest," Dillard uses rhetorical strategies to develop the theme of the essay. Dillard uses figurative language and rhetorical questions to show that the world is both dangerous and beautiful—sometimes at the same time. It's hard for humans to understand, but Dillard tries to make the questions clearer for herself and for her readers.

Dillard starts with the death of a frog. The giant water bug has sucked the life out of the frog, which is probably a horrible way to die. Dillard tries to understand the meaning of the frog's death by using similes to tie the death to the question of human existence. Some of the images make the dying frog seem beautiful, as if the frog were a work of art. Dillard's use of figurative language shows that she is trying to understand not just the frog's death but death in general. She writes, "The spirit vanished from his eyes as if snuffed." Because most people think only of humans losing "spirit" when they die, this image shows that Dillard is thinking about the question of human death. When Dillard writes that "his very skull seemed to collapse and settle like a kicked tent," and that he "was shrinking before my eyes like a deflating football," she is using ordinary objects, a tent and a football, to help herself deal with that question. Beautiful images that contrast with the death of the frog help create a sense of tension. The frog's skin is beautiful even as the frog is dying, which is confusing, and Dillard is trying to help readers understand that she is struggling to find an explanation. Her use of ordinary images helps show that death is common and natural. The beautiful images show tension. Dillard uses the figurative language to make the question of death more understandable and less horrific.

In the last paragraph, Dillard uses rhetorical questions and repetition to show that she is trying to understand what life means for both humans and other forms of life. She asks seven rhetorical questions about the meaning of life in that paragraph. No one expects an answer to rhetorical questions; instead, their purpose is to provoke thought. Dillard is asking the reader to think about life and what it means. She repeats the same question but in different words, as if she is brainstorming. The process might generate ideas, but it won't offer an answer, and Dillard doesn't say she has an answer, either. By using rhetorical questions, Dillard wants readers to think. The act of thinking about life is important, even if no one has the answers.

Dillard uses the death of a frog as a way to get readers to think about the big questions about life. She uses the rhetorical strategies of figurative language, rhetorical questions, and repetition to show the beauty and the harshness of life and death. She also uses them to help her and readers think about the meaning of life and death and the place of every form of life in the universe.

Commentary. This response earns a score of 7 through its solid, if not particularly insightful, analysis. It notes Dillard's use of rhetorical strategies but is not as thorough or creative as a higher scoring paper. The student's evidence and support are appropriate. The prose is generally clear but is not sophisticated, borders on redundancy, and is often choppy.

Score Point 5

This essay is about a frog's death, but the author implies that it is about human death, too. The writer, Annie Dillard, uses figurative language and rhetorical questions to make the reader think about larger issues. Maybe the giant water bug is Fate or God or Death. Whatever the bug may represent, Dillard's essay invites readers to consider bigger things than the death of a frog. Some of the essay's language makes the dead frog sound beautiful. Lots of people don't think a live frog is beautiful, but Dillard makes the frog a symbol for life in general. That's the theme of "Heaven and Earth in Jest"—the meaning of life. There isn't a clear answer, but Dillard leads people to think about the subject.

The dead frog inspires Dillard to think about life and what it means. She describes the frog so that readers understand that she's writing about life in general. The frog's skin is all that's left, like a shell. Dillard uses similes to make the frog seem ordinary and natural. Some of the similes also make the frog's skin seem beautiful, like life. Yet life is confusing. The frog's "spirit vanished" when he died, like the spirit of a human. Dillard also compares the dying frog to a tent and a football that loses air. This makes the death seem ordinary, not horrible. It's something we all have to deal with. Dillard is still trying to understand this, and her essay leads readers to want to understand, too. Death is natural however it comes, and it's part of nature. No one lives forever. Dillard uses figurative language to try to help readers accept this.

Dillard also uses a lot of rhetorical questions. The questions show that she doesn't have all the answers. She's thinking about the meaning of life, and she wants readers to think about it, too. When listeners hear a question, they are driven to search for an answer. They might not wind up with that answer, but the question prompts them to think. This is how Dillard wants readers to react. Why did the frog die? Why did he die this way? Why do we die? Dillard knows that it's important to think about life because that's the best way to come up with personal goals. Some people never think about anything, and that's why there are so many problems in the world. So Dillard asks questions to get us to think about the most important issues, like "What is life?" Her rhetorical questions force readers to consider those issues, even if no one will find clear answers.

The frog's death makes readers think about the big questions about life. Dillard uses figurative language to show that even death can be beautiful. It can also be ugly and cruel. Dillard uses questions to help her and readers think about the meaning of existence. The symbolic use of the dead frog and Dillard's rhetorical strategies generate questions about the meaning of life, exactly as Dillard intended them to do.

Commentary. This response earns a score of 5 by adequately noting the use of figurative language and rhetorical questions, but the analysis is incomplete and lacks adequate support or depth. The writing shows acceptable but somewhat immature control of language.

Strategies for Timed Writing

The idea of writing a response to an essay question in a limited time can be intimidating. However, a few basic strategies can make timed writing manageable.

Analyzing the Prompt

To get off to the right start in timed writing, be sure that you understand what the **writing prompt,** or question, is asking you to do. Read the prompt below.

> Read the following poem. Then, write an essay in which you analyze the poem's tone. Consider stylistic devices such as rhyme, rhythm, diction, and figurative language.

The Boy and the Wolf

A boy employed to guard the sheep
Despised his work. He liked to sleep.
And when a lamb was lost, he'd shout,
"Wolf! Wolf! The wolves are all about!"

The neighbors searched from noon till
   nine,
But of the beast there was no sign,
Yet "Wolf!" he cried next morning when
The villagers came out again.

One evening around six o'clock
A real wolf fell upon the flock.
"Wolf!" yelled the boy. "A wolf indeed!"
But no one paid him any heed.

Although he screamed to wake the dead,
"He's fooled us every time," they said,
And let the hungry wolf enjoy
His feast of mutton, lamb—and boy.

The moral's this: The man who's wise
Does not defend himself with lies.
Liars are not believed, forsooth,*
Even when liars tell the truth.

         —Louis Untermeyer

*__forsooth:__ old-fashioned word meaning "truly."

"The Boy and the Wolf" from *The Magic Circle* by Louis Untermeyer. Copyright 1952 by Harcourt, Inc. and renewed © 1980 by Brian I. Untermeyer. Reproduced by permission of **Harcourt, Inc.** and electronic format by permission of **Laurence S. Untermeyer by arrangement with the Estate of Louis Untermeyer, Norma Anchin Untermeyer c/o Professional Publishing Services Company.**

To analyze the prompt, look for key words. Most prompts will contain one **key verb** (or give you two or more to choose from, such as *agree or disagree*). In literary analysis prompts like the one above, you must also identify the **key literary concepts** that the prompt requires you to discuss. Keep the following points in mind:

- The prompt may provide very broad guidance (for example, "analyze **literary devices**").

- Alternatively, it may name a specific literary effect that you are asked to explain (for example, "explain how literary devices contribute to the **somber tone**").

- Sometimes the prompt will note specific devices or literary elements to analyze but will not name the specific effect. In these cases, you must identify and then analyze the effect. This is the case with the prompt in the example. Here are the key words from that prompt:

| **KEY VERB** | analyze |
| **KEY LITERARY CONCEPTS** | tone; stylistic devices (rhyme, rhythm, diction, figurative language) |

To respond to the prompt in the example above, you must first identify the poem's **tone.** Only then can you begin to consider the stylistic devices used to create that tone. The words *such as* in the prompt are important: They tell you that you can choose from the list of stylistic devices, but you don't have to consider *all* of these devices.

The chart below defines some of the more common key verbs for timed writing prompts.

Key Verbs That Appear in Essay Questions

Key Verbs	Task	Sample Question
defend, challenge, or qualify	Take a stand on an issue stated in the prompt or on an idea in a quotation or selection that follows the prompt. (To *qualify* is to agree with the position only under certain circum-stances; the circumstances must be explained in the body of your essay.)	Write an essay in which you **defend, challenge, or qualify** the saying "No good deed goes unpunished."
agree or disagree	See defend, challenge, or qualify	**Agree or disagree** with the speechwriter's central point. Support your posi-tion with evidence from your experience, observa-tion, or reading.
analyze	Examine the various parts of a work and explain how they interact.	**Analyze** how the literary devices used in Alfred Noyes's poem "The Highwayman" create a particular mood.
explain	Give reasons and examples.	Read the poem below. In a well-organized essay, **explain** how the poem's imagery reflects the speaker's attitude.

describe	Give a picture in words. When this verb is included in a prompt, it will usually be the first step in a two-step task.	**Describe** how the protagonist changes, and explain how this change reflects the novel's theme of renewal.
identify	Point out; name. When this verb is included in a prompt, it will usually be the first step in a two-step task.	**Identify** the story's theme, and explain how the author uses symbols to express the theme.
discuss	*See analyze.*	**Discuss** how the author's diction and use of figurative language create suspense.
compare and contrast	Point out similarities and differences.	**Compare and contrast** the two poems. Analyze how each poet's diction helps characterize the poem's speaker.
consider	Take into account to support an analysis. This verb usually describes a secondary task.	Analyze how the poet establishes the speaker's laid-back attitude. **Consider** the following stylistic devices: word choice, imagery, and sentence structure.
demonstrate (*also* show)	Provide examples to support a point.	Read the passage below. **Demonstrate** how the author's word choices reflect a shift in tone from despairing to hopeful.
synthesize	Use information or ideas from several sources to take a position on an issue.	Read the three selections above, and study the political cartoon. **Synthesize** the ideas to develop a position on the topic they address.

Writing a Thesis Statement

Once you have analyzed the writing prompt, you can begin to form a thesis—your "big idea" in response to the prompt. Developing a strong thesis is half the battle in writing a successful response. Therefore, you should expect to spend a fair amount of time doing it.

The thesis statement is not merely the naming of a topic. Nor is it just a statement of fact. Instead, the thesis gives the topic *plus* what you have to say about the topic—your opinion about or position on the topic. Notice the difference between the three examples below. All relate to the poem "The Boy and the Wolf," but only the third example does more than name a topic or state a fact. It takes a position.

TOPIC	Louis Untermeyer's literary devices
STATEMENT OF FACT	Louis Untermeyer uses literary devices.
THESIS STATEMENT	Louis Untermeyer uses literary devices to create a parental tone.

In timed writing, your choices about the topic are limited. Your topic and your thesis must respond to the prompt. For the sample prompt on page 45, the thesis should

- identify the poet's tone
- identify the literary devices that reveal that tone

A thesis statement that merely restates the prompt is vague and weak. By making your thesis statement as specific as possible, you will set the course for a successful response.

WEAK, VAGUE THESIS	In "The Boy and the Wolf," Louis Untermeyer uses literary devices to reveal his tone.
STRONG, SPECIFIC THESIS	In "The Boy and the Wolf," Louis Untermeyer uses simple rhymes and rhythm, straightforward words, and humorous understatement to create a parental tone.

The second thesis above shows that the writer has a plan for writing. It provides an informal outline for the essay. The reader can expect that the essay will discuss rhyme and rhythm and what makes them simple, the words and what makes them straightforward, the humor that comes from understatement, and how all these elements work together to create a parental tone.

Writing Introductions

Some writing experts advise students to get right to the point in introductions. In other words, answer the entire prompt in the introduction—but save specific examples for the body of your essay. For many writing prompts, this means starting off by explaining the relationship between the author's techniques and an overall literary effect.

The example of a strong thesis statement above does just that: It identifies the literary effect (parental tone) and the techniques that create it (simple rhymes and rhythm, straightforward words, and so on). What is missing, and what would appear in the body of the essay, are specific examples from the poem, with explanations of how they support the thesis.

Be aware that answering an entire prompt in a thesis can lead to overly complicated sentences. One approach to writing an introduction is to **state the thesis and then explain it.** In the example introduction below, notice how the writer of the strong thesis statement on the previous page has unpacked some of the details in the original thesis to create a strong, clear introduction.

> In "The Boy and the Wolf," Louis Untermeyer uses several stylistic devices to convey a parental tone. The simple rhymes and singsong rhythm have the same quality as Mother Goose verses that are used to teach children. Straightforward language leaves little room for confusion, mirroring the direct language parents use when giving warnings. Understated details provide comic relief. All of these techniques contribute to the tone, a tone that warns clearly but does not frighten, one that parents have used to deliver warnings for as long as little children have misbehaved.

This introduction answers the whole prompt. It also raises many questions: What are the simple rhymes? What makes them sound singsong? What is the straightforward language that is referred to? How is it parental? What details are understated, and why are they funny? These questions can all be answered and explained fully in the body paragraphs.

Other Approaches to the Introduction

In a timed-writing situation, an introduction must always answer the prompt. For literary-analysis prompts, a straightforward introduction that states the thesis and then explains it is the most effective type. In responding to more open-ended prompts, however, you may want to begin with something other than your thesis. By opening with something unusual—a question or a quotation, for example—you capture your audience's attention. By delaying the thesis, you stir your reader's curiosity.

The chart below provides some suggestions for creating attention-grabbing introductions for open-ended writing prompts. The examples all refer to the following prompt:

> In *The Picture of Dorian Gray,* the Irish writer Oscar Wilde writes, "There is only one thing in the world worse than being talked about, and that is not being talked about." Write a well-organized persuasive essay, agreeing or disagreeing with this statement.

Technique	Example
Begin with an anecdote.	The other day I did a Web search for myself. I entered my name in a popular search engine to see if it turned up on the Internet. I wasn't sure at first whether to be relieved or disappointed that the only hit was a mention in our local paper of my making the honor roll.

Begin with an analogy or a contrast.	Most people would probably be very unhappy to find that their photograph had been imprinted at the center of a dartboard and sold at a chain store. Yet many teenagers do not hesitate to post photos of themselves on Web sites whose sole purpose is to get "feedback" from the general Web-surfing public.
Use an appropriate quotation.	A wise person once asked, "If a tree falls in a forest, and no one is there to hear it, does it make a sound?" If no one notices or talks about something you have accomplished, why bother trying at all?
Ask a question.	If you could read your best friend's diary, including—no, especially—those entries concerning you, would you?

Incorporating Quotations and Text Citations

In a response to any reading passage, you should plan to use quotations from that passage to support your point. The chart below lists some guidelines for using quotations effectively during timed writing. The example to the right of the chart shows how an essay writer might follow those guidelines.

1. **Make sure the quotation supports your thesis.** If your thesis states that an author uses figurative language to create an impression of majestic power, make sure that you quote a passage that both (1) includes figurative language and (2) conveys majestic power. The quotation selected for the example at right fulfills both conditions.	In "The Eagle," Alfred, Lord Tennyson, uses figurative language to show the majesty of his subject. Our first image of the eagle shows the eagle at rest on a cliff. The speaker says the eagle is "Close to the sun in lonely lands" (line 2). Of course, in reality, the eagle is not much closer to the sun than a worm is. By using the figure of speech of hyperbole, the poet raises the eagle to a high level, like a king on a throne.
2. **Introduce a quotation by providing background information that the reader might need.** In the example at right, the writer provides the context for the first quotation.	
3. **Add a line number in parentheses after the quotation.** The line number should follow the closing quotation and appear in parentheses. Add a period after the closing parenthesis.	
4. **Explain how the quotation relates to your thesis or the topic sentence of the paragraph.** In the example at right, the two sentences that follow the quotation explain what type of figurative language is used in the quotation and how it creates an impression of majesty—two ideas mentioned in the topic sentence.	

To make the meaning of a quotation clear to the reader, you will sometimes need to edit the text. Here are two techniques you might use, followed by an example using both.

- Use brackets to add or substitute text. A common type of substitution is replacing a pronoun with the noun to which it refers. When adding or substituting text, enclose the new text in brackets.

- Use ellipses (. . .) to show where text has been omitted.

> "As the twilight drew on, [the dog's] eager yearning for the fire mastered it. . . . Then it turned and trotted up the trail in the direction of the camp it knew . . ." (lines 130–139).
>
> —Jack London, "To Build a Fire"

Writing Conclusions

In wrapping up your timed writing, leave time to compose a conclusion. Your conclusion should do two things:

1. **Leave the reader with a sense of completeness.** Most readers don't like to be left hanging. Writing a conclusion is like saying a formal goodbye.

2. **Reinforce the thesis.** The conclusion should bring your readers back to your thesis.

One sure-fire strategy for writing a conclusion, especially for a literary analysis, is to refer to your introduction, particularly your thesis and major points. But your conclusion should also go a step beyond restating the thesis. One strategy is to pose a question or speculate about a point related to your thesis, leaving your reader with food for thought.

> Through literary devices and humor, the poet conveys a tone that children recognize immediately as the voice of parental authority. The poem strikes just the right note for anyone who has tried to warn a small child about a potential danger without giving the child nightmares. Perhaps that is why parents have turned to the story of the boy who cried wolf for centuries and why Untermeyer chose to make the classic folk tale the subject of a modern poem.

Many other concluding strategies are useful, especially in answering open-ended prompts. The examples in the chart on the following page refer to the Oscar Wilde prompt on page 49.

Technique	Example
Conclude with a look to the future.	Yes, most teenagers would probably agree at first with Oscar Wilde that the only thing worse than being talked about is not being talked about. But in an age of high-speed communication, where "talk" can spread faster than wildfire, they may wish more to be quietly respected than to be widely discussed.
End with a statement of the subject's overall significance.	No one would agree more with Oscar Wilde's quotation than a teenager. After all, most teenagers are looking somewhere for acceptance, and the first step to acceptance is being recognized—being talked about. Unfortunately, teenagers who are the subject of mean gossip may feel the need to change in order to get the acceptance they want.
Use a final illustration or anecdote.	My family has a rule that on weeknights after 7:30, no one can use the phone or e-mail or visit chat rooms or have friends over. As drastic as this rule seems, I sometimes look forward to this quiet time, when I don't have to worry about who's saying what about me, and I can just be me.

There are many other ways to wrap up your essay, such as including

- a call to action
- a prediction
- a reason for dismissing an opposing idea
- a solution to a problem
- an analogy that clarifies a key point
- a strong contrast
- a warning
- a quotation that applies to the topic

Be careful not to wander too far from your thesis when you write your conclusion. A further speculation or an unanswered question can offer an intriguing glimpse of a future writing topic. However, if you elaborate on these topics in your conclusion, your audience will wonder why they are not part of the body of your essay.

Modifying AP Writing Prompts

The released writing prompts available from the College Board can guide your instruction. Reviewing prompts from AP English exams will help you focus on developing the key analytical skills students need. However, you may want to avoid having your students respond to released AP prompts, even as guided practice in class. In particular, younger students may not be prepared for

- high-level vocabulary used in prompts
- conceptually packed sentences
- analyzing multiple elements at one time
- the advanced reading level of test passages
- sophisticated thematic analysis

Notice the factors listed above at work in this released AP prompt:

> **EXAMPLE** Read the following poem carefully. Then, in a well-organized essay, analyze how the speaker uses the varied imagery of the poem to reveal his attitude toward the nature of love.

In the course of the school year, you can gradually help students become more comfortable with AP-style prompts by scaffolding in the following ways.

Define terminology or substitute age-appropriate words. You will need to decide whether you want to teach new terms within a prompt or limit the prompt to assessing students' skills.

> **DEFINITION** Analyze how the speaker—the character the poet has created to address the audience—uses imagery, or language that appeals to the five senses, in the following poem.

> **SUBSTITUTION** Read the following poem, and analyze how the character speaking in the poem uses language that appeals to the five senses.

Break prompts into shorter, simpler sentences. Even if your students know all the terminology in a prompt, long sentences may hinder understanding.

> **EXAMPLE** Read the following poem carefully. Consider the various types of imagery the speaker uses. How do these images reflect the speaker's attitude toward love? Explain your response in a well-organized essay.

Limit prompts to one or two concepts at a time. Use focused prompts to assess students' analyses of individual concepts, especially early in the year. Later in the school year, students may be able to weave together analyses of multiple concepts that they have already mastered in isolation.

> **EXAMPLE 1** Read the following poem, and consider the kinds of imagery the poet uses. What is the effect of these images?
>
> **EXAMPLE 2** Read the following poem. Then, write an essay in which you explain the poet's attitude toward his subject—love.

Replace reading selections with age-appropriate works or passages. Remember that the selections chosen for AP exams reflect college-level reading. Even if your students grasp the vocabulary and diction of a college-level passage, they may not be ready for the complex themes and nuances of such material. Instead, have younger students respond to selections or passages that focus on one or two key themes or concepts. Your choices may be on or above grade level and should be sufficiently rich, well written, and ambiguous to invite analysis and debate.

Simplify the intellectual tasks required. Help younger students develop their abstract thinking skills one step at a time. For example, use prompts that ask guiding questions to help students grasp a literary concept as part of their analysis.

> **EXAMPLE** Read the following poem carefully. Who do you think is doing the "talking" in this poem? What clues does the poem give you about this person? What is he or she talking about? How does he or she feel about this subject, and how can you tell?

The types of modifications you use will depend on the needs and abilities of your students. Early in the year, you might use modified prompts as much for discussion as for writing. By the end of the school year, your students may be ready to write essays in response to prompts as complex as those on AP exams.

Writing prompts appear in every Lesson Plan in this book—some requiring AP-style analysis and others equally rigorous but more creative in nature. In addition, the Test Practice features each include a writing prompt, a detailed rubric, and a sample response. Have students analyze and respond to the prompts in this book, and give them feedback on how well they address the various parts of the prompts.

Collection Resources

Elements of Literature selection

The Leap
by Louise Erdrich

Literary Focus

The coverage of **flashback** below builds on the instruction in the Student Edition. You may want to introduce the additional skill of analyzing **foreshadowing** when teaching this story to advanced students.

Flashback

Much of "The Leap" uses **analepsis,** the telling of an event or story after later events have been related. *Analepsis* is an umbrella term that includes **flashback,** retrospection, and other techniques. There are many instances of flashback in "The Leap," such as the narrator's recollection of the fire that almost took her life. Throughout the story, the narrator uses retrospection, or contemplation of the past, to tie disparate events together. For example, she notes that "the catlike precision of her [mother's] movements in old age might be the result of her early training." Have students analyze how the story's temporal "leaps" support theme and tone. You might also use the story to provide additional examples of flashback and retrospection.

Author Focus. Louise Erdrich is perhaps best known for her lyrical prose, her reliance on her own Native American heritage, and her Faulknerian gift for creating a cross-generational, cross-textual cast of characters and intriguing stories. Interestingly, Erdrich may be viewed as part of an oral tradition: She collaborates, recites stories about past events, and interprets myths—all of which activities are characteristic of oral storytelling. You might discuss with students why foreshadowing and flashback often figure heavily in oral tales.

Foreshadowing: Prolepsis

In her work, Erdrich makes extensive use of **prolepsis:** She narrates or refers to events or stories that lie in the narrative present's future. Prolepsis, like analepsis, is an umbrella term that includes foreshadowing, flash-forward, and anticipation. In "The Leap," the narrator uses foreshadowing when she mentions "the disaster that put our town smack on the front page." Words and phrases that increase our anticipation of events are also sprinkled through the story. Erdrich's description of the "sudden roll of drums" preceding her mother's leap is an excellent illustration of this technique.

SKILLS FOCUS

Literary Skill
Analyze flashback and foreshadowing.

Advanced Skill
Analyze prolepsis.

As students explore **flashback** and **foreshadowing (prolepsis),** remind them not to look at these elements in isolation but to consider how they contribute to our understanding of **character, tone,** and **theme.**

Collection Resources

Related Works

Consider teaching one of the works below from *Elements of Literature* with "The Leap."

Analyzing flashback:
"Night Calls" by Lisa Fugard

Analyzing foreshadowing (prolepsis):
"R.M.S. Titanic" by Hanson W. Baldwin

Close Reading

Metacognitive Strategy: Reading Journals

Students might be confused by the use of **flashback** in the story. Have students copy into the left-hand columns of their readers' logs sentences that introduce temporal "leaps" backward. Ask students to write answers to the following questions in the right-hand column:

- How does the author alert us that the story is shifting into the past?

- Does the author attempt to make the flashback understandable or logical? How does she do so?

- Do you find the time change confusing? Why or why not?

Close-Reading Practice: Foreshadowing

Have students re-read the sixth paragraph of the story. Then, discuss these questions to analyze Erdrich's use of foreshadowing:

- What detail tells you that Harold Avalon's death is imminent? What is the effect of this detail? *[The narrator quotes a newspaper article that says that the Avalons' lips were "destined never again to meet." Erdrich uses the image of kissing lips symbolically; the image helps convey the couple's love, their passion for taking risks (kissing in midair), and the sense of loss following Harry's death.]*

- What sounds foreshadow events to come? What tone do these sounds help create? *[The howling wind, the "rumble of electrical energy," and the "sudden roll of drums" foreshadow the oncoming, powerful storm and Harry's fall. These details establish a suspenseful, threatening tone.]*

Vocabulary: Antonyms

Erdrich employs many powerful descriptive words in the story's lengthy **flashbacks**. By reviewing the antonyms of these potent words, students can think analytically about the word choices Erdrich makes.

Activity. In her long flashback to the fire, the narrator uses the words in the margin. Have students discuss or write down the antonym of each word and consider the context in which each word appears. Finally, have them write a few sentences explaining why the author chose the word and not its antonym. Ask them to analyze how each word contributes to the flashback and tone of the story.

*[Sample responses: **Gutted** has the antonym restored. In this context, gutted means "destroyed." The author chose this word to emphasize the disastrous nature of the fire. Gutted communicates the dire nature of the flashback's events and creates an ominous tone. **Massive** has the antonym tiny. In this context, massive means "huge." The author chose this word to portray the gargantuan tree. Massive is an exaggerated word that contributes to Anna's almost mythic feat and the scene's dramatic tone. **Vigorous** has the antonym lifeless. In this context, vigorous means "full of life." The author chose this word to imply that the tree is full of*

Resources

For information on **reading journals** and other metacognitive strategies, see page 16 of this book.

Close Reading

The close-reading passage is on page 44 of the Student Edition.

Vocabulary

Before assigning this activity, make sure your students have mastered the Vocabulary words on page 41 of the Student Edition.

Words for the Activity

gutted, p. 47

massive, p. 48

vigorous, p. 48

ascended, p. 48

looming, p. 48

Collection Resources

life; like the narrator's mother, who leaps from it, the tree helps to save a life. Vigorous *contributes to the flashback's dramatic tone.* **Ascended** *has the antonym* descended. *In this context,* ascended *means "rose." The author chose this word to describe the narrator's mother racing up the ladder.* Ascended *contributes to the flashback's mythic quality by making the mother appear supernaturally strong; it also supports the tone of exaltation.* **Looming** *has the antonym* receding. *In this context,* looming *means "coming forward." The author may have chosen this word to connect the watching crowd with a demanding audience.* Looming *contributes to the dramatic language of the flashback and its magical tone.]*

Postreading

Discussion Method: Reading Conference

Have students discuss the story's use of **flashbacks** in a reading conference. Ask them to prepare for the conference by drafting a time line of the story's events. In groups, have them finalize their time lines and discuss why Erdrich reveals events out of order. Use the following questions to prompt students' thinking:

- The narrator "sees" the past for her mother. How does her mother's blindness—and her reluctance to discuss the past—make the story's structure necessary? *[The author uses flashback to reconstruct the narrator's mother's past because the narrator's mother wouldn't otherwise reveal it. To deepen readers' understanding of the narrator and her mother, the author also uses flashback as a parallel device, disclosing the speaker's own past.]*

- How do the "leaps" of flashback support the story's tone and theme? *[The leaps underscore the physical leap taken by the mother, the leap of imagination implicit in the mother's reading, and the leap to save the narrator. They also support the reverential tone and theme.]*

Writing

Have students write a short story that responds to the prompt below.

> **Flashbacks** and **foreshadowing (prolepsis)** are techniques authors use to sustain interest and create suspense. Write a short story that uses both flashbacks and foreshadowing to convey the story's events and reveal information about its characters. Make an outline of your plot before you begin writing, and be sure to develop character, tone, and theme. Use fresh images to make your story come alive.

Resources

For information on **reading conferences** and other discussion methods, see page 20 of this book.

Collection Resources

Criteria for Success

A successful response
- creatively uses flashbacks and foreshadowing
- shows insight into character, tone, and theme
- incorporates fresh images
- uses language effectively

Elements of Literature selection

The Pedestrian
by Ray Bradbury

SKILLS FOCUS

Literary Skill
Analyze setting and mood.

Advanced Skill
Analyze science fiction.

As students explore **setting** and **mood** and **science fiction,** remind them not to look at these elements in isolation but to consider how they contribute to our understanding of **character, tone,** and **theme.**

Collection Resources

Related Works

Consider teaching one of the works below from *Elements of Literature* with "The Pedestrian."

Analyzing setting and mood:
"Where Have You Gone, Charming Billy?" by Tim O'Brien

Analyzing science fiction:
· "All Watched Over by Machines of Loving Grace" by Richard Brautigan

Literary Focus

The coverage of **setting** and **mood** below builds on the instruction in the Student Edition. You may want to introduce the additional skill of analyzing the genre of **science fiction** when teaching this story to advanced students.

Setting and Mood

The **mood,** or atmosphere, of "The Pedestrian" is gloomy and apocalyptic; the story often alludes to physical, spiritual, and intellectual death. The tale's setting supports this mood; the story takes place on an evening in November, the month before the year's end. Leonard Mead travels in a "westerly direction," or toward the setting sun. Dozens of details refer to death, tombs, graveyards, and darkness (a leaf, for example, bears a "skeletal pattern"). The television-obsessed people in their "tomblike houses" are "dead," and Mead ends up in a "little black jail." Discuss with students other examples of funereal images and allusions. Ask them to consider how those descriptions contribute to the story's dark theme and pessimistic tone.

Author Focus. Much of Ray Bradbury's work features a bleak mood or atmosphere that complements his investigation of how technology mechanizes and dehumanizes his characters. Television is sometimes a central villain. In his novel *Fahrenheit 451,* for instance, the character Mildred—like the anonymous neighbors in "The Pedestrian"— watches television almost constantly, resembles a corpse, and lives in a house like a "mausoleum." Bradbury himself fears such a fate. A genuine technophobe, he refuses to drive a car or use a computer.

Science Fiction

Science fiction is frequently confused with fantasy literature. Isaac Asimov provided perhaps the best distinction between the two genres: Science fiction is possible; fantasy is not. To clarify that distinction, ask students to explore differences between the *Star Trek* and *Lord of the Rings* movies.

Science fiction is a complex genre that includes a host of subgenres, ranging from space opera to cyberpunk. Ask students to identify subjects of science fiction in "The Pedestrian," such as artificial intelligence, technology run amuck, overpopulation, a bleak future, dehumanization, and persecution of nonconformity.

Close Reading

Metacognitive Strategy: Ladder of Questions

Have students work as a class or in groups to paraphrase the story. Then, have them analyze **setting,** including **mood,** by answering the following questions:

Literal Questions

1. Where does Mead walk? Which details establish the mood of the scene?

2. How are other people described? What tone is used? Why?

Interpretive Questions

1. What is the mood when Mead is captured? Support your answer with examples from the text. Why do you think Bradbury chose that mood?

2. How are sounds incorporated into the setting? Analyze how these sounds contribute to the theme of the story.

Experiential Questions

1. Is Bradbury's pessimism about humanity justified? Why or why not?

2. Have you ever felt your humanity crushed by technology? Explain.

Close-Reading Practice: Science Fiction

Have students re-read the passage from "Your name?" to "For what?" Then, discuss answers to these questions to explore characteristics of **science fiction:**

- How does Bradbury describe the police car's voice? How is the description characteristic of science fiction? *[The voice is a "metallic whisper" that sounds as if it is "talking to itself." It is also a "phonograph voice, hissing." The voice, which ordinarily would come from a human police officer, sounds as if it is produced by a computer. Fear of human displacement by technology is a topic characteristic of science fiction writing.]*

- How does the police car respond to the information that Mead is a writer? How does that response support the story's theme? How is that response characteristic of science fiction? *[The police car ignores Mead's creative job because it is no longer relevant in a purely technological society. Apparently, human beings have become so mechanistic that literature is not necessary. This concern for technological impact often surfaces in science fiction writing.]*

Vocabulary: Connotation

When Bradbury describes the sidewalk as "buckling" from lack of repair, he shows how ordinary human activities, such as walking, have vanished from the **setting.** He also establishes an atmosphere of decay. Thinking critically about Bradbury's word choices can give students insight into setting and **mood.**

Resources

For information on **ladders of questions** and other metacognitive strategies, see page 16 of this book.

Close Reading

The close-reading passage is on page 60 of the Student Edition.

Vocabulary

Before assigning this activity, make sure your students have mastered the Vocabulary words on page 56 of the Student Edition.

Collection Resources

Words for the Activity

tomblike, p. 57

squads, p. 59

scarab, p. 59

lone, p. 59

riverbed, p. 61

Collection Resources

Activity. Bradbury uses the words in the margin as he describes the story's setting. Have students discuss or write down the connotations of each word, consider the context in which each word appears, and explain how each word contributes to the story's mood.

[Sample responses: **Tomblike** *connotes the stillness of death; in this context, it creates a somber mood.* **Squads** *connotes militarism, perhaps military rule and ruthless soldiers; in this context, it contributes to an oppressive mood. In Egyptian mythology, the scarab is associated with death. Here,* **scarab** *also connotes the nonhumanity of insects; in this context, it contributes to the story's dark, alienated mood.* **Lone** *connotes solitude; in this context, it supports the ominous and impersonal mood.* **Riverbed** *connotes the regenerative power of flowing water; in this context,* riverbed *is used to describe the street; however, the street is empty, which underscores the lifelessness of the setting, contributing to the pessimistic mood.]*

Postreading
Discussion Method: Fishbowl Discussion

Have students discuss the story's classification as **science fiction** in a fishbowl discussion. Arrange students in inner and outer circles; then, ask the students in the inner circle *one* of the following questions:

- Prepare a list of "clues" in the story that indicate that the story falls into the genre of science fiction. How do these clues also support theme and tone? *[The setting is a barren suburban or urban landscape populated by housebound zombies. Mead's sole interaction is with a machine. These and other elements are typical of science fiction. They also support the theme that alienation from nature and the arts may lead to humanity's downfall; they also provide a foundation for the story's pessimistic tone.]*

- Could the story be told effectively in any other genre? Why or why not? *[Responses will vary, but students should present and support their arguments with detailed examples.]*

After students trade seats, ask a question suggested by responses to the first question, or ask a different question from the list above.

Writing

Have students respond to the prompt below in an essay.

> Bradbury clearly considers literature to be an essential part of civilization. Do you think the story convincingly supports his position? Why or why not? Consider **setting, mood,** character, tone, and theme as you formulate an opinion. Then, write a persuasive essay in which you analyze and evaluate the story's case for a literate society. Use details and examples to support your points.

Resources

For information on **fishbowl discussions** and other discussion methods, see page 20 of this book.

Link to Media

A prolific writer, Ray Bradbury wrote screenplays for a number of classic science fiction films. Invite students to watch videos of some of his more famous films, including *It Came from Outer Space* (1953), *The Beast from 20,000 Fathoms* (1953), and *Something Wicked This Way Comes* (1983). Have students note **mood, setting,** and **science fiction** elements in the films.

Criteria for Success

A successful response

- states persuasive reasons for the student's choice
- supports the choice with apt examples
- shows insight into setting, mood or atmosphere, theme, character, and tone
- uses language effectively

Section I: Multiple-Choice Questions

Directions: Carefully read the following excerpt from "My Daily Dives in the Dumpster®" by Lars Eighner. Then, choose the *best* answer to each question.

from "My Daily Dives in the Dumpster®"

I began scavenging by pulling pizzas out of the Dumpster behind a pizza delivery shop. In general, prepared food requires caution, but in this case I knew what time the shop
5   closed and went to the Dumpster as soon as the last of the help left.

Because the workers at these places are usually inexperienced, pizzas are often made with the wrong topping, baked incorrectly,
10 or refused on delivery for being cold. The products to be discarded are boxed up because inventory is kept by counting boxes: A boxed pizza can be written off; an unboxed pizza does not exist. So I had a steady sup-
15 ply of fresh, sometimes warm pizza.

The area I frequent is inhabited by many affluent[1] college students. I am not here by chance; the Dumpsters are very rich. Students throw out many good things, in-
20 cluding food, particularly at the end of the semester and before and after breaks. I find it advantageous to keep an eye on the academic calendar.

A typical discard is a half jar of peanut
25 butter—though non-organic peanut butter does not require refrigeration and is unlikely to spoil in any reasonable time. Occasionally I find a cheese with a spot of mold, which, of course, I just pare off, and
30 because it is obvious why the cheese was discarded, I treat it with less suspicion than an apparently perfect cheese found in similar circumstances. One of my favorite finds

is yogurt—often discarded, still sealed, when
35 the expiration date has passed—because it will keep for several days, even in warm weather.

I avoid ethnic foods I am unfamiliar with. If I do not know what it is supposed to
40 look or smell like when it is good, I cannot be certain I will be able to tell if it is bad.

No matter how careful I am I still get dysentery[2] at least once a month, oftener in warm weather. I do not want to paint too
45 romantic a picture. Dumpster diving has serious drawbacks as a way of life.

Though I have a proprietary feeling[3] about my Dumpsters, I don't mind my direct competitors, other scavengers, as much
50 as I hate the soda-can scroungers.[4]

I have tried scrounging aluminum cans with an able-bodied companion, and afoot we could make no more than a few dollars a day. I can extract the necessities of life from
55 the Dumpsters directly with far less effort than would be required to accumulate the equivalent value in aluminum. Can scroungers, then, are people who *must* have small amounts of cash—mostly drug ad-
60 dicts and winos.

I do not begrudge them the cans, but can scroungers tend to tear up the Dumpsters, littering the area and mixing the contents. There are precious few courtesies among
65 scavengers, but it is a common practice to

---

[1] **affluent** *adj.:* wealthy.
[2] **dysentery** *n.:* illness that affects the intestines and causes diarrhea and abdominal pain.
[3] **proprietary feeling:** a sense of ownership.
[4] **scroungers** *n.:* people who hunt for free goods or materials.

Collection Resources

set aside surplus items: pairs of shoes, clothing, canned goods, and such. A true scavenger hates to see good stuff go to waste, and what he cannot use he leaves in good condition in plain sight. Can scroungers lay waste to everything in their path and will stir one of a pair of good shoes to the bottom of a Dumpster to be lost or ruined in the muck. They become so specialized that they can see only cans and earn my contempt by passing up change, canned goods, and readily hockable items.

Can scroungers will even go through individual garbage cans, something I have never seen a scavenger do. Going through individual garbage cans without spreading litter is almost impossible, and litter is likely to reduce the public's tolerance of scavenging. But my strongest reservation about going through individual garbage cans is that this seems to me a very personal kind of invasion, one to which I would object if I were a homeowner. . . .

Dumpster diving is outdoor work, often surprisingly pleasant. It is not entirely predictable: things of interest turn up every day, and some days there are finds of great value. I am always very pleased when I can turn up exactly the thing I most wanted to find. Yet in spite of the element of chance, scavenging, more than most other pursuits, tends to yield returns in some proportion to the effort and intelligence brought to bear.

I think of scavenging as a modern form of self-reliance. After ten years of government service, where everything is geared to the lowest common denominator, I find work that rewards initiative[5] and effort refreshing. Certainly I would be happy to have a sinecure[6] again, but I am not heartbroken to be without one.

I find from the experience of scavenging two rather deep lessons. The first is to take what I can use and let the rest go. I have come to think that there is no value in the abstract. A thing I cannot use or make useful, perhaps by trading, has no value, however fine or rare it may be. (I mean useful in the broad sense—some art, for example, I would think valuable.)

The second lesson is the transience[7] of material being. I do not suppose that ideas are immortal, but certainly they are longer-lived than material objects.

The things I find in Dumpsters, the love letters and rag dolls of so many lives, remind me of this lesson. Many times in my travels I have lost everything but the clothes on my back. Now I hardly pick up a thing without envisioning the time I will cast it away. This, I think, is a healthy state of mind. Almost everything I have now has already been cast out at least once, proving that what I own is valueless to someone.

I find that my desire to grab for the gaudy bauble has been largely sated.[8] I think this is an attitude I share with the very wealthy—we both know there is plenty more where whatever we have came from. Between us are the rat-race millions who have confounded their selves with the objects they grasp and who nightly scavenge the cable channels looking for they know not what.

I am sorry for them.

Excerpts from "My Daily Dives in the Dumpster" from *Travels with Lizbeth: Three Years on the Road and on the Streets* by Lars Eighner. Copyright © 1993 by Lars Eighner. Reproduced by permission of **St. Martin's Press, LLC.**

[5] **initiative** *n.:* enterprise.
[6] **sinecure** *n.:* job requiring little or no work.
[7] **transience** *n.:* quality of being temporary or impermanent.
[8] **sated** *v.:* satisfied.

1. The function of the first three paragraphs (lines 1–23) is to
   (A) set up an extended analogy
   (B) re-create a moment from the author's past
   (C) create a sense of time and place
   (D) establish the author's argument
   (E) describe the author's daily experience

2. The central contrast in paragraphs 8–10 (lines 51–88) is that between the
   (A) materialism of the wealthy and the poverty of the scavengers
   (B) goals of Dumpster divers and the goals of can scroungers
   (C) opinion of the public and the needs of homeless people
   (D) desires of homeowners and the actions of can scroungers
   (E) contents of individual trash cans and the contents of shared trash bins

3. Which statement best paraphrases a dumpster diver's philosophy, according to the author?
   (A) Never let anything go to waste.
   (B) Don't eat ethnic food.
   (C) Take everything you can carry.
   (D) Take only cans and leave the rest.
   (E) Show respect for homeowners.

4. The central idea of paragraphs 11 and 12 (lines 89–106) is that
   (A) scavengers often find valuable objects
   (B) many jobs do not require much work
   (C) scavenging rewards hard work and thought
   (D) not having a regular job depressed the writer
   (E) some jobs give small rewards for hard work

5. In lines 120–121, the "love letters and rag dolls" symbolize
   (A) essentials for a homeless person
   (B) things that can scroungers hate
   (C) the author's sensitive character
   (D) the temporary nature of existence
   (E) the wasteful behavior of most people

6. The phrase "gaudy bauble" (line 131) is an example of
   (A) asyndeton
   (B) allusion
   (C) alliteration
   (D) assonance
   (E) analogy

7. The word "rat-race" (line 135) is an allusion to
   (A) laboratory animals
   (B) reckless consumer spending
   (C) the lives of the rich and famous
   (D) competition in the working world
   (E) urban wildlife

8. What is the antecedent of "them" in line 140?
   (A) "gaudy bauble" (line 131)
   (B) "very wealthy" (lines 132–133)
   (C) "rat-race millions" (line 135)
   (D) "objects they grasp" (lines 136–137)
   (E) "cable channels" (line 138)

9. The reader can infer from the conclusion of the passage that
   (A) modern society is destined for collapse
   (B) television is overrated
   (C) life on the streets is competitive
   (D) homelessness is a terrible condition
   (E) the author rejects materialistic values

10. The tone of the passage as a whole is best described as
    (A) intensely sincere
    (B) determinedly objective
    (C) hopelessly pedantic
    (D) frankly philosophical
    (E) deeply ironic

For information about how to analyze a **writing prompt** and other strategies for timed writing, see page 45 of this book.

Section II: Essay

Directions: Read the following prompt carefully. Then, present your response in a well-developed essay.

> Homelessness and joblessness prompted Eighner to develop his own philosophy about meeting one's needs and enjoying personal freedom. At one point he explains, "I think of scavenging as a modern form of self-reliance" (lines 99–100). What are the implications of Eighner's observation about the relationship between living on the street and self-reliance? Consider how free and self-supporting Eighner is compared to people with homes and jobs. Then, write a carefully reasoned essay that explores the validity of Eighner's assertion. Use examples from your reading, observations, or experiences to develop your position.

Scoring Guidelines

9–8 These essays fully explore the validity and reasoning behind Eighner's assertion. They present coherent, well-reasoned arguments about the relationship between self-reliance and life as a homeless person. They support their arguments with comprehensive evidence from the passage and from personal observations or experiences. The students exhibit a sophisticated control of language.

7–6 These essays adequately evaluate the validity of Eighner's assertion. They present sound arguments and make insightful observations using appropriate evidence but may be less thorough, perceptive, or specific than essays in the 9–8 range. The students' prose is clear but may contain a few errors in diction or syntax.

5 These essays acknowledge the validity and drawbacks of Eighner's assertion and make clear claims, but their arguments may be unevenly developed or may contain limited or incorrect evidence. The students' control of language is adequate.

4–3 These essays present an inadequate response to the prompt. The students may misunderstand Eighner's assertion or may have difficulty establishing their own position and use inappropriate or insufficient evidence. The students demonstrate an inconsistent control over such elements of writing as diction and syntax.

2–1 These essays do not successfully respond to the prompt. The students may fail to understand the prompt, respond tangentially, or substitute a simpler task, such as merely summarizing Eighner's position. The students' prose reveals consistent weaknesses in such elements of writing as organization, grammar, and diction.

0 These essays present a response that receives no credit. They may simply paraphrase the prompt, for example.

Sample Response

The following essay represents a high-scoring response to the writing prompt.

In the passage from "My Daily Dives in the Dumpster," author Lars Eighner claims that he is self-reliant because he satisfies his needs by taking things that other people have thrown away. By invoking the mantra "self-reliance," Eighner implies that his lifestyle includes the traditional American values of personal freedom, independence, and initiative. There are contradictions in his philosophy, though, because he actually relies on others and could not maintain his lifestyle without their help.

Eighner claims that he has more freedom than most people, implicitly comparing his life to that of pioneers. He says, "I think of scavenging as a modern form of self-reliance." However, Eighner's form of personal freedom mainly shows freedom from a sense of civic responsibility. He does not hold a paying job, and he does not support a family, a sharp contrast to the traditional pioneers who worked to expand the nation and to create better lives for their families. Eighner speaks disparagingly of "the rat-race millions" who work for a living, and he ends the passage by saying that he feels "sorry for them." He contrasts his own freedom with their lack of freedom and their mindless quest for material things. Yet he admits that his lifestyle carries dangerous hazards, not the least of which is illness, the dysentery he suffers "at least once a month." Readers may not agree that a life that is dependent upon the excesses of others and that exposes Eighner to illness is "free."

Because he searches through garbage looking for what he needs, Eighner considers himself to be independent. Like an early American pioneer, he perceives a world full of possibilities and endless resources. However, instead of the land and natural resources used by pioneers, a trash bin full of food, clothes, and other supplies will provide for Eighner's needs. He is living on the fringes of urban society, and he is dependent upon numerous people. He knows that "there is plenty more where whatever we have came from" only because other people are spending money on things they don't want or need. While he need not meet the expectations of society, he is still, as he concedes, dependent upon at least the tolerance of that society. He worries that the irresponsible behavior of can scavengers might lead to restrictions on his own access to trash and garbage. What happens to Eighner's independence if the city imposes restrictions or he becomes seriously ill? He will become dependent upon resources or health services supplied by "the rat-race millions." Eighner scavenges in times of abundance and makes no provision for times of trouble. Eighner's lack of planning may burden society when he eventually becomes too frail, injured, or ill to scavenge.

Scavenging, Eighner says, "rewards initiative." The harder and smarter a scavenger works, the greater the chance that he or she will find good food and usable supplies. In that respect, Eighner's efforts echo those of the pioneers. However, pioneers were motivated by the belief that they were building new and better lives for their families, not to mention a new and better nation. Eighner, in contrast, is working to support only himself, and he does only what is necessary to survive. Eighner's sense of initiative ignores necessary long-term planning to provide for natural disasters, injuries, and illness—crises suffered by many individuals and their communities.

Eighner may feel free from the responsibilities that burden people and families who struggle to get by, but he is still part of urban society. He relies on the resources available to him only because other people are out there working, consuming, and building. His personal freedom, independence, and initiative are dependent upon not only the material excesses of others but also their tolerance and eventual support. He may be performing a public service by using castoff items, but his definition of self-reliance would be unrecognizable to most pioneers.

Everyday Use
by Alice Walker

Literary Skill
Analyze character traits.

Advanced Skill
Analyze historical influences.

As students explore **character traits** and **historical influences,** remind them not to look at these elements in isolation but to consider how they contribute to our understanding of **character, tone,** and **theme.**

Related Works

Consider teaching one of the works below from *Elements of Literature* with "Everyday Use."

Analyzing character traits:
"Two Kinds" by Amy Tan

Analyzing historical influences:
from "Hands: For Mother's Day" by Nikki Giovanni

Literary Focus

The coverage of **character traits** below builds on the instruction in the Student Edition. You may want to introduce the additional skill of analyzing **historical influences** when teaching this story to advanced students.

Character Traits

The characters in "Everyday Use" are fully drawn, and some literary critics consider the story to be Alice Walker's best. Using both direct and indirect characterization, Walker creates a dense patchwork of **character traits.** Walker's descriptions of characters' appearances, mannerisms, gestures, actions, emotions, histories, and relationships with setting reveal an abundance of distinct traits. Still, Walker's dialogue may be her most effective technique for breathing life into her characters. The story's dialogue and its related tags avoid overt authorial intrusion, thus allowing readers to analyze the characters with seeming objectivity. Use the story to help students analyze how Walker "stitches" together character traits and dialogue, achieving a cohesive "quilt" that displays characters as individuals who reside together within a shared familial and historical context.

Author Focus. The **character traits** presented in "Everyday Use" are replete with parallels to Alice Walker's life. Walker was raised in a setting similar to that of the story—a dilapidated shack in the Deep South. Her mother and father were sharecroppers; racial segregation was legal (and enforced). Like Maggie, Walker was physically scarred (the result of a gunshot wound) and shy, and like Dee, Walker went away to a prestigious college.

Historical Influences

The **historical influences** that shape Walker's story are also quiltlike. As with the African American experience of piecing together lost elements of personal and cultural history, creating a quilt involves cobbling together diverse fragments of material in order to create something new and relevant. The story's central conflict reflects the tensions that naturally arise in the impulse to reclaim an abstract historical and intellectual heritage without losing contact with an immediate, personal history and context.

Close Reading

Metacognitive Strategy: Thinking Notes

As students read, have them annotate with **thinking notes,** focusing on **character traits** and **dialogue.** To help students identify character traits, remind them of the many ways that authors reveal character. You might also review an excerpt of the story's dialogue, pointing out how diction helps reveal traits of character. Have students annotate with thinking notes, marking instances in which dialogue reveals that

- the character is sad
- the character is happy
- the character is angry
- the character is frightened
- the character is worried
- the character is proud

Close-Reading Practice: Character Traits

Have students re-read the passage beginning with "Can I have these old quilts?" and ending with "thing you *could* do with quilts." Then, discuss answers to the following questions to explore **character traits** in the story:

- What does Mama's observation that "these old things was just done by me and Big Dee from some tops your grandma pieced before she died" indicate about her character? *[Mama's observation indicates that she may be astute and somewhat evasive. She casts the quilts in a negative light, hoping that Dee will change her mind, but Mama clearly values the quilts and, having promised them to Maggie, does not want Dee to take them.]*

- What traits of Dee's character emerge when she remarks that Maggie would "probably be backward enough to put them to everyday use"? *[Dee's remark indicates that she feels superior to Maggie and to her own family. Dee considers use of the quilts inappropriate. For Dee, her immediate, living heritage is less worthy of preservation than a static, intellectualized heritage.]*

- How does Maggie's response, "She can have them, Mama . . , I can 'member Grandma Dee without the quilts," help define Maggie's character? *[Maggie's response emphasizes her sense of personal subordination to her sister, hinting that Maggie may consistently avoid confrontation. Her response also indicates that Maggie, unlike Dee, relies on her memory to participate in her family's heritage; she does not need to adopt an icon in order to feel contact with that heritage.]*

Vocabulary: Historical Influences

Walker uses many details in the story that both establish setting and reveal **historical influences.** Thinking critically about Walker's word choices can give students insight into the world she depicts.

Activity. Walker uses the words in the margin to help establish the story's tone. Have students use a dictionary to define each word in the context of the story. Then, have students write a sentence explaining how the word helps establish context and contributes to characterization.

Resources

For information on **thinking notes** and other metacognitive strategies, see page 16 of this book.

Close Reading

The close-reading passage is on page 108 of the Student Edition.

Collection Resources

Vocabulary

Before assigning this activity, make sure your students have mastered the Vocabulary words on page 102 of the Student Edition.

Words for the Activity
organdy, p. 105
rawhide, p. 105
lye, p. 105
chitlins, p. 107
snuff, p. 109

*[Sample responses: **Organdy** is a thin, stiff, and expensive fabric often used for formal dresses in the past. The narrator provides this detail to indicate Dee's fancy childhood tastes. **Rawhide** is rough, untanned cattle hide. It is used to hold the shutters up because other materials, such as wire, are unaffordable or unavailable. This detail helps convey the resourcefulness and relative poverty of Maggie and her mother. **Lye** is a chemical solution used to make soap. The detail indicates that Mama is wary of Dee's caustic sense of humor. **Chitlins** are pigs' small intestines. Poverty encouraged people to use and eat every scrap of a pig. Dee's delight with chitlins and the rest of the food indicates that she is making a showy point of appreciating the kinds of food her family regularly eats. **Snuff** is powdered tobacco. In the rural South, snuff has been a low-cost indulgence; Maggie's use of snuff is a detail that helps establish her economic and social status.]*

Resources

For information on **timed discussions** and other discussion methods, see page 20 of this book.

Postreading

Discussion Method: Timed Discussion

Explain to students that Walker uses **character traits** and **dialogue** to explore the negative aspects of misusing language. Blustery Dee, for instance, prefers even inappropriate language over silence. Organize students into groups of five. Ask them to discuss the interplay between **character traits** and **dialogue** in the story. Then, have one student from each group provide timed responses to the following questions:

- How would you describe Dee's dialogue? How does it reflect her character traits? *[Dee's dialogue is usually aggressive, prideful, self-important, oppressive, and dismissive. It is similar to her character traits—she wears "loud" clothes, ignores others' remarks, etc.]*

- In the climactic scene, the narrator expresses herself by rejecting dialogue in favor of action. Why do you think she makes that choice? *[Mama is rejecting dialogue because Dee has misused it so terribly. She snatches the quilts and gives them to Maggie as a silent but eloquent expression of her faith in "everyday use" and honesty.]*

Writing

Have students write an essay responding to the prompt below.

Criteria for Success

A successful response
- states persuasive reasons for the student's analysis of fire imagery and characterization
- supports the reasons with apt examples
- shows insight into theme, character, and tone
- uses language effectively

> Mama often uses words associated with fire to describe Dee. How do those associations help establish Dee's character? Consider **historical influences, character traits,** tone, and theme as you gather evidence for your views. Then, write an essay in which you explain how fire imagery helps characterize Dee.

Elements of Literature selection

Two Kinds
by Amy Tan

Literary Focus

The coverage of **conflict** and **motivation** below builds on the instruction in the Student Edition. You may want to introduce the additional skill of analyzing **symbols** when teaching this story to advanced students.

Conflict and Motivation

Conflict in a story causes characters to take action, to reflect on their situation, and to grow. Without conflict, characters would have little motivation. "Two Kinds" is replete with conflict. The story's most evident conflicts are between the mother and daughter (the external conflict) and between the daughter and herself (the internal conflict). Yet other conflicts are also at work. Both mother and daughter experience conflict with Auntie Lindo as well as with the culture of the United States. Use the story to show students how the characters' internal and external conflicts contribute to the story's theme.

Author Focus. Tan's stories and novels often return to the theme of cultural and familial conflicts. Her characters' conflicts reflect situations she herself experienced—struggles to integrate Chinese and American values, to be a good daughter yet true to herself, and to express herself while honoring her heritage.

Symbol

A **symbol** is a person, place, thing, or event that stands for both itself and for something beyond itself. In literature, a writer develops symbols that are specific to the story. Objects, actions, and words take on meanings beyond the literal. Point out that in "Two Kinds," the movie icon Shirley Temple, the narrator's piano, the recital, and the mother's twin babies all serve as symbols. Explain that these people, events, and objects develop special meanings and significance over the course of the story and come to stand for something beyond themselves.

Close Reading

Metacognitive Strategy: Ladder of Questions

To help students identify and analyze the internal and external conflicts in "Two Kinds," encourage them to ask literal, interpretive, and

Literary Skill
Analyze conflict and motivation.

Advanced Skill
Analyze symbols.

As students explore **conflict, motivation,** and **symbol,** remind them not to look at these elements in isolation but to consider how they contribute to our understanding of **character, plot, tone,** and **theme.**

Collection Resources

Related Works

Consider teaching one of the works below from *Elements of Literature* with "Two Kinds."
Analyzing conflict:
"The Bass, the River, and Sheila Mant" by W. D. Wetherell
Analyzing motivation:
"The Tale of Sir Launcelot du Lake" by Sir Thomas Malory, retold by Keith Baines
Analyzing symbols:
"Stopping by Woods on a Snowy Evening" by Robert Frost

Resources

For information on **ladders of questions** and other metacognitive strategies, see page 16 of this book.

experience-based questions. Help students get started by offering them the following questions. Encourage students to write and answer at least three more questions of each type on their own.

- **Literal:** Why does the mother believe her daughter can be a prodigy? *[She believes that in the United States a person can be anything he or she wants.]*

- **Interpretive:** Do you think the narrator deliberately plays badly during her piano lessons? *[I think she deliberately plays badly to prove that no one can make her play the piano against her will.]*

- **Experience-based:** What is the most valuable skill you have? Is that skill the result of talent, of determination, or of a combination of the two? *[Students may relate skills and report opinions about the relationship of talent and determination to developing those skills.]*

Close-Reading Practice: Conflict

Have students re-read the passage near the end of the story, from "I assumed my talent-show fiasco" to "thin, brittle, lifeless." Then, discuss these questions to explore Tan's use of internal and external conflict:

- What does the narrator's remark that "this wasn't China" reveal about her conflict with her mother? *[The remark reveals that their conflict represents more than a dispute between parent and child; the conflict between Jing-mei and her mother also represents a clash of cultures: Jing-mei rejects the cultural assumption that she should obediently fulfill her mother's wishes.]*

- What similes does Tan use to describe how Jing-mei feels as she disobeys her mother? How do the similes explain her long delay in confronting her mother? *[After her outbursts, Jing-mei feels "as if my true self had emerged" and says that her words felt "like worms and toads and slimy things crawling out of my chest." The similes reveal that she has had to overcome internal constraints and guilt; although she desires autonomy and freedom from her mother's perfectionist demands, the confrontation reveals an "awful side" of her, a powerful, personally repugnant, yet desirable self.]*

- What figurative language describes the mother's reaction to Jing-mei's shout "I wish I were dead! Like them!"? What does this language tell you about the conflict between Jing-mei and her mother? *[Several similes describe the reaction: It is abrupt, "as if I had said the magic words." The mother, shocked, backs away "as if she were blowing away" "like a small brown leaf, thin, brittle, lifeless." The mother is compared to the victim of a spell and to a dead leaf; clearly Jing-mei has crossed a significant line and hurt her mother deeply.]*

Vocabulary: Connotation

The author chooses her words carefully to build scenes fueled by **internal** and **external conflict.** Tan often uses words that convey sensory

Close Reading

The close-reading passage is on page 132 of the Student Edition.

Vocabulary

Before assigning this activity, make sure your students have mastered the Vocabulary words on page 124 of the Student Edition.

experience. Thinking critically about Tan's word choices can give students insight into the conflicts her characters experience.

Activity. Tan uses the words in the margin to reveal the story's conflict. Have students discuss or write down the connotations of each word and decide which of the five senses relates to each word. Finally, have students write a few sentences explaining how each word affects their impression of the narrator's character and point of view.

[Sample responses: **Embraceless** *means "without embrace"; that is, "without holding on to someone." It connotes loneliness and relates to the sense of touch.* **Squabbling** *means "quarreling noisily" and carries a negative connotation. It relates to the sense of hearing.* **Squawked** *means "uttered a harsh cry." It also has a negative connotation and relates to the sense of hearing.* **Gawkers** *means "those who stare stupidly or rudely." The word has a negative connotation and relates to the sense of sight.* **Shrilly** *means "in a high-pitched and annoying manner." It has a negative connotation and relates to the sense of hearing. The words' negative connotations help the narrator convey the sense of unhappiness she felt during this time in her life.]*

Postreading

Discussion Method: Reading Conference

Have students discuss the **symbol** of the piano in a reading conference. Ask them to prepare for the conference by re-reading the sections of the story in which the piano appears. Ask students to draw conclusions about what the piano means for both the mother and the daughter. Use the following questions to prompt students' thinking:

- What does the piano symbolize for the narrator's mother? *[It is a symbol of her daughter's potential talent. It is also a symbol of her own pride and of how hard she worked to save money to buy it.]*

- What does the piano symbolize for the daughter, first as a child and then as an adult? *[The piano is a symbol of betrayal to her. By playing badly, the narrator betrays her mother's hopes and her own talent. Later, the piano is a symbol not only of her mother's hopes in the United States but also of her own childhood and of beauty.]*

Writing

Have students respond to the prompt below in an essay.

> Identify a person, place, event, or thing (other than the piano) that serves as a **symbol** in the story. In an essay, tell what the symbol means literally and how it takes on symbolic importance in the story. Discuss the characters and their **internal** and **external conflicts** as well as the story's theme in your essay. Use details and examples to support your points.

Words for the Activity

embraceless, p. 128
squabbling, p. 129
squawked, p. 130
gawkers, p. 131
shrilly, p. 132

Collection Resources

Resources

For information on **reading conferences** and other discussion methods see page 20 of this book.

Criteria for Success

A successful response

- identifies a symbol in the story and explains its meaning and significance
- supports the choice with apt examples
- shows insight into character, conflict, and theme
- uses language effectively

Section I: Multiple-Choice Questions

Directions: Carefully read the following poem by Alberto Ríos. Then, choose the *best* answer to each question.

Collection Resources

Nani[1]

Sitting at her table, she serves
the *sopa de arroz*[2] to me
instinctively, and I watch her,
the absolute *mamá*, and eat words
5 I might have had to say more
out of embarrassment. To speak,
now-foreign words I used to speak,
too, dribble down her mouth as she serves
me *albóndigas*.[3] No more
10 than a third are easy to me.
By the stove she does something with
    words
and looks at me only with her
back. I am full. I tell her
I taste the mint, and watch her speak
15 smiles at the stove. All my words
make her smile. Nani never serves
herself, she only watches me
with her skin, her hair. I ask for more.

I watch the *mamá* warming more
20 tortillas for me. I watch her
fingers in the flame for me.
Near her mouth, I see a wrinkle speak
of a man whose body serves
the ants like she serves me, then more
    words
25 from more wrinkles about children, words
about this and that, flowing more
easily from these other mouths. Each
    serves
as a tremendous string around her,
holding her together. They speak
30 Nani was this and that to me
and I wonder just how much of me
will die with her, what were the words
I could have been, was. Her insides speak
through a hundred wrinkles, now, more
35 than she can bear, steel around her,
shouting, then, What is this thing she
    serves?

She asks me if I want more.
I own no words to stop her.
Even before I speak, she serves.

[1] **Nani** (NAH NEE): a term of endearment for a grandmotherly figure.
[2] **sopa de arroz** (SOH pah de ah ROHS): cooked rice that is later steamed.
[3] **albóndigas** (ahl BOHN dee GAHS): spicy meat-balls.

1. In line 4, what does the speaker mean by "eat words"?
   (A) The speaker regrets having said something embarrassing.
   (B) The food is so rich that it inspires the speaker to write a poem.
   (C) The speaker has forgotten most of the Spanish he or she had learned as a child.
   (D) The meal reminds the speaker of a conversation.
   (E) The speaker eats soup instead of saying anything.

2. Which of the following groups of words adds details to show that Nani serves the speaker "instinctively" (lines 1–3)?
   (A) "dribble down her mouth" (line 8)
   (B) "I taste the mint" (line 14)
   (C) "watches me / with her skin, her hair" (lines 17–18)
   (D) "warming more / tortillas for me" (lines 19–20)
   (E) "her / fingers in the flame" (lines 20–21)

3. Nani equates love with which of the following?
   (A) the speaker's poetry
   (B) acts of service
   (C) conversation with friends
   (D) the wisdom of age
   (E) sitting silently together

4. "I see a wrinkle speak" (line 22) is an example of
   (A) simile
   (B) metaphor
   (C) symbolism
   (D) personification
   (E) synecdoche

5. For the speaker, Nani's wrinkles symbolize which of the following?
   (A) life's missed possibilities
   (B) linguistic barriers between the two
   (C) Nani's pride in her ethnicity
   (D) Nani's deceased husband
   (E) children from Nani's past

6. In the lines "They speak / Nani was this and that to me" (lines 29–30), what is the antecedent of "They"?
   (A) mouth (line 22)
   (B) wrinkle (line 22)
   (C) body (line 23)
   (D) ants (line 24)
   (E) words (line 25)

7. In line 38, what words is the speaker unable to say?
   (A) "No more food."
   (B) "Thank you."
   (C) "I love you."
   (D) "Tell me family stories."
   (E) "Sit down and eat."

8. The mood of the final stanza (lines 37–39) is best described as
   (A) scornfully aloof
   (B) helplessly loving
   (C) cruelly callous
   (D) unexpectedly funny
   (E) cheerfully polite

9. Which of the following best describes Nani's character?
   (A) meekly subservient
   (B) quietly suffering
   (C) lovingly officious
   (D) angrily resigned
   (E) determinedly strong

10. Which of the following quotations best illustrates the poem's theme?
    (A) "more / out of embarrassment" (lines 5–6)
    (B) "she does something with words" (line 11)
    (C) "fingers in the flame" (line 21)
    (D) "I wonder just how much of me / will die with her" (lines 31–32)
    (E) "before I speak, she serves" (line 39)

Section II: Essay

Directions: Read the following prompt carefully. Then, present your response in a well-developed essay.

Resources

For information about how to analyze a **writing prompt** and other strategies for timed writing, see page 45 of this book.

In the poem "Nani" by Alberto Ríos, the speaker's feelings about the culture and language of his or her childhood are tied to feelings for Nani, a grandmotherly figure. Notice how the poem's speaker struggles with language and with feelings for Nani. Pay attention to the use of poetic devices such as meter, line endings, diction, images, and repetition. Then, in a well-written essay, analyze two or more of the devices and their role in expressing the theme of the poem.

Scoring Guidelines

9–8   These essays fully explore the relationship between two or more poetic devices and the theme of Ríos's poem. They present coherent, well-written analyses supported by comprehensive evidence. The students exhibit a sophisticated control of language.

7–6   These essays adequately evaluate the relationship between two or more poetic devices and theme in Ríos's poem. They present sound analyses using appropriate evidence, although the analyses may not be as precise, thorough, and accurate as essays in the 9–8 range. The students' prose is clear but may contain a few errors in diction or syntax.

5   These essays acknowledge Ríos's use of poetic devices and theme and make clear claims, but their ideas may be unevenly developed or contain limited evidence. The students' control of language is adequate.

4–3   These essays present an inadequate response to the prompt. The students may incorrectly identify poetic devices or misinterpret the theme of the poem. They may have difficulty establishing a point of view and may use inappropriate or insufficient evidence. The students demonstrate an inconsistent control over such elements of writing as diction and syntax.

2–1   These essays do not successfully respond to the prompt. The students may fail to understand the prompt, respond tangentially, or substitute a simpler task, such as merely summarizing the poem. The students' prose reveals consistent weaknesses in such elements of writing as organization, grammar, and diction.

0   These essays present a response that receives no credit. They may simply paraphrase the prompt, for example.

Sample Response

The following essay represents a high-scoring response to the writing prompt.

The poem "Nani" by Alberto Ríos serves as a loving memorial to a grandmotherly figure. In the poem, repeated key words and the use of images of service indicate that the speaker understands that actions and gestures can express one's feelings as effectively as words can, especially when the feelings are as complicated as those shared by Nani and the speaker.

Because the speaker no longer comfortably speaks Nani's language, neither of them can rely on speech to convey their feelings for each other or to renew their relationship. Their worlds have slipped apart. Instead, the two communicate primarily through action—Nani feeds the speaker without pausing, and the speaker continues to eat, unable to refuse her offers.

At first, as if mimicking the speaker's inability to communicate his or her feelings, no conventional structure is apparent in the poem. Ríos uses no rhyme scheme or regular meter. However, the poet's repetition of words, combined with their placement at the end of lines, reveals a governing structure. Each line ends with one of the following six words: serves, me, words, more, speak, or her. In the poem's thirty-nine lines, her, serves, and more end seven lines; me and speak end six lines, and words ends six lines. Because these key words are repeated at the end of lines, readers are more likely to pay attention to them, noting that the speaker conflates service with language. Together, the words emphasize the poem's events, but more important, the insistent, if not always predictable, repetition hints at the poem's theme: Service communicates love just as effectively as words can. An action, the repetition seems to tell readers, can be as eloquent as the use of words.

Similarly, Ríos's images of Nani serving food to the speaker support the theme. Nani's service is a repeated, insistent and affectionate action overpowering the speaker, leaving him or her unable to speak. Nani "instinctively" serves the speaker rice, rises to warm "more / tortillas," and talks without the speaker's full understanding. As if her full responsibility is to the speaker, she "never serves / herself," puts "her / fingers in the flame," and leads the speaker to "wonder just how much of me / will die with her." The two comfortably share only "a third" of what is spoken aloud, yet they share much more.

The two share a past with which the speaker has lost touch, knowing that "Nani was this and that to me." This past, as the speaker reveals, speaks from each wrinkle on Nani's face as easily as it would from her mouth and relates her personal history. Without relying on words, Nani's wrinkles tell of the loss of a love, "a man whose body serves / the ants like she serves me," and hints at the interrupted relationship with the speaker, "what were the words / I could have been, was." Still, the two love each other. Nani speaks "smiles at the stove," and all of the speaker's words "make her smile." In turn, the speaker, although full, does not refuse the food, noting the taste of mint and owning "no words to stop her." Despite barriers of language, the two effectively communicate their affection for each other.

By repeating key words and developing the image of Nani as she serves love in the form of food, Alberto Ríos shows that actions are at least as effective at expressing love as are words.

Elements of Literature selection

By the Waters of Babylon
by Stephen Vincent Benét

Literary Skill
Analyze first-person point of view. Analyze setting.

Advanced Skill
Analyze allusions.

As students explore **first-person point of view, setting,** and **allusion,** remind them not to look at these elements in isolation but to consider how they contribute to our understanding of **character, tone,** and **theme.**

Collection Resources

Related Works

Consider teaching one of the works below from *Elements of Literature* with "By the Waters of Babylon."

Analyzing first-person point of view:

"From a Lifeboat" by Mrs. D. H. Bishop

"The Leap" by Louise Erdrich

Analyzing setting:

"Where Have You Gone, Charming Billy?" by Tim O'Brien

Analyzing allusion:

"Lamb to the Slaughter" by Roald Dahl

Literary Focus

The coverage of **first-person point of view** and **setting** below builds on the instruction in the Student Edition. You may want to introduce the additional skill of analyzing **allusions** when teaching this story to advanced students.

First-Person Point of View and Setting

Authors sometimes use first-person point of view and setting to engage readers' interest in strange new worlds. In first-person narratives, the author may adopt an identity, or **persona.** This identity allows the author to present the setting through a distinct character's eyes. Stephen Vincent Benét, author of "By the Waters of Babylon," uses an engaging persona to introduce his readers to a bizarre future world. Readers, who are unfamiliar with this world, must trust Benét's persona, John, to guide them and point out significant details. Use the story to show how persona and setting work to immerse readers in a novel place and time.

Allusion

An **allusion**—or reference to a statement, person, place, thing, or event from another text or from history or culture—is effective only when readers are familiar with what is being alluded to. Authors generally trust readers to recognize or to discover the connection between a given allusion and its purpose within a piece of writing. An allusion adds a level of meaning to a work of literature, connecting the work's ideas to a memorable person, place, thing, event, statement, or context. As students read, have them think about how Benét's allusion in the title contributes to the story's meaning.

Author Focus. In part, Stephen Vincent Benét's fascination with history and literature explains the use of allusion in his writing. Much of Benét's poetry and fiction retells past events through the eyes of a firsthand witness. In some cases, Benét updated ancient stories by setting them in more recent times.

Close Reading

Metacognitive Strategy: Thinking Aloud

Ask students to read aloud with partners or in small groups. At the end of each page, students should pause to reflect on the story and to ask and answer questions that will help them clarify the text and appreciate the author's use of **first-person point of view, persona,** and **setting.** Suggest the following questions as a starting point. Encourage students to develop other reflective questions as they read.

- When and where is the narrator now?

- Who is the narrator? What do I know about him?

- What are the narrator's limitations in describing the setting?

Close-Reading Practice: First-Person Point of View and Setting

Have students re-read the passage near the middle of the story from "I do not know the customs" to "Everywhere there are the ruins of the high towers of the gods" and discuss these questions to explore Benét's use of setting and first-person point of view.

- The narrator asserts that he does "not know the customs of rivers" and that he "thought the river meant to take me past the place of the Gods." What do these assertions indicate about his perceived relationship with the setting? *[By personifying the river, the narrator indicates that he perceives the natural setting to have a distinct willfulness. When he grows angry and speaks, he believes that his words have an effect on the setting: "The current changed itself."]*

- What is the effect of John's report that "it felt like ground underfoot; it did not burn me," and that "everywhere in it there are god-roads, though most are cracked and broken"? *[John's report establishes a contrast between the narrator's knowledge of what he sees and the reader's knowledge of the setting. John is puzzled by the things he sees in the ruined city, yet he provides descriptions that savvy readers quickly recognize. For example, readers may infer that the "ground underfoot" had once been burned or contaminated and that "god-roads" are simply highways or sidewalks. To John these aspects of the setting are among the mysteries of the "Place of the Gods."]*

Vocabulary: Context

The author artfully makes the language of the character John sound archaic and strange. Readers will recognize the language as English, but the context and subject matter make it feel unfamiliar.

Activity. As Benét tells the story of John's rediscovery of the ruins of a modern civilization, he uses the words in the margin. Have students discuss the meanings of the words and their context. Finally, have students write a few sentences explaining how each word contributes to the story's tone.

Resources

For information on **thinking aloud** and other metacognitive strategies, see page 16 of this book.

Close Reading

The close-reading passage is on page 179 of the Student Edition.

Vocabulary

Words for the Activity
purification, p. 176
enchantments, p. 179
anteroom, p. 181
tongues, p. 181
company, p. 184

Collection Resources

[Sample responses: **Purification** *usually means "the removal of pollutants"; the word has a religious or ritualistic meaning here; it refers to the cleansing of the narrator's spirit.* **Enchantments** *are things that charm or are charming. The word in this context refers to actual magic spells.* **Anteroom** *has only one meaning: "a room that leads to a larger room." It is an old-fashioned word that is rarely used today.* **Tongues** *has several meanings, including "the organ attached to the floor of the mouth" and "languages." In this context, the meaning is "languages."* **Company** *means "companions," "a group," "a business," "visitors or guests," and "a military unit." The context here suggests the meaning "a military unit." All the words sound old-fashioned, particularly as they are used in the story. Their meanings in the story are not the most modern meanings. The words create an archaic feeling or tone.]*

Postreading

Discussion Method: Literature Circle

Have students discuss the story's **allusions** in a literature circle. Ask them to prepare for the circle by joining groups and selecting roles. Use the following questions to prompt students' discussion:

- The story contains both biblical and modern allusions. How does the title's biblical allusion add to the story? *[The title refers to Psalm 137, which concerns the sorrow of Jews taken captive and exiled to Babylon. The psalm is a lament for Jerusalem, the city from which the Jews were exiled. The title's allusion leads readers to understand that John's people, although apparently happy, are exiles. The allusion, because it refers to a religious text, also helps establish the story's religious tone and vaguely foreshadows John's discovery of "newyork," the ruined city of his ancestors.]*

- Identify at least three modern allusions in the story. To what do they refer? How do they add to the story? *[Modern allusions include a statue marked "ASHING," the gods Lincoln and Biltmore and Moses, and the name newyork. Each alludes to a monument or person important to New York City and the United States. The statue is of George Washington; the Biltmore is a hotel; Lincoln refers to Abraham Lincoln; and Robert Moses was a city planner and builder. The allusions provide readers with clues to the fallen city's identity and suggest that the city was destroyed during the twentieth century.]*

Writing

Have students write an essay responding to the prompt below.

What is the theme of the story "By the Waters of Babylon"? Consider the narrator's **persona** as well as the setting, characters, plot, and tone as you decide on the story's theme. Then, write an essay in which you identify the theme and explain how the other elements in the story support it. Use details and examples to support your points.

Collection Resources

Resources

For information on **literature circles** and other discussion methods, see page 20 of this book.

Criteria for Success

A successful response

- states a theme that is supported by other elements in the story
- uses appropriate textual evidence to develop the analysis of theme
- shows insight into theme, character, and tone
- uses language effectively

Typhoid Fever
by Frank McCourt

Literary Focus

The coverage of **voice, diction,** and **tone** below builds on the instruction in the Student Edition. You may want to introduce the additional skill of analyzing **stream of consciousness** when teaching this narrative to advanced students.

Voice, Diction, and Tone

Diction and **tone** are two elements a writer needs in order to create a unique **voice.** A writer's choice of words (diction) and the attitude he or she reveals to the audience (tone) help forge a voice that sounds like no other. McCourt's voice in "Typhoid Fever" is actually a **persona,** or mask: As an adult, McCourt has assumed the identity of himself as a child, re-creating a voice that reflects the character, experiences, and feelings of his younger self. This voice captures the cadences, or rhythms, and diction of informal speech and dialect as heard through the ears of a child. McCourt's diction and voice help convey a distinct time and place (Ireland in the 1930s) along with young Frank's emotions during his stay in a hospital.

Author Focus. Frank McCourt has said that his Irish childhood was enlivened by the oral sharing of stories, poetry, and songs. As a result, McCourt's writing possesses distinct qualities of speech. In "Typhoid Fever," McCourt's use of a child's voice allows him to tell his story freely and honestly, without imposing direct judgment on the people who were part of his distant but often painful past.

Stream of Consciousness

Stream of consciousness is a technique developed by modern writers to convey the flow of a character's inner experiences, including the flood of impressions, thoughts, feelings, and memories that cycle continuously through a person's mind. Stream-of-consciousness narratives often embrace experimental techniques, distinguishing them from straightforward narratives. For example, "Typhoid Fever" is not constrained by traditional punctuation, such as using quotation marks. The narrative simply moves from each character's dialogue to the narrator's thoughts and back again. This lack of quotation marks helps emphasize the narrator's inner world: Without them, dialogue and impressions seem to flow directly from the narrator's consciousness.

SKILLS FOCUS

Literary Skill
Analyze the writer's voice, diction, and tone.

Advanced Skill
Analyze stream of consciousness.

As students explore **writer's voice, diction, tone,** and **stream of consciousness,** remind them not to look at these elements in isolation but to consider how they contribute to our understanding of **persona** and **theme.**

Collection Resources

Related Works

Consider teaching one of the works below from *Elements of Literature* with "Typhoid Fever."

Analyzing writer's voice and tone:
"Eating Together" by Li-Young Lee

Analyzing diction:
"Geraldo No Last Name" by Sandra Cisneros

Analyzing stream of consciousness:
"Where Have You Gone, Charming Billy" by Tim O'Brien

For information on **reading aloud** and other metacognitive strategies, see page 16 of this book.

Close Reading

The close-reading passage is on pages 228–229 of the Student Edition.

Vocabulary

Before assigning this activity, make sure your students have mastered the Vocabulary words on page 227 of the Student Edition.

Words for the Activity

apparatus, p. 229
desperate, p. 229
huffy, p. 230
blathering, p. 231
twinge, p. 231

Close Reading

Metacognitive Strategy: Reading Aloud

Thanks to its roots in an oral tradition and its emphasis on the speaker's voice and experiences, Frank McCourt's "Typhoid Fever" is an excellent selection for students to read aloud. Ask students to form groups and to take turns reading sections of the narrative. Have them mark the text with cues about how to read aloud. Have them consider the following questions after they complete each section:

• How would you describe the character's tone of voice here?

• What do you notice about the rhythm and volume of Frank's words?

• What words are unfamiliar? What do they mean?

Close-Reading Practice: Stream of Consciousness

One method by which McCourt creates stream-of-consciousness elements in his narrative is to omit quotation marks and tags (such as *he said*) in retelling this episode from his childhood.

Activity. Have students re-read the beginning of the story, from "The room next to me is empty" to "find you talking." Have students consider the effect of the absence of quotation marks by answering the following questions:

• What effect is created by not using conventional punctuation to distinguish speakers? *[Although different characters speak, all the words seem to come directly from the narrator, drawing attention to the fact that the narrative arises from the memory of the narrator. The speaker is remembering conversations, not necessarily quoting the speakers, and his memories are filtered by his adult consciousness.]*

• How would the narrative's impact change if the author were to use standard punctuation? *[The narrative would look more like many other stories or autobiographies. The uniqueness of the speaker's voice might be lost, and readers might lose the sense of immediacy and empathy gained through contact with the speaker's consciousness.]*

Vocabulary: Context

The speaker's voice is a unique mixture of childish and adult language that reflects each of the characters he is recalling. McCourt carefully chooses words to create a tone that is childlike yet mature.

Activity. McCourt uses the words in the margin in recalling a sad time in his life. Have students discuss the context and meanings of each word and use context to classify the word as one an adult or a child might use. Finally, have students explain how each word adds to the speaker's voice.

*[Sample responses: **Apparatus** means "machinery" or "tools," but here it refers to organs in the body. The word is one used by an adult, and it is used euphemistically. **Desperate** has several meanings, but here it means "having little chance for improvement." The word does not sound like a*

word a child would use to describe his or her illness. Again, the speaker uses a word he has heard used by an adult. **Huffy** *means "offended." The speaker uses it to describe Patricia's reaction. It is a term that a child or an adult might use.* **Blathering** *means "nonsensical talk" or "babble." Altlough the word is informal or slangy, the nurse uses it to characterize the speaker's conversation.* **Twinge** *means "pang" or "sudden sharp pain." The word is used by the nurse. The context of the words indicates whether they are originally spoken by children or by adults, but used together, they help create a mixed, childlike yet mature, tone. The words also contribute to the chatty, conversational tone of the selection.]*

Postreading

Discussion Method: Threaded Discussion

Have students discuss the speaker's voice in a threaded discussion. Students should write at least one paragraph in response to the questions below. After each student has posted a response, he or she should respond in writing to another student's ideas.

Resources

For information on **threaded discussions** and other discussion methods, see page 20 of this book.

Collection Resources

- How does the speaker's choice of words reflect the ages, nationality, time, and place of the characters? *[The speaker uses language that reflects the voices of the people who are speaking. For example, Patricia and Seamus speak in a dialect that sometimes drops letters like final g's. The nurse speaks in haughty tones and uses euphemisms. The speaker's own voice becomes clear when he recalls his feelings.]*

- How does McCourt's use of stream of consciousness affect a reader's understanding of the speaker's experiences? *[Students may report that the lack of quotation marks and tags makes it difficult to recognize who is speaking. They may also suggest that the lack of descriptive details makes it difficult to picture the characters. The lack of quotation marks and tags helps speed up the story's pace and reflects the youthful understanding of the narrator. The lack of descriptive detail draws attention to the narrator's isolation and inability to see much of what transpires.]*

Writing

Have students write an essay that responds to the prompt below.

> How effective do you think author Frank McCourt's use of voice is in "Typhoid Fever"? Consider the stylistic and literary elements of **diction, tone, stream of consciousness,** character, and speaker in your evaluation. Then, write an essay in which you explain and support your opinion. Use details and examples to support your points.

Criteria for Success

A successful response
- takes a stand on the effectiveness of the writer's use of voice
- supports the choice with apt examples from the text
- shows insight into voice, diction, speaker, and tone
- uses language effectively

Elements of Literature workshop

Writing Workshop: Analyzing Problems and Solutions

Writing Skill
Write a problem-solution essay.

As students explore **persuasive writing**, remind them that expository writing, like all forms of writing, gains power from attention to literary elements such as **diction, figurative language, tone,** and **voice.**

Resources

For more information on **generalization** and other aspects of **reasoning,** see the Handbook of Rhetorical Concepts in this book.

Resources

For information on **counterarguments,** see the Handbook of Rhetorical Concepts in this book.

Resources

For more information on **phrases** and **clauses,** see the Handbook of Grammatical Concepts in this book.

Collection Resources

Prewriting
Advanced Prewriting Strategy

Build an Argument. Explain to students that their essay's purpose is to suggest and promote future actions. In their arguments, students must demonstrate sound reasoning. **Induction** is one type of sound reasoning. Tell students that inductive reasoning begins with a specific set of facts or observations. After studying those facts or observations, a writer reaches a general conclusion. Induction moves from the specific to the general. Here is an example:

Fact: This year, tenth-graders' grade-point averages fell 5 points.

Fact: This year, more than half of all tenth-graders held part-time jobs.

Fact: The number of tenth-graders with jobs jumped by twenty percent.

Inductive Generalization: Because more tenth-graders are taking part-time jobs, their overall grades are declining.

Writing
Advanced Writing Skills

Addressing Counterclaims. Remind students that an essential part of an effective persuasive essay is the treatment of counterclaims. Explain to students that there are three parts to answering a counterclaim. First, a writer must acknowledge that a counterclaim exists. Next, a writer should consider the validity of the counterclaim. Finally, the writer needs to refute the counterclaim with solid evidence and reasoning.

Activity. To help students consider and disprove counterclaims, have them answer the following questions as they draft their papers:

- What counterclaims could be made against my argument?

- What valid and reasonable points do those counterclaims raise?

- What evidence can I use to prove each counterclaim wrong?

Grammar Solutions. As students begin to think about how to address **counterclaims,** remind them that careful placement of **phrases** and **clauses** is a useful grammatical tool. Phrases and clauses may be used to modify, or describe, a word or word group. If those phrases or clauses are misplaced, they can confuse readers and undermine students' claims and logic. Discuss the following examples:

MISPLACED PHRASE	*Researchers were pleased to see that grade averages had climbed after scanning the reports.*
CORRECT PHRASE PLACEMENT	*After scanning the reports, researchers were pleased to see that grade averages had climbed.*

The grammatical structure of the first sentence suggests that the grade averages scanned the reports, which is not possible. The second sentence correctly places the modifying phrase in front of the word it modifies *(researchers)*. As students draft their essays, remind them to pay attention to the logical placement of modifying phrases and clauses.

Evaluating and Revising
Revising for Style
Using Active Voice. Encourage students to use mostly active voice in their writing and to avoid the unintentional use of passive voice. Active voice is usually stronger because it places emphasis on a sentence's subject and the subject's action. In passive voice, the subject receives the action, de-emphasizing the subject's role in the action. Here are examples of the two voices:

Passive voice: A new policy has been adopted by school administrators.

Active voice: School administrators have adopted a new policy.

Activity. Ask students to read through their essays and to locate examples of passive voice in their writing. Remind them that active voice sounds stronger and more direct and will usually be more persuasive to readers.

Publishing and Reflecting

Exchanging Ideas. To allow students to share their ideas and benefit from their classmates' responses, have students take turns reading their essays aloud. Ask students to offer constructive evaluations and suggestions for improvement. Students should evaluate the strength of arguments or the feasibility of proposed solutions.

Self-Evaluation. Finally, have students reflect on their essays. Instruct them to write responses to the following questions:

- What **generalizations** did you make in your essay? Were they based on inductive reasoning that included solid facts?

- What **counterclaims** did you address? Were you successful in answering them? Why or why not?

- Did you have difficulty in consistently using **active voice**? Why or why not?

Literature Link

Before students begin revising to add active voice, encourage them to re-read Penny Parker's "Double Daddy" or Sue Shellenbarger's "Diary of a Mad Blender" to see how these authors use active voice to convey a sense of strength and action in their writing.

Collection Resources

Section I: Multiple-Choice Questions

Directions: Carefully read the following excerpt from "Tobermory," a short story by Saki. Then, choose the *best* answer to each question.

from "Tobermory"

"And do you really ask us to believe," Sir Wilfrid was saying, "that you have discovered a means for instructing animals in the art of human speech, and that dear old Tobermory
5 has proved your first successful pupil?"

"It is a problem at which I have worked for the last seventeen years," said Mr. Appin, "but only during the last eight or nine months have I been rewarded with glim-
10 merings of success. Of course I have experimented with thousands of animals, but latterly only with cats, those wonderful creatures which have assimilated[1] themselves so marvelously with our civilization while re-
15 taining all their highly developed feral[2] instincts. Here and there among cats one comes across an outstanding superior intellect, just as one does among the ruck[3] of human beings, and when I made the ac-
20 quaintance of Tobermory a week ago I saw at once that I was in contact with a 'Beyond-cat' of extraordinary intelligence. I had gone far along the road to success in recent experiments; with Tobermory, as you call him, I
25 have reached the goal."

Mr. Appin concluded his remarkable statement in a voice which he strove to divest of a triumphant inflection. No one said "Rats," though Clovis's lips moved in a
30 monosyllabic contortion which probably invoked those rodents of disbelief.

"And do you mean to say," asked Miss Resker, after a slight pause, "that you have taught Tobermory to say and understand
35 easy sentences of one syllable?"

"My dear Miss Resker," said the wonder-worker patiently, "one teaches little children and savages and backward adults in that piecemeal fashion; when one has once
40 solved the problem of making a beginning with an animal of highly developed intelligence one has no need for those halting methods. Tobermory can speak our language with perfect correctness."

45 This time Clovis very distinctly said, "Beyond-rats!" Sir Wilfrid was more polite, but equally skeptical.

"Hadn't we better have the cat in and judge for ourselves?" suggested Lady Blemley.

50 Sir Wilfrid went in search of the animal, and the company settled themselves down to the languid[4] expectation of witnessing some more or less adroit[5] drawing-room ventriloquism.[6]

55 In a minute Sir Wilfrid was back in the room, his face white beneath its tan and his eyes dilated with excitement.

"By Gad,[7] it's true!"

His agitation was unmistakably genuine,
60 and his hearers started forward in a thrill of awakened interest.

---

[1] **assimilated** *v.:* adjusted; fit in with.
[2] **feral** *adj.:* wild; untamed.
[3] **ruck** *n.:* the masses; the common people.
[4] **languid** *adj.:* listless; indifferent.
[5] **adroit** *adj.:* clever; skillful.
[6] **ventriloquism** *n.:* art of speaking so that the speaker's voice seems to come from elsewhere.
[7] **by Gad:** mild British oath.

Collapsing into an armchair he continued breathlessly: "I found him dozing in the smoking-room and called out to him to come for his tea. He blinked at me in his usual way, and I said, 'Come on, Toby; don't keep us waiting'; and, by Gad! he drawled out in a most horribly natural voice that he'd come when he dashed[8] well pleased! I nearly jumped out of my skin!"

Appin had preached to absolutely incredulous[9] hearers; Sir Wilfrid's statement carried instant conviction. A Babel-like[10] chorus of startled exclamation arose, amid which the scientist sat mutely enjoying the first fruit of his stupendous discovery.

In the midst of the clamor Tobermory entered the room and made his way with velvet tread and studied unconcern across to the group seated round the tea-table.

A sudden hush of awkwardness and constraint fell on the company. Somehow there seemed an element of embarrassment in addressing on equal terms a domestic cat of acknowledged dental ability.

"Will you have some milk, Tobermory?" asked Lady Blemley in a rather strained voice.

"I don't mind if I do," was the response, couched in a tone of even indifference. A shiver of suppressed excitement went through the listeners, and Lady Blemley might be excused for pouring out the saucerful of milk rather unsteadily.

"I'm afraid I've spilt a good deal of it," she said apologetically.

"After all, it's not my Axminster,"[11] was Tobermory's rejoinder.[12]

Another silence fell on the group, and then Miss Resker, in her best district-visitor manner, asked if the human language had been difficult to learn. Tobermory looked squarely at her for a moment and then fixed his gaze serenely on the middle distance. It was obvious that boring questions lay outside his scheme of life.

"What do you think of human intelligence?" asked Mavis Pellington lamely.

"Of whose intelligence in particular?" asked Tobermory coldly.

"Oh, well, mine for instance," said Mavis, with a feeble laugh.

"You put me in an embarrassing position," said Tobermory, whose tone and attitude certainly did not suggest a shred of embarrassment. "When your inclusion in this house-party was suggested Sir Wilfrid protested that you were the most brainless woman of his acquaintance, and that there was a wide distinction between hospitality and the care of the feeble-minded. Lady Blemley replied that your lack of brain-power was the precise quality which had earned you your invitation, as you were the only person she could think of who might be idiotic enough to buy their old car. You know, the one they call 'The Envy of Sisyphus,'[13] because it goes quite nicely uphill if you push it."

Lady Blemley's protestations would have had greater effect if she had not casually suggested to Mavis only that morning that the car in question would be just the thing for her down at her Devonshire home.

---

[8] **dashed:** mild British oath.

[9] **incredulous** *adj.:* unable to believe.

[10] **Babel-like:** Babel is a biblical city. The people of Babel were said to have tried to build a tower high enough to reach heaven. God is said to have thwarted the plan by making the people speak different languages so that they could no longer understand each other.

[11] **Axminster:** expensive British woolen carpet.

[12] **rejoinder** *n.:* answer to a question or response to a comment.

[13] **Sisyphus:** figure from Greek mythology whom the gods were said to have condemned to spend eternity repeatedly pushing a heavy boulder to the top of a hill only to have it roll back down again.

1. Mr. Appin's attitude toward his audience in lines 36–44 is one of
   (A) condescension
   (B) triumph
   (C) reconciliation
   (D) humility
   (E) mockery

2. Which phrase below provides the context clue for the meaning of the word "skeptical" (line 47)?
   (A) "say and understand easy sentences" (lines 34–35)
   (B) "speak our language with perfect correctness" (lines 43–44)
   (C) "judge for ourselves" (line 49)
   (D) "went in search of the animal" (line 50)
   (E) "dilated with excitement" (line 57)

3. The description of Sir Wilfrid's return to the drawing room (lines 55–61) has the effect of
   (A) providing unexpected comic relief
   (B) returning the story's focus to Sir Wilfrid
   (C) reinforcing the story's tone
   (D) increasing the sense of suspense
   (E) foreshadowing the story's ending

4. The main effect of the allusion to the city of Babel (line 73) is to
   (A) show that the narrator is well read
   (B) emphasize the characters' confusion
   (C) underscore the theme of the story
   (D) establish the mood of the scene
   (E) make the scene more humorous

5. In lines 73–88, the mood in the drawing room changes from one of
   (A) confusion to enlightenment
   (B) hilarity to moroseness
   (C) derision to delight
   (D) excitement to restraint
   (E) optimism to despair

6. Tobermory's speech and manner, as shown in lines 89–106, are best described as
   (A) acutely cruel
   (B) stridently defensive
   (C) surprisingly nostalgic
   (D) coolly aloof
   (E) deeply humble

7. Which of the following is the best example of verbal irony?
   (A) "Appin had preached to absolutely incredulous hearers." (lines 71–72)
   (B) "I don't mind if I do." (line 89)
   (C) "A shiver of suppressed excitement went through the listeners." (lines 90–92)
   (D) "After all, it's not my Axminster." (line 97)
   (E) "You put me in an embarrassing position." (lines 113–114)

8. The effect of the allusion to Sisyphus in lines 127–129 is to
   (A) remind the reader of the story's message
   (B) make a connection between the story and mythology
   (C) indicate a change in the speaker's tone
   (D) darken the mood of the scene
   (E) introduce a comic image

9. What irony is at the center of the story?
   (A) The cat learns to speak the English language better than most humans do.
   (B) The cat is better loved than the humans in the story.
   (C) The value of a talking cat is dubious when the cat is insensitive and offensive.
   (D) The humans are more catty and selfish than the cat is.
   (E) The humans do not believe the cat can speak until they hear it.

10. The tone of the passage can *best* be described as
    (A) optimistic and kind
    (B) reflective and earnest
    (C) moralistic and indignant
    (D) arch and ironic
    (E) deliberate and detached

Section II: Essay

Directions: Read the following prompt carefully. Then, present your response in a well-developed essay.

Resources

For information about how to analyze a **writing prompt** and other strategies for timed writing, see page 45 of this book.

> In the excerpt from "Tobermory," a story written by Saki (H. H. Munro) in the early twentieth century, a cat that has learned to speak English amazes and offends an English hostess and her guests. Consider the story's setting, characters, tone, and theme. Then, in a well-written essay, analyze and discuss how two of these literary elements reveal the author's attitude toward humans and the things they value, such as wealth, possessions, social standing, and personal pride.

Scoring Guidelines

9–8 These essays fully explore the author's attitude toward human beings and the things they value. The essays present coherent, well-written analyses supported by comprehensive evidence. The students exhibit a sophisticated control of language.

7–6 These essays adequately explore the author's attitude toward human beings. They make clear connections and present sound evidence, although the students' work may not be as precise, thorough, or perceptive as essays in the 9–8 range. The students' prose is clear but may contain a few errors in diction or syntax.

5 These essays demonstrate an understanding of the author's attitude toward human beings and make clear claims, but their analysis may be unevenly developed or contain limited evidence. The students' control of language is adequate.

4–3 These essays present an inadequate response to the prompt. The students may misidentify the author's attitude or may have difficulty establishing their own viewpoint and use inappropriate or insufficient evidence. The students demonstrate an inconsistent control over such elements of writing as diction and syntax.

2–1 These essays do not successfully respond to the prompt. The students may fail to understand the prompt, respond tangentially, or substitute a simpler task, such as merely commenting on the author's presentation of the characters. The students' prose reveals consistent weaknesses in such elements of writing as organization, grammar, and diction.

0 These essays do not address any part of the prompt. They may simply paraphrase the prompt, for example.

Collection Resources

Sample Response

The following essay represents a high-scoring response to the writing prompt.

In the excerpt from "Tobermory," Saki's talking cat comments upon the flaws of English society. Saki's ironic, mocking tone and his exposure of human character flaws serve as social commentary, indicating that humans erroneously value superficialities.

Saki begins by exposing flaws in the characters with the highest social standing or with more intelligence or education. The hostess and host, Lady Blemley and Sir Wilfrid, are revealed as superficial, silly, and, in the case of Lady Blemley, mean-spirited. She calculatingly takes advantage of the gullibility of one of her guests, Mavis Pellington, who becomes flustered when Tobermory speaks to her. The scientist, Mr. Appin, has a condescending, superior attitude that reveals that he is not aware of the problems his research may cause. Clovis, the aloof doubter, is barely mentioned and then only as a skeptic who makes cryptic critical remarks about the scientist's assertions. Events quickly contradict his expectations.

Even though they may have less education and social standing, the remaining guests are not exempt from the author's sharp wit. Miss Resker attempts to engage Tobermory in polite parlor conversation, but he is not willing to waste time in idle chitchat and coldly rebuffs her, ignoring her question. Tobermory's remarks emphasize the silliness of Mavis Pellington, although Saki displays some sympathy for her. When Tobermory reveals that Lady Blemley and Sir Wilfrid have noted Pellington's lack of intelligence, Lady Blemley is revealed to be dishonest and coldhearted. She has invited Pellington to take advantage of her by selling her a car that does not run well.

Ironically, the most active and the most sympathetic character is Tobermory, the cat. While he makes pointed and perhaps tactless remarks about humans, he also reveals unpleasant truths that may echo the author's opinions about social position, wealth, intellectual hubris, desire for social acceptance, and greed. However, Saki also hints that Tobermory lacks kindness: The cat is indifferent to the feelings of the targets of his remarks, as in his response to Mavis's question. It might be better that Mavis not learn how little regard Lady Blemley has for her. The unvarnished truth can be unkind, especially when people can do little or nothing about the characteristics being ridiculed (such as Mavis's dimwittedness).

The tone of the excerpt emphasizes the author's attitude toward human society in general. The narrator sets the ironic tone by describing the way the characters speak. By telling readers that Mr. Appin spoke "in a voice which he strove to divest of triumphant inflection," the narrator indicates that Mr. Appin hasn't been successful in trying to speak modestly of his accomplishment. When Sir Wilfrid informs the other characters of Tobermory's ability to speak English, the reaction of the humans is described as "Babel-like," as though everyone is talking at once, each in a language that the others cannot understand. The narrator creates an indisputable sense of the cat's superiority by contrasting the humans' unease with the cat's undeniable dignity and poise as he enters the room "with velvet tread and studied unconcern." Both Tobermory's diction and his mannerisms are aristocratic, in humorous contrast to the behavior of the humans.

Saki uses characters—both human and feline—and tone to comment upon the flaws in human society. The ironic tone is not unrelenting, because Saki leaves hints that he disapproves of the predatory, greedy behavior of Lady Blemley. Such behavior is not acceptable even when the person being victimized is foolish and is herself eager to be seen in what she considers better society. Having Tobermory the cat serve as a spokesperson, demonstrating dignity and decorum exceeding that of the humans, satirically emphasizes human character flaws, forcing readers to laugh at the characters' many foibles.

Elements of Literature selection

And of Clay Are We Created
by Isabel Allende

Ill-Equipped Rescuers Dig Out Volcano Victims
by Bradley Graham

Literary Focus

The coverage of **genre, theme,** and **purpose** below builds on the instruction in the Student Edition. You may want to introduce the additional skill of analyzing **narrative structure** when teaching these works to advanced students.

Genre, Theme, and Purpose

Genre is the category under which a work of literature is classified. The genres include fiction, nonfiction, poetry, drama, and myth. All genres express **themes,** underlying insights about life. The theme of a piece of fiction is usually conveyed by the words, actions, and thoughts of the characters or narrator. The theme of a piece of nonfiction is often stated outright, sometimes even in the title. Expressing a theme is one **purpose,** or reason, an author writes. Use the selections to show that although the two works share the same subject, the genres, themes, and authors' purposes differ.

Author Focus. The school of writing with which Allende is most often associated, magic realism, mixes fantasy and reality. In her stories and novels, Allende weaves fiction and nonfiction in order to express themes about the strength of the human spirit. Although "And of Clay Are We Created" is not an example of magic realism, have students notice similarities between her account of the fictional Azucena and the article about the real Omaira Sanchez.

Narrative Structure

Allende's narrative structure is nonlinear, using flashbacks and other narrative shifts to change the story's focus, time, and place. For example, the story begins with the discovery of Azucena, shifts back to the landslide, and then shifts forward to Rolf Carlé's departure. Later, the story shifts back from Azucena's predicament to Carlé's childhood and then shifts from Azucena to the narrator. Allende uses these narrative shifts to show how Azucena's fate affects different people.

SKILLS FOCUS

Literary Skill
Analyze fiction and nonfiction genres. Analyze theme and purpose.

Advanced Skill
Analyze narrative structure.

As students explore **fiction** and **nonfiction genres, theme, purpose,** and **narrative structure,** remind them not to look at these elements in isolation but to consider how they contribute to our understanding of **voice, tone,** and **diction.**

Related Works

Consider teaching one of the works below from *Elements of Literature* with "And of Clay Are We Created" and "Ill-Equipped Rescuers Dig Out Volcano Victims."

Analyzing genre:
from *The Vietnam War: An Eyewitness History,* edited by Sanford Wexler, and "Where Have You Gone, Charming Billy?" by Tim O'Brien

Analyzing theme:
"Catch the Moon" by Judith Ortiz Cofer

Analyzing narrative structure:
"Night Calls" by Lisa Fugard

For information on **annotating text** and other metacognitive strategies, see page 16 of this book.

The close-reading passage is on page 309 of the Student Edition.

Before assigning this activity, make sure your students have mastered the Vocabulary words on page 304 of the Student Edition.

Words for the Activity
putrefying, p. 306
viscous, p. 306
stagnated, p. 308
impotence, p. 309
immobility, p. 310

Close Reading

Metacognitive Strategy: Annotating Text

As students read, have them annotate the story, focusing on its **narrative structure**—the flow of its scenes. As students read, encourage them to pay attention to sudden shifts in the narrative. Have students answer the following questions as they read:

- Where does the narrative suddenly shift from one place or time to another?

- What is the new time and place? How does it relate to the previous scene?

- What is the effect of the narrative shift?

Close-Reading Practice: Narrative Structure

Have students re-read the passage near the middle of the story, from "'Don't leave me alone,'" to "dead for a million years," and discuss these questions to explore the story's narrative structure:

- What is the effect of opening the passage by focusing on Azucena at the end of her first day trapped in the mud? *[By opening in Azucena's present, Allende creates a sense of immediacy that generates empathy for both Azucena and Carlé: Their situation has yet to resolve, and the scene's hopefulness moves the narrative forward.]*

- At what point does the narrative shift? How does its effect support the story's theme? *[The narrative shifts to Carlé's thoughts. As he learns the details of Azucena's life, he is "buoyed by a premature optimism" and is "convinced that everything would end well." The shift hints that the story will end tragically, but Carlé's concern for gifts appropriate to Azucena during her hospital recuperation underscores the theme that tragic events inspire powerful hopes, regrets, and strengths.]*

Vocabulary: Word Roots

The translator of Allende's text is careful to choose words that reflect the horror of the setting. Thinking critically about Allende's (and her translator's) choice of words can give students deeper insight into the world Allende depicts.

Activity. Allende uses the words in the margin in describing the events and setting of the story. Have students consult a dictionary to learn the origins and meanings of the words. Then, have students explain how each word contributes to the story's theme.

[Sample responses: **Putrefying** *means "rotting," and its origin is the Latin word* putrefacere, *meaning "to make putrid or rotten."* **Viscous** *means "sticky," and its origin is the Latin word* viscum, *which is a sticky substance used to catch birds.* **Stagnated** *means "became foul due to lack of circulation." It comes from the Latin word* stagnum, *which means "pool" or "swamp."* **Impotence** *means "lack of strength or power." It comes from the Latin word* potens, *which means "having power."*

Immobility *is the lack of the ability to move. The word comes from the Latin* mobilis, *which means "movable." All of the words have Latin origins and have tactile or kinesthetic components. Each of the words deals with sensation or movement, giving the story a physical quality that supports its theme that the forces of nature often seem harsh, overwhelming, and disgusting to humans.]*

Postreading

Discussion Method: Fishbowl Discussion

Have students form two groups for a fishbowl discussion in which they consider the effectiveness and limitation of two **genres**— nonfiction and fiction. Use the following questions to prompt students' thinking:

Resources

For information on **fishbowl discussions** and other discussion methods, see page 20 of this book.

- How might the fictional account of Azucena be considered more emotionally effective than the nonfiction article about Omaira Sanchez? *[By shifting points of view and settings, the author shows the deep emotional impact Azucena had on people. By showing Azucena up close and revealing her thoughts and fears, Allende allows readers to build an attachment to her and feel strongly about her. The article, while sympathetic to Omaira, uses her to illustrate the point that the disaster was overwhelming and that no life was any more important or meaningful than any other.]*

- How is the nonfictional account more objectively effective than the story? *[The article provides the facts in a logical, straightforward order. The article more effectively provides an objective snapshot of events at that particular point in time. The report answers basic factual questions without attempting to communicate emotional responses to the disaster.]*

- Which account did you prefer? Why? *[Students' responses will vary. They may suggest that they prefer the story because it is more emotionally engaging and descriptive. Or they may prefer the objective, more factually accurate account of the article.]*

Writing

Have students write an essay that responds to the prompt below.

> The story and the article use various narrative structures and techniques. What narrative technique do you think is especially effective? Consider **setting, character, tone,** and **theme** as you re-read the story and article to make your choice. Then, write an essay in which you explain how this technique is important to the story or article. Use details and examples to support your points.

Criteria for Success

A successful response
- states persuasive reasons explaining the importance of the chosen narrative technique
- supports the choice with apt textual examples
- shows insight into setting, character, tone, theme, and narrative structure
- uses language effectively

The Man in the Water
by Roger Rosenblatt

SKILLS FOCUS

Literary Skill
Analyze personal essays.
Analyze the main idea.

Advanced Skill
Analyze generalization.

As students explore **personal essays, main idea,** and **generalization,** remind them not to look at these elements in isolation but to consider how they contribute to our understanding of **voice, tone,** and **theme.**

Collection Resources

Literary Focus

The coverage of **personal essays** below builds on the instruction in the Student Edition. You may want to introduce the additional skill of analyzing **generalization** when teaching this essay to advanced students.

Personal Essay

As a literary form, the personal or informal essay is a relatively recent development. The sixteenth-century French writer Michel de Montaigne gave the essay its name when he used the word *essai* (which means "trying out") to describe his attempts to explore ideas and express himself. His works are considered the first modern essays. Since then, the essay has been a form that writers sometimes use to reflect on humanity, its flaws, and its potential. The freestyle form of the modern essay allows writers to experiment with voice and style. You can use Rosenblatt's essay to show students how the essay form is suited to exploring the best aspects of humanity.

Generalization

A **generalization** is a broad statement that applies to or covers many individuals, experiences, situations, observations, or texts. A valid generalization is a conclusion drawn from consideration of as many specific facts as possible, and it expresses a larger, general understanding. Point out that the author of this essay bases his generalization about ordinary people on specific facts about the actions of one anonymous man.

Author Focus. The author, Roger Rosenblatt, a journalist who has covered issues such as the effects of war on children, shifts from objective reporting in his essay "The Man in the Water." Instead, Rosenblatt looks at the heroism of one person and considers what the man's actions reveal about every individual's capacity for brave and selfless action.

Related Works

Consider teaching one of the works below from *Elements of Literature* with "The Man in the Water."
Analyzing personal essays and main idea:
"A State Championship Versus Runner's Conscience" by John Christian Hoyle
Analyzing generalization:
"Ill-Equipped Rescuers Dig Out Volcano Victims" by Bradley Graham

Close Reading

Metacognitive Strategy: Reading Aloud

Because the selection is a personal essay, students may benefit from working in small groups to read it aloud, paragraph by paragraph. As students read, have them consider the following questions:

Resources

For information on **reading aloud** and other metacognitive strategies, see page 16 of this book.

- How would you describe the author's voice? For example, is it conversational? Is it difficult or easy to understand?

- What do you notice about the author's sentences? Are they long and complicated, short and direct, or a mixture of both?

- Describe the tone of voice that you used in reading aloud.

Close-Reading Practice: Grammar and Syntax

Rosenblatt is a sophisticated writer who mixes simple and complex sentences in his essay. He adds complexity by using sentence **modifiers**—phrases or clauses that add meaning but cannot stand alone—and **appositives**, words or phrases that identify nouns in the sentence.

Activity. Have students re-read the first two paragraphs of the essay, from "As disasters go" to "rose to the occasion." Then, have students discuss these questions about the author's syntax and style:

- What impact do the sentence modifiers "As disasters go," "of course," "for the moment," and "to be sure" have on the author's effectiveness in conveying the main idea? *[The sentence modifiers establish a conversational tone; they also help underscore the essay's main idea: The disaster, which is relatively unremarkable, is not the central focus; instead, the focus is on the human response to that disaster.]*

- How do the two sentence fragments at the beginning of the second paragraph affect the essay's tone? What is their purpose? *[The fragments provide conversational answers to the question posed in the last line of the first paragraph ("Why, then, the shock here?"); they also focus attention on the answers, both of which stress aspects of the essay's main idea: The disaster reveals something shocking and marvelous about human nature.]*

Vocabulary: Connotation

In describing a scene of chaos and tragedy, Rosenblatt chooses his words carefully. Thinking critically about Rosenblatt's word choices can give students insight into his tone.

Activity. As he grapples with the meaning of one person's sacrifice, Rosenblatt uses the words in the margin. Have students discuss or write down the meaning and connotation of each word. Then, have students write a few sentences explaining how each word contributes to the author's tone. *[Sample responses: A **roster** is a list, usually one that shows duties or assignments. The word is associated with the military but has a neutral connotation here. **Aesthetic** means "related to beauty, art, or good taste." It is a formal word with a neutral connotation. A **casualty** is an accident, a victim, or someone who is injured. It is a formal term that has a neutral connotation. **Universal** means "including or related to everything." Again, the word has a neutral connotation.*

Close Reading

The close-reading passage is on page 322 of the Student Edition.

Collection Resources

Vocabulary

Before assigning this activity, make sure your students have mastered the Vocabulary words on page 320 of the Student Edition.

Words for the Activity
roster, p. 322
aesthetic, p. 322
casualty, p. 323
universal, p. 323
impersonal, p. 325

*Impersonal means "without personal feelings" and has a neutral conno-
tation. The words all have relatively neutral connotations. By avoiding
positive or negative connotations, the writer is able to describe a chaotic
event and his own search for meaning without embracing obvious, overly
sentimental, or hackneyed ideas.]*

Postreading
Discussion Method: Timed Discussion

Have students discuss the author's choice of form—the **personal
essay**—and his use of **generalization** in a timed discussion. Ask them
to prepare for the discussion by reviewing the essay and considering
the author's purpose for writing. Use the following questions to
prompt students' thinking:

- How does the form of the personal essay affect the author's tone?
  How is the essay's form effective? *[The form allows the author to use
  and exploit a comfortable tone that carries the full rhetorical impact
  of a personally appealing, creative voice. In a personal essay, the
  writer can express opinions and reach conclusions without necessarily
  having to generate logical supporting arguments or a fully reasoned
  defense of his or her ideas.]*

- What generalization does the author reach in the essay? Based on
  the essay's evidence, what other generalizations might he have
  reached? *[The author generalizes about the man in the water as a
  symbol of human capabilities—the man represents the human ability
  to struggle against both nature and the impulse for self-preservation
  in order to preserve the lives of fellow human beings. Students may
  suggest other generalizations, such as "technology, when it goes wrong,
  can harm us more than it helps us" or "nature is simply too strong for
  individuals to beat."]*

Writing

Have students write an essay that responds to the prompt below.

In his **personal essay** "The Man in the Water," the author Roger
Rosenblatt considers one man's selfless actions and makes a
generalization about humanity. Think of a specific experience from
your own life in which one person's actions reveal an important aspect of human nature. Then, in a well-written essay, explain your
generalization and tell how you reached it. Use details and examples
to support your points.

Resources

For information on **timed
discussion** and other discussion
methods, see page 20 of this
book.

Collection Resources

Criteria for Success

A successful response
- states a generalization based
  on a specific experience
- supports the generalization
  with clear facts, examples, or
  observations
- shows insight into generalization and the essay form
- uses language effectively

Writing Workshop: Writing a Persuasive Essay

Prewriting

Advanced Prewriting Strategy

Emotional Appeal. Explain to students that there are many emotions to which a persuasive essay can appeal, including joy, anger, pity, sympathy, empathy, and hope. Here are some tips on using emotional appeals in a persuasive essay:

- **Know the audience.** A writer should understand which emotional reactions readers are likely to have and then appeal to those emotions.

- **Think about the connotations.** Connotations play an important role in establishing the tone and mood of an essay. For example, an essay that describes a law as *heinous* will have a different impact than one that describes it as *annoying*.

- **Be prudent.** Emotional appeals should be used sparingly and subtly. Readers may feel manipulated if an argument relies too much on transparently emotional appeals.

Writing

Advanced Writing Skills

Preparing an Effective Conclusion. Students may already know that their conclusion should review the main ideas and include a call to action. Remind them that the conclusion should also do the following:

Inspire the audience. The facts and ideas in the body should stand by themselves, but the conclusion's emotional appeals can help motivate readers to act.

Connect with readers. The conclusion is an effective place to employ ethical appeals that forge a final connection with readers.

Emphasize the most important point. The conclusion is a good place to remind readers of the essay's most important point and to tie this point to the call to action.

Activity. To help students draft effective conclusions, have them answer the following questions:

- What emotional words can I use to inspire the audience and forge a connection?

SKILLS FOCUS

Writing Skill
Write a persuasive essay.

As students explore **persuasive writing,** remind them that persuasive writing, like all forms of writing, gains power from attention to literary elements, such as **diction, figurative language, tone,** and **voice.**

Resources

For more information on **emotional appeals,** see the Handbook of Rhetorical Concepts in this book.

Resources

For more information on types of appeals (such as logical appeals), see the Handbook of Rhetorical Concepts in this book.

Collection Resources

- What one thing do I want my readers to remember?
- How can I make sure the audience remembers it?

Grammar Solutions. As students think about how to prepare an effective conclusion, they should remember that compound subjects and verbs should agree in number. Compound subjects (two or more subjects joined by *and*) take a plural verb. When singular subjects are joined by *or,* the verb should also be singular. When *or* joins a singular and a plural subject, the verb agrees with the number of the subject closest to it.

SUBJECTS JOINED BY *AND*	*Animal rights **activists and** their **opponents agree** that leash laws help save pets' lives.*
SINGULAR SUBJECTS JOINED BY *OR*	*A pet **owner** or an animal shelter **worker wants** every animal to have a good home.*
SINGULAR AND PLURAL SUBJECTS JOINED BY *OR*	*If your neighbors or a police **officer asks** you to put a leash on your dog, you should do so. If a police officer or your **neighbors ask** you to put a leash on your dog, you should do so.*

Revising and Publishing

Revising for Style

Vary Sentence Beginnings. The basic structure of a sentence in English is a subject followed by a verb. However, if the pattern is repeated too often in a piece of writing, the text can be monotonous. Varying sentence beginnings adds variety to writing.

Activity. Ask students to read their essays and to locate sentences that contain embedded phrases or clauses that can be moved to the beginning of the sentence to add variety. As they revise, students should consider the rhythm and meaning of their new sentences.

Publishing and Reflecting

Exchanging Ideas. To allow students to share their ideas and benefit from their classmate's responses, have students work in pairs to review each other's essays. Students should consider the validity of the writers' arguments, the soundness of evidence, and the effectiveness of appeals. Ask students to give constructive feedback to their partners.

Self-Evaluation. Finally, have students reflect on their essays. Instruct them to write responses to the following questions:

- How does **varying your sentence beginnings** affect the rhythm and sound of your essay? Does it make your writing more interesting? Why or why not?

- Did you use **emotional appeals** in your essay? Where? Do you think they are effective?

- Is your **conclusion** effective? Why or why not?

Resources

For more information on **compound subjects,** see the Handbook of Grammatical Concepts in this book.

Collection Resources

Literature Link

Before students begin revising to vary sentence beginnings, encourage them to re-read Edgar Lee Masters's "Lucinda Matlock" or Stephen Vincent Benét's "By the Waters of Babylon" to see how these authors vary sentences to make reading interesting.

Section I: Multiple-Choice Questions

Directions: Carefully read the following passage from a speech by Helen Keller, who, as a toddler, contracted a disease that left her blind and deaf. Then, choose the *best* answer to each question.

from Three Days to See

If, by some miracle, I were granted three seeing days, to be followed by a relapse into darkness, I should divide the period into three parts.

5   On the first day, I should want to see the people whose kindness and gentleness and companionship have made my life worth living. First I should like to gaze long upon the face of my dear teacher, Mrs. Anne
10 Sullivan Macy, who came to me when I was a child and opened the outer world to me. I should want not merely to see the outline of her face, so that I could cherish it in my memory, but to study that face and find in it
15 the living evidence of the sympathetic tenderness and patience with which she accomplished the difficult task of my education. I should like to see in her eyes that strength of character which has enabled her to stand
20 firm in the face of difficulties, and that compassion for all humanity which she has revealed to me so often.

I do not know what it is to see into the heart of a friend through the "window of
25 the soul," the eye. I can only "see" through my fingertips the outline of a face. I can detect laughter, sorrow, and many other obvious emotions. I know my friends from the feel of their faces. But I cannot really picture
30 their personalities by touch. I know their personalities, of course, through other means, through the thoughts they express to me, through whatever of their actions are revealed to me. But I am denied that deeper
35 understanding of them which I am sure would come through sight of them, through watching their reactions to various expressed thoughts and circumstances, through noting the immediate and fleeting
40 reactions of their eyes and countenance.

Friends who are near to me I know well, because through the months and years they reveal themselves to me in all their phases; but of casual friends I have only an incom-
45 plete impression, an impression gained from a handclasp, from spoken words which I take from their lips with my fingertips, or which they tap into the palm of my hand.

How much easier, how much more satis-
50 fying it is for you who can see to grasp quickly the essential qualities of another person by watching the subtleties of expression, the quiver of a muscle, the flutter of a hand. But does it ever occur to you to use
55 your sight to see into the inner nature of a friend or acquaintance? Do not most of you seeing people grasp casually the outward features of a face and let it go at that?

For instance, can you describe accurately
60 the faces of five good friends? Some of you can, but many cannot. As an experiment, I have questioned husbands of long standing about the color of their wives' eyes, and often they express embarrassed confusion
65 and admit that they do not know. And, incidentally, it is a chronic complaint of wives that their husbands do not notice new dresses, new hats, and changes in household arrangements.

70 The eyes of seeing persons soon become accustomed to the routine of their surroundings, and they actually see only the startling and spectacular. But even in viewing the most spectacular sights the eyes are 75 lazy. Court records reveal every day how inaccurately "eyewitnesses" see. A given event will be "seen" in several different ways by as many witnesses. Some see more than others, but few see everything that is within the 80 range of their vision.

Oh, the things that I should see if I had the power of sight for just three days!

The first day would be a busy one. I should call to me all my dear friends and 85 look long into their faces, imprinting upon my mind the outward evidences of the beauty that is within them. I should let my eyes rest, too, on the face of a baby, so that I could catch a vision of the eager, innocent 90 beauty which precedes the individual's consciousness of the conflicts which life develops.

And I should like to look into the loyal, trusting eyes of my dogs—the grave, canny 95 little Scottie, Darkie, and the stalwart, understanding Great Dane, Helga, whose warm, tender, and playful friendships are so comforting to me.

On that busy first day I should also view 100 the small simple things of my home. I want to see the warm colors in the rugs under my feet, the pictures on the walls, the intimate trifles that transform a house into a home. My eyes would rest respectfully on the

105 books in raised type which I have read, but they would be more eagerly interested in the printed books which seeing people can read, for during the long night of my life the books I have read and those which have 110 been read to me have built themselves into a great shining lighthouse, revealing to me the deepest channels of human life and the human spirit.

In the afternoon of that first seeing day, I 115 should take a long walk in the woods and intoxicate my eyes on the beauties of the world of Nature, trying desperately to absorb in a few hours the vast splendor which is constantly unfolding itself to those who 120 can see. On the way home from my woodland jaunt my path would lie near a farm so that I might see the patient horses plowing in the field (perhaps I should see only a tractor!) and the serene content of men liv- 125 ing close to the soil. And I should pray for the glory of a colorful sunset.

When dusk had fallen, I should experience the double delight of being able to see by artificial light, which the genius of man 130 has created to extend the power of his sight when Nature decrees darkness.

In the night of that first day of sight, I should not be able to sleep, so full would be my mind of the memories of the day.

1. Which of the following rhetorical devices does the speaker use in paragraph 2 (lines 5–22)?
   (A) Allusion
   (B) Parallelism
   (C) Antithesis
   (D) Euphemism
   (E) Understatement

2. Paragraph 3 (lines 23–40) assumes that
   (A) readers do not know that Keller is blind
   (B) some aspects of character are communicated through sight alone
   (C) individuals with sight readily detect "obvious emotions"
   (D) the sense of hearing is less important than that of sight
   (E) the speaker's experiences with friends have been greatly limited

3. Lines 49–58 contrast
   (A) the speaker's understanding of sight's value with seeing individuals' understanding
   (B) nonverbal communication with speech
   (C) intrinsic characteristics of personality with extrinsic characteristics
   (D) an awareness of "essential qualities" with casual awareness
   (E) conditions of life for sighted individuals with conditions of life for the blind

4. The rhetorical questions in paragraph 5 (lines 54–58) indicate that the speaker
   (A) feels angry and confused by her condition
   (B) longs to understand the experiences of people who are able to see
   (C) believes herself to have a superior understanding of human nature
   (D) doubts that sighted individuals take full advantage of sight
   (E) seeks reconciliation with friends and acquaintances

5. The quotation marks around *eyewitness* and *seen* in lines 76 and 77 indicate that the speaker is
   (A) using verbal irony
   (B) quoting terms used in court records
   (C) relying on words with which she is unfamiliar
   (D) building a case for improving the quality of admissible evidence
   (E) alluding to the adage "Seeing is believing"

6. The speaker's exclamation, "Oh, the things that I should see if I had the power of sight for just three days!" (lines 81–82) serves as
   (A) an assertion
   (B) a digressive aside
   (C) an ethical appeal
   (D) a metaphorical element
   (E) a transitional device

7. The speaker uses "intimate trifles" (lines 102–103) to
   (A) establish the significance of her rugs and pictures
   (B) provide a context clue for the meaning of the phrase "small simple things" (line 100)
   (C) convey her attitude toward printed books
   (D) associate "warm colors" (line 101) with household objects
   (E) clarify the connotation for *home* (line 103)

8. *Intoxicate* in line 116 suggests that sight of the natural world would
   (A) muddle the speaker
   (B) distract the speaker
   (C) excite the speaker
   (D) stupefy the speaker
   (E) frighten the speaker

9. The tone of lines 120–126 is best described as
   (A) contemplative and optimistic
   (B) confident and forthright
   (C) clinical and detached
   (D) moralistic and strident
   (E) reverent and sentimental

10. "In the night of that first day of sight, I should not be able to sleep, so full would be my mind of the memories of the day" (lines 132–134) is
    (A) a simple sentence
    (B) a compound sentence
    (C) a complex sentence
    (D) a compound-complex sentence
    (E) an imperative sentence

Section II: Essay

Directions: Carefully read the following prompt. Then, present your response in a well-developed essay.

For information about how to analyze a **writing prompt** and other strategies for timed writing, see page 45 of this book.

> Carefully read the passage from "Three Days to See" by Helen Keller. As you read, notice how the speaker uses rhetorical strategies—such as rhetorical questions, description, parallelism, and voice—to create her tone and to make her points. Then, in a well-written essay, analyze how Keller uses two of these rhetorical strategies to serve her purpose.

Scoring Guidelines

9–8 These essays fully explore two of the rhetorical strategies Keller uses to support her purpose. They show insight into the speaker's ability to use techniques to make her points. They present coherent, well-written analyses supported by comprehensive evidence. The students exhibit a sophisticated control of language.

7–6 These essays adequately analyze the rhetorical strategies employed by the speaker. They offer insight into the effectiveness of the techniques, but their analyses are less thorough, perceptive, or specific than essays in the 9–8 range. The students' prose is clear and mostly free of major errors in diction or syntax.

5 These essays offer clear analyses of the speaker's use of rhetorical strategies in making her points, but their analyses may be unevenly developed or may contain limited evidence. The students' control of language is adequate.

4–3 These essays present an inadequate response to the prompt. The students may fail to comprehend the rhetorical strategies used by the speaker, have difficulty explaining how the strategies are used, and use inappropriate or insufficient evidence. The students demonstrate an inconsistent control over such elements of writing as diction and syntax.

2–1 These essays do not successfully respond to the prompt. The students may fail to understand the prompt, respond tangentially, or substitute a simpler task, such as merely summarizing Keller's speech. The students' prose reveals consistent weaknesses in such elements of writing as organization, grammar, and diction.

0 These essays present a response that receives no credit. They may simply paraphrase the prompt, for example.

Sample Response

The following essay represents a high-scoring response to the writing prompt.

In her speech "Three Days to See," Helen Keller joyfully lists the things she would like to see—her teacher Anne Sullivan Macy, her friends, a baby, her dogs, her home, and a woodland path. However, Keller's purpose is not to think about things that will always be invisible to her; instead, she wants hearers to realize that sighted people do not always enjoy sight. They don't "see" what is essential. Keller carefully uses rhetorical questions and vivid descriptive details to build an inviting tone, and she calls on her hearers to think about the many possibilities of sight and to begin noticing the world's beauty. Keller argues that seeing is a miraculous gift.

Keller establishes her central purpose by posing rhetorical questions that prompt her hearers to ask themselves whether they recognize sight's full value. Keller phrases these questions as accusations because she wants the audience to think about things they usually overlook. She asks, "does it ever occur to you to use your sight to see into the inner nature of a friend or acquaintance?" and "can you describe accurately the faces of five good friends?" Answers to her questions are less important than the fact that she feels like she has to ask them. Most people have never thought about her questions at all. Can sight show "more than meets the eye"? Do we know what sight shows us about the world's beauty? As Keller implies, members of her audience are probably too "accustomed to the routine of their surroundings" to bother thinking about sight at all.

Her purposes established, Keller uses descriptive details to help hearers understand what sight can be, if people use it the way they should. First, she points out that sight reveals character. Because Keller has to rely on touch alone, she has an "incomplete impression" of people. If she were able to see Mrs. Macy, she would not merely "see the outline of her face," as most people would, but she would find "the living evidence of the sympathetic tenderness and patience" of Macy's personality. Keller points out that sighted people see more than they realize. They are able to note "reactions to various expressed thoughts and circumstances," "immediate and fleeting reactions of [others'] eyes and countenance," and "subtleties of expression, the quiver of a muscle, the flutter of a hand." These highly specific details invite Keller's audience to think about how sight reveals character quickly—and marvelously.

Next, Keller uses descriptive details to point out how much unacknowledged beauty lies in everyday items and experiences. She says that "even in viewing the most spectacular sights the eyes are lazy." Then, ironically, she describes sights that she <u>cannot</u> see to an audience that probably <u>does</u> <u>not</u> see. Keller wants to look into her dogs' eyes, to see the "warm colors" in her rugs, to view the pictures on her walls, and to read the pages of printed books. She would love to see "patient horses plowing in the field" and gets excited at the thought of seeing a tractor. She would even pray "for the glory of a colorful sunset." Finally, she asks hearers to think about "the double delight of being able to see by artificial light." Keller loves the fact that lights "extend the power of [human] sight when Nature decrees darkness." Although she does not "see" the world around her, Keller is more aware of the miracle of its visibility than sighted people are.

"Three Days to See" is not a grief-stricken lament about Keller's years of "darkness." Instead, the speech is a powerful reminder that sight is an extraordinary gift. Keller's use of rhetorical questions helps her hearers understand that they often take sight for granted, and her use of description points to sight's possibilities. Together, these two rhetorical techniques emphasize the fact that the people, things, and events of our lives deserve more attention than we often offer. Keller is right: Sight is indeed a miraculous gift.

Elements of Literature selection

Lamb to the Slaughter
by Roald Dahl

Collection Resources

Related Works

Consider teaching one of the works below from *Elements of Literature* with "Lamb to the Slaughter."
Analyzing situational irony and dramatic irony:
"The Cold Equations" by Tom Godwin
Analyzing historical context:
"Typhoid Fever" by Frank McCourt

Literary Focus

The coverage of **irony** below builds on the instruction in the Student Edition. You may want to introduce the additional skill of analyzing **historical context** when teaching this story to advanced students.

Irony

The picture of domestic contentment in "Lamb to the Slaughter" quickly degenerates into a view of a murder scene. Roald Dahl takes readers by surprise with his use of situational irony, unexpectedly fabricating a calculating killer from a most unpromising source—an apparently devoted, pregnant wife. Dahl's wit ensures that his tale is not a simple mystery. His use of dramatic irony creates humor at an unexpected moment: The murderer, Mary Maloney, hides her weapon in plain sight, and detectives bungle the case by eating the evidence. Use the story to show students how Dahl's use of irony builds suspense and shapes reader expectations about what will happen next.

Historical Context

Dahl's murderous protagonist is a complacent 1950s housewife until the moments before she kills her husband. Dahl expertly paints the historical context of the post-World War II period by illustrating rigid gender roles. When Patrick, the family's breadwinner, announces his betrayal, Mary's cocktail-mixing homemaking days are over. Details hinting at period and location—an ice bucket, a deep freezer, footsore police officers, a neighborhood grocer who closes at six, use of *spanner* for *wrench*—help place Dahl's characters in a specific historical place. More telling, though, are the author's descriptions of male and female roles and expectations. Discuss with students Mary Maloney's behavior and how her sudden reaction marks a rejection not just of her husband's betrayal, but also of the "feminine" passivity expected in her time and culture.

Author Focus. With their surprise endings, Dahl's works are often compared to those of O. Henry and Saki, writers famous for twists at the end of their stories. Dahl is famous for his children's stories such as *James and the Giant Peach* and *Charlie and the Chocolate Factory.* His own childhood was rather bleak, marked by the death of his father and "days of horrors" in regimented British boarding schools. Little wonder, then, that children in his stories often wreak gleeful revenge on adults who have wronged them.

Close Reading

Metacognitive Strategy: Thinking Notes

As students read, have them annotate the text with **thinking notes,** focusing on instances of **irony.** To help students differentiate between situational and dramatic irony, have them mark examples in which the reader is surprised by events (situational irony) and those in which the reader knows more about events than some characters do (dramatic irony). In addition, have students mark the language and details that indicate the story's context—both its British setting and examples of its historical context. Have them annotate these details with thinking notes to indicate the following:

- unexpected and surprising events
- circumstances readers are aware of but characters are not
- indications that the story is set in Great Britain
- clues as to the story's historical context

Close-Reading Practice: Irony

Have students re-read the passage from "This is going to be a bit of a shock to you" to "back of his head," and discuss the following questions to explore Dahl's use of irony:

- What does Patrick's speech reveal about him? How does what he says contribute to the passage's dramatic irony? *[Phrases such as "I hope you won't blame me too much," "I know it's kind of a bad time," and "wouldn't be very good for my job" indicate that Patrick gives little thought to his pregnant wife's emotional or intellectual state. He is leaving her, yet he asks her to avoid fuss that would affect his job. His businesslike attitude and lack of concern for his wife lead him to ignore or fail to recognize the possibility that she will take action. She catches him totally off guard.]*

- Mary strikes Patrick "without any pause." Does the narrator indicate that she gives any thought to her actions? *[By telling readers that Mary "sat very still" with "a kind of dazed horror," that she denies what she has heard, fancying that she "imagined the whole thing," and that her actions become "automatic," the narrator indicates that Mary's action is not premeditated. This description contributes to the passage's situational irony; the reader, like Mary, is ill-equipped to predict what she is going to do.]*

- How do the passage's instances of irony contribute to the narrative's effectiveness? *[Because the story begins by describing Mary's devotion to her husband, the sudden change from passivity to violence makes the passage especially dramatic. Mary's change comes as a shock to the story's readers: Situational and dramatic irony help build the scene's drama, improving its effectiveness.]*

Resources

For information on **thinking notes** and other metacognitive strategies, see page 16 of this book.

Close Reading

The close-reading passage is on pages 381–382 of the Student Edition.

Collection Resources

Words for the Activity

tranquil, p. 379

punctually, p. 380

blissful, p. 380

content, p. 380

quietly, p. 380

Collection Resources

Resources

For information on **fishbowl discussions** and other discussion methods, see page 20 of this book.

Vocabulary: Connotations

The cozy scene that opens Dahl's story sets up an ironic contrast with the tale that follows. Focusing on the word choices describing Mary's home life can give students insight into her sudden change in behavior.

Activity. The words in the margin describe the Maloney household before Patrick announces that he is leaving. Have students discuss or write down the connotations of each word and its context. Then, have students explain how each word contributes to the situational irony.

[Sample responses: **Tranquil** *connotes passivity, suggesting that Mary is submissive; she proves to be active.* **Punctually** *suggests routine, implying that the characters will act according to habit. The break with habit adds irony to Patrick's bombshell and Mary's response.* **Blissful** *indicates a joyful fulfillment, the opposite of the betrayal.* **Content** *connotes completeness and perfection. Until Patrick's announcement, Mary appears to be content in her role.* **Quietly** *carries connotations of restfulness and calmness. Mary has no reason to expect a disruption of her domestic bliss.]*

Postreading

Discussion Method: Fishbowl Discussion

Have students discuss the story's use of **irony** in a fishbowl discussion. Arrange students in inner and outer circles; then, ask the students in the inner circle one of the following questions:

- Is Mary Maloney's act the perfect crime? Explain why or why not. *[Mary Maloney has no known motive, creates an alibi, explains her whereabouts, and eliminates evidence. She is unlikely to be accused.]*

- How does dramatic irony help make Mary's ability to conceal her crime more believable? *[Because readers know facts that the detectives do not, the story is more believable. Readers know Mary's motive; know that she is, in part, able to conceal her crime because her husband, a detective, has shared information about crime solving; and know her murder weapon. The detectives have little reason to suspect Mary.]*

After students trade seats, ask a question suggested by student responses or a different question from the list above.

Writing

Have students write an essay that responds to the prompt below.

Criteria for Success

A successful response

- analyzes the use of situational irony in the story
- develops the analysis with appropriate textual support
- shows insight into theme, character, and tone
- uses language effectively

> Mary Maloney "luxuriates" in her husband's presence as she serves him his cocktails. Consider the **historical context** of Dahl's post-World War II setting. Then, write an essay explaining how the story's use of **situational irony** critiques the traditional roles of men and women.

Elements of Literature selection

R.M.S. Titanic
by Hanson W. Baldwin

Literary Focus

The coverage of **objective** and **subjective writing** below builds on the instruction in the Student Edition. You may want to introduce the additional skill of analyzing **point of view** when teaching this article and accompanying eyewitness accounts to advanced students.

Objective and Subjective Writing

This objective fact about the *Titanic's* sinking gives a measure of the tragedy: More than 1,500 people died. Objective details, including the names of passengers and their activities, the number of rescue boats, the types of emergency signals, and the number of survivors, help place the deaths in a historical context. Equally telling, though, are **subjective details,** for example, "boat crews had been slow in reaching their stations; launching arrangements were confused . . . ; passengers were loaded into the boats haphazardly." Baldwin's choice of details reveals the character of the people aboard the unlucky ship, helping readers appreciate the courage, cowardice, and foolhardiness of the survivors and victims of the disaster.

Point of View

Each passenger aboard the *Titanic* saw events from his or her particular point of view. In his first-person narrative, "A Fireman's Story," Harry Senior describes the preference given to rich passengers as he is beaten back with an oar. Similarly, in "From a Lifeboat," Mrs. D. H. Bishop uses first person to describe the ship's final minutes and the cries of victims. In contrast, Hanson Baldwin, in "R.M.S. Titanic," relies on an omniscient narrator to recount the tragedy. Baldwin's narrator tells of multiple events, including their causes and results. Point out that while the first-person eyewitness accounts may lack the breadth of Baldwin's thoughtful analysis, their immediacy may better convey the terror and confusion of the disaster.

Author Focus. Throughout his long career, Baldwin crafted technical information into accounts accessible to the average reader. He specialized in writing about the U.S. military and covered military issues from World War II to the Vietnam War. For his newspaper articles about U.S. military bases in the South Pacific, Baldwin received the 1943 Pulitzer Prize for foreign correspondence. In addition to articles, he wrote many books about military and defense topics.

SKILLS FOCUS

Literary Skill
Analyze objective and subjective writing.

Advanced Skill
Analyze point of view.

As students explore **objective** and **subjective writing** and **point of view,** remind them not to look at these elements in isolation but to consider how they contribute to our understanding of **character, tone,** and **theme.**

Related Works

Consider teaching one of the works below from *Elements of Literature* with "R.M.S. Titanic."
Analyzing objective and subjective writing:
"Ill-Equipped Rescuers Dig Out Volcano Victims" by Bradley Graham
Analyzing point of view:
"Diary of a Mad Blender" by Sue Shellenbarger

Collection Resources

Close Reading

Metacognitive Strategy: Reading Journal

Resources

For information on **reading journals** and other metacognitive strategies, see page 16 of this book.

As students read, have them make notes about **objective** and **subjective writing** in the three *Titanic* selections, closely considering the impact of details. Have students note details related to the following:

* the effect of each writer's point of view
* the technical and human reasons for the disaster
* emotional and reasoned responses, including judgments

Students should add their own comments, analyses, and questions to their notes. Have students share entries to spur discussion about how objective and subjective details affect each story's impact.

Close-Reading Practice: Point of View

Close Reading

The close-reading passage is on pages 403–404 of the Student Edition.

Have students re-read the passage from "One of the collapsible boats" to "just died away then," and discuss the following questions to explore point of view in "R.M.S. Titanic":

* The passage states that the men "stood knee-deep in water in the freezing air" and that their "soaked clothing clutched their bodies in icy folds." How does the point of view bring the mens' experience to life? [*The omniscient point of view allows the narrator to add sensory details that otherwise might be lost or forgotten in a first-person recounting of events. Also, the point of view casts these details as facts rather than as subjective experiences or memories of the past.*]

* The narrator states that only a few of the rescue boats had lights and only one of those "was of any use to the *Carpathia*." The narrator also relates the radio message sent from *La Provence* to *Celtic*. What effect does point of view have on the narrative of events? [*Because the narrator has access to information from all the ships, the narrator can describe events that occurred at several places and times. The point of view offers a more complete vision of what took place than a limited point of view could offer.*]

Vocabulary: Context Clues

Vocabulary

Before assigning this activity, make sure your students have mastered the Vocabulary words on page 391 of the Student Edition.

Words for the Activity

knots, p. 394

steerage, p. 394

aft, p. 395

crow's-nest, p. 396

dynamos, p. 399

"R.M.S. Titanic" uses nautical terms to describe the ship and its operation. Although some of these words may be unfamiliar to students, their context helps reveal their meaning. Discuss with students how the author's use of marine terms helps support the effect of the narrative's **point of view.**

Activity. In his descriptions of the *Titanic*, Baldwin uses the words in the margin. Have students explain which context clues helped them understand the meaning of these words. Then, have students write down what they think each word means. When students have finished, have them check their definitions against those in a dictionary.

[*Sample responses: The story says that the* Titanic *could travel at twenty-three* knots. Knots *refers to the speed of a ship. The* **steerage** *class had "plain wooden cabins," and the people in these cabins were immigrants.*

Steerage must be plain accommodation for poorer people. People re-
treated to the **aft.** *Because the word* retreated *is used, the aft must be a*
section to the rear. The lookouts were stationed in the **crow's-nest,** *gaz-*
ing down at the water. A crow's-nest must be a high place from which
sailors look for threats. The **dynamos** *were located in the engine rooms,*
where they whirred until the ship sank. Because of their location and
sound, dynamos must provide electrical power.]

Postreading

Discussion Method: Reading Conference

Have students discuss the selections' **objective** and **subjective details**
in a reading conference. Ask students to prepare for the conference by
reviewing the stories and identifying facts—times, dates, and numbers. Then, have students look for details that reveal the writers' opinions about these facts. In groups, have students discuss the effect of
each type of writing on the description of the *Titanic* disaster.

- The liner *Californian* had "some message" about three icebergs that
the *Titanic*'s radio operator at first "didn't bother" to take down.
When J. Bruce Ismay received the information, he "stuffed it into
his pocket." How does Baldwin's diction affect his tone? *[Some,*
bother, and stuffed *give the impression of arrogance, implying that*
members of the Titanic*'s crew should have been carefully attentive.]*

- Harry Senior's tale is told in dispassionate language. However, details reveal his sense of why upper-class passengers were more
likely to survive than lower-class passengers. Is Senior's writing objective or subjective? *[Some students may say that Senior objectively*
describes the collision and evacuation. Others may say that Senior's
inclusion of the detail about the presence of millionaires in the first
lifeboat reveals his belief that wealthy people were given preferential
treatment.]

Writing

Have students respond to the prompt below in an essay.

Historical information is shaped and interpreted according to an author's **point of view.** Write an essay in which you compare and contrast the three accounts of the *Titanic* disaster. Consider how
perspective shapes the **objective** and **subjective** details that authors
include, and analyze how those details enhance readers' understanding of the event. Support your points with examples that reveal each
author's point of view.

Resources

For information on **reading**
conferences and other discussion methods, see page 20 of this
book.

Collection Resources

Criteria for Success

A successful response
- analyzes how the authors'
perspectives shape details
- supports the analysis with
apt examples
- shows insight into theme,
character, and tone
- uses language effectively

Section I: Multiple-Choice Questions

Directions: Carefully read the following speech by Mark Twain. Then, choose the *best* answer to each question.

Advice to Youth

Being told I would be expected to talk here, I inquired what sort of a talk I ought to make. They said it should be something suitable to youth—something didactic, in-
5 structive, or something in the nature of good advice. Very well. I have a few things in my mind which I have often longed to say for the instruction of the young; for it is in one's tender early years that such things will
10 best take root and be most enduring and most valuable. First, then, I will say to you, my young friends—and I say it beseech-ingly, urgingly—

Always obey your parents, when they are
15 present. This is the best policy in the long run, because if you don't they will make you. Most parents think they know better than you do, and you can generally make more by humoring that superstition than
20 you can by acting on your own better judg-ment.

Be respectful to your superiors, if you have any, also to strangers, and sometimes to others. If a person offends you, and you
25 are in doubt as to whether it was intentional or not, do not resort to extreme measures; simply watch your chance and hit him with a brick. That will be sufficient. If you shall find that he had not intended any offense,
30 come out frankly and confess yourself in the wrong when you struck him; acknowledge it like a man and say you didn't mean to. Yes, always avoid violence; in this age of charity and kindliness, the time has gone by for

35 such things. Leave dynamite to the low and unrefined.

Go to bed early, get up early—this is wise.[1] Some authorities say get up with the sun; some others say get up with one thing,
40 some with another. But a lark is really the best thing to get up with. It gives you a splendid reputation with everybody to know that you get up with the lark; and if you get the right kind of a lark, and work at
45 him right, you can easily train him to get up at half past nine, every time—it is no trick at all.

Now as to the matter of lying. You want to be very careful about lying; otherwise you
50 are nearly sure to get caught. Once caught, you can never again be, in the eyes of the good and the pure, what you were before. Many a young person has injured himself permanently through a single clumsy and
55 illfinished lie, the result of carelessness born of incomplete training. Some authorities hold that the young ought not to lie at all. That, of course, is putting it rather stronger than necessary; still, while I cannot go quite
60 so far as that, I do maintain, and I believe I am right, that the young ought to be tem-perate in the use of this great art until prac-tice and experience shall give them that confidence, elegance, and precision which
65 alone can make the accomplishment grace-ful and profitable. Patience, diligence, painstaking attention to detail—these are the requirements; these, in time, will make

[1]**Go to bed early, get up early—this is wise:** An allusion to Benjamin Franklin's aphorism "Early to bed and early to rise makes a man healthy, wealthy, and wise," published in *Poor Richard's Almanack* in 1735.

the student perfect; upon these, and upon these only, may he rely as the sure foundation for future eminence. Think what tedious years of study, thought, practice, experience, went to the equipment of that peerless old master who was able to impose upon the whole world the lofty and sounding maxim that "truth is mighty and will prevail"[2]—the most majestic compound fracture of fact which any of woman born has yet achieved. For the history of our race, and each individual's experience, are sown thick with evidence that a truth is not hard to kill and that a lie told well is immortal. There is in Boston a monument of the man who discovered anesthesia; many people are aware, in these latter days, that the man didn't discover it at all, but stole the discovery from another man. Is this truth mighty, and will it prevail? Ah no, my hearers, the monument is made of hardy material, but the lie it tells will outlast it a million years. An awkward, feeble, leaky lie is a thing which you ought to make it your unceasing study to avoid; such a lie as that has no more real permanence than an average truth. Why, you might as well tell the truth at once and be done with it. A feeble, stupid, preposterous lie will not live two years— except it be a slander upon somebody. It is indestructible, then, of course, but that is no merit of yours. A final word: begin your practice of this gracious and beautiful art early—begin now. If I had begun earlier, I could have learned how. . . .

There are many sorts of books; but good ones are the sort for the young to read. Remember that. They are a great, an inestimable, an unspeakable means of improvement. Therefore be careful in your selection, my young friends; be very careful; confine yourselves exclusively to Robertson's Sermons,[3] Baxter's *Saint's Rest*,[4] *The Innocents Abroad*,[5] and works of that kind.

But I have said enough. I hope you will treasure up the instructions which I have given you, and make them a guide to your feet and a light to your understanding. Build your character thoughtfully and painstakingly upon these precepts, and by and by, when you have got it built, you will be surprised and gratified to see how nicely and sharply it resembles everybody else's.

---

[2]**"truth is mighty . . .":** This statement is credited to Thomas Brooks (1608–1680), an English Puritan minister famous for his sermons and morally instructive books.

[3]**Robertson's Sermons:** Frederick William Robertson (1816–1853) was an English minister who was considered one of the greatest preachers of the nineteenth century. His published works include five volumes of sermons.

[4]**Baxter's *Saint's Rest*:** Richard Baxter (1615–1691) was a popular English minister whose books, including *The Saints' Everlasting Rest*, were still widely read in the late nineteenth century.

[5]***The Innocents Abroad*:** Published in 1869, *The Innocents Abroad; or, The New Pilgrim's Progress* is based on Twain's experiences on a trip to Europe and the Middle East. In the book, Twain satirizes his traveling companions and irreverently describes traditional tourist and pilgrimage sites.

1. The second paragraph can best be described as an example of
   (A) regionalism
   (B) satire
   (C) foreshadowing
   (D) realism
   (E) personification

2. Paragraph three (lines 22–36) includes all of the following rhetorical strategies except
   (A) exaggeration
   (B) irony
   (C) analogy
   (D) humor
   (E) oversimplification

3. When discussing lying, Twain does all of the following except
   (A) describe follies as virtues
   (B) practice ironic understatement
   (C) attempt to instruct through ridicule
   (D) engage in mockery and innuendo
   (E) use mimicry to praise and glorify

4. In the next to last paragraph (lines 104–112), the main effect of recommending his own book is to
   (A) encourage listeners to read sermons
   (B) show that he values spiritual insight
   (C) maintain the humorous tone
   (D) introduce factual information
   (E) increase sales of his own books

5. What indicates that Twain's speech is a parody?
   (A) It includes jokes, riddles, and puns.
   (B) It mocks people who wake up early.
   (C) It uses irony to satirize character traits.
   (D) It ridicules another type of speech.
   (E) It is a philosophical exploration of manners.

6. What describes an audience's most likely reaction to the speech?
   (A) Admiration
   (B) Anxiety
   (C) Affection
   (D) Amusement
   (E) Apathy

7. Which of the following quotations best reveals Twain's tone?
   (A) "Always obey your parents. . . . This is the best policy." (lines 14–15)
   (B) "Go to bed early, get up early—this is wise." (lines 37–38)
   (C) "Many a young person has injured himself permanently through a single clumsy and illfinished lie." (lines 53–55)
   (D) "There are many sorts of books; but good ones are the sort for the young to read." (lines 104–105)
   (E) "Build your character thoughtfully and painstakingly upon these precepts." (lines 116–118)

8. What is Twain's primary purpose in the speech?
   (A) To inform and educate
   (B) To investigate and reveal
   (C) To research and analyze
   (D) To discourage and dismiss
   (E) To entertain and enlighten

9. By adopting a persona, Twain
   (A) increases his credibility as an advisor
   (B) more effectively appeals to his audience
   (C) practices a different narrative voice for his fiction
   (D) uses allusions to the Bible and literature to emphasize his seriousness
   (E) avoids verbal attacks by those who might disagree with him

10. Which statement is the best clue that this is a graduation address?
    (A) "They said it should be something suitable to youth." (lines 3–4)
    (B) "If a person offends you, . . . do not resort to extreme measures." (lines 24–26)
    (C) "If you get the right kind of a lark . . . you can easily train him." (lines 43–45)
    (D) "An awkward, feeble, leaky lie is a thing which you ought . . . to avoid." (lines 91–93)
    (E) "A final word: begin your practice of this gracious and beautiful art early." (lines 100–102)

Section II: Essay

Directions: Carefully read the following prompt. Then, present your response in a well-developed essay.

> Some public libraries and schools have banned some of Twain's books because their characters were considered poor role models. What is the overall effect of Twain's "Advice to Youth" on young people? Consider how allusions, exaggeration, irony, understatement, and humor shape Twain's message for his audience. Imagine that officials who have seen a draft of Twain's speech claim that it encourages students to be disobedient, violent, lazy, and dishonest, and that it should therefore be banned. Write a well-developed essay in which you defend, challenge, or qualify the claim. Use examples from the speech and your reading, observation, or experience to develop a carefully reasoned argument.

For information about how to analyze a **writing prompt** and other strategies for timed writing, see page 45 of this book.

Scoring Guidelines

9–8   These essays fully explore the complexity of the issue. They competently defend, challenge, or qualify the proposal. They present coherent, well-reasoned arguments supported by comprehensive evidence. The students exhibit a sophisticated control of language.

7–6   These essays explore the complexity of the issue. They defend, challenge, or qualify the proposal. They present sound arguments using appropriate evidence. The students' prose is clear but may contain a few errors in diction or syntax.

5   These essays acknowledge the complexity of the issue and make clear claims, but their arguments may be unevenly developed or may contain limited evidence. The students' control of language is adequate.

4–3   These essays present an inadequate response to the prompt. The students may misunderstand the issue or may have difficulty establishing their own position. They might use inappropriate or insufficient evidence. The students demonstrate an inconsistent control over such elements of writing as diction and syntax.

2–1   These essays do not successfully respond to the prompt. The students may fail to understand the prompt, respond tangentially, or substitute a simpler task, such as merely summarizing the position of the officials. The students' prose reveals consistent weaknesses in such elements of writing as organization, grammar, and diction.

0   These essays present a response that receives no credit. They may simply paraphrase the prompt, for example.

Sample Response

The following essay represents a high-scoring response to the writing prompt.

Mark Twain models "Advice to Youth" on conventional inspirational and instructional speeches for young people. However, Twain's distortion of conventional advice may alarm officials, moving them to ban its presentation. Misunderstanding Twain's purpose, those officials may mistakenly think that Twain advises young people to be disobedient, violent, lazy, and dishonest. This is not the case. Twain's humorous, ironic presentation of advice is more likely to hold the attention of young people than a sermon might, so his speech is exactly what young people should hear.

Twain's introduction establishes the expectation that the speech will follow a familiar instructive model. However, Twain uses humor and irony to overturn that expectation. The second paragraph begins, "Always obey your parents"; however, Twain inserts a comma, a pause long enough for the audience to assume that this is another sermon. He then adds, "when they are present." Undoubtedly, Twain's young audience will laugh, recognizing their own attitudes about their parents' rules. Twain's strategy, therefore, is to prevent his audience from tuning out. They are likely to listen to one of their own. In a subtle twist of verbal irony, Twain drops in his true point: His audience will "make more" by following their parents' advice. Twain's advice to "disobey" is turned on its head; the audience is listening to common advice—that they might otherwise ignore.

Twain treats violence similarly. He structures the beginning of the third paragraph with conventional advice ("Be respectful to your superiors") and undermines it in mid-sentence ("if you have any"). He then provides an irony-laden example of violence: Hitting someone with a brick—especially when the insult is unintentional—is a ridiculous response to insult. Violence, Twain suggests, cannot solve the problem; an injured person is unlikely to accept an apology and excuse ("you didn't mean to"). Twain's speech, far from condoning violence, directs attention to its shortcomings: If we fail to respect each other, anger leads to insults, which in turn lead to violence.

In his fourth paragraph, Twain sounds almost as if he advocates laziness, but once again, his point is ironic. He uses one of Benjamin Franklin's most famous aphorisms, "Early to bed and early to rise makes a man healthy, wealthy, and wise," but he does not invert or qualify the aphorism. Here, Twain agrees with Franklin. The pursuit of laziness, as the audience is likely to understand, may take more effort than it's worth. Twain's young listeners are likely to recognize that training a lark to sleep until 9:30 would involve far more effort than getting up early would.

When Twain discusses lying, the central focus of his speech, he is once again ironic. He speaks as if he is giving advice about how to lie successfully, but his point is that people should avoid lies altogether. Lying may be a "great art," but Twain draws attention to significant problems with lying. Only with "practice and experience" can people become proficient liars. Liars are always in danger of getting caught. Liars threaten others. Lies distort historical truth. In case the audience needs an additional reason to avoid lying, Twain admits that despite years of practice, he is still a bad liar. Good lying takes a lot of work. By using humor, Twain attempts, like parents and ministers alike, to convince young people to stop lying.

Despite the unconventional treatment of common advice Twain's speech includes sound advice about character. Because Twain presents the advice humorously and with irony that appeals to young people they are likely to listen. Hearing Twain's speech could benefit not just young people but everyone else, too.

Through the Tunnel
by Doris Lessing

Literary Focus

The coverage of **symbolic meaning** below builds on the instruction in the Student Edition. You may want to introduce the additional skill of analyzing **climax** and **denouement** when teaching this story to advanced students.

Symbolic Meaning

The young protagonist in "Through the Tunnel" faces a difficult transition: To gain a sense of maturity, he must gain independence from his mother. For this reason, the task he sets for himself—swimming through an underwater tunnel—is weighted with particular significance. More than an obstacle, the tunnel symbolizes Jerry's fearful and dramatic transition from childhood dependence to teenaged autonomy. His drift from the safety of his mother's beach to a rocky island to the mysterious and beckoning tunnel takes on symbolic meaning, showing that Jerry has adopted the dangerous personal independence of a teen.

Climax and Denouement

As readers follow Jerry's passage through the story's disturbingly threatening tunnel, they may find themselves holding their breath with anticipation and worry. The heart-stopping description of the boy's journey forms the story's **climax,** or most intense moment. Tensions that have grown throughout the story, beginning with Jerry's adoption of a foolhardy plan to gain acceptance with the local boys, finally come to a head. In the story's **denouement,** or resolution, Jerry recovers from his swim and nosebleed and silently considers what has happened. This resolution indicates that Jerry's physical test has brought him a new emotional maturity and sense of independence: He no longer needs to prove himself to anyone.

Author Focus

A citizen of the far-flung British Empire, Doris Lessing was born in Persia (Iran) and raised in Southern Rhodesia (Zimbabwe). She claims that growing up in Africa formed her perspective as a writer; it was a place, she said, one could "wake up every morning with one's eyes on fresh evidence of inhumanity." Lessing's work often exposes injustices, including racism, terrorism, and environmental destruction.

SKILLS FOCUS

Literary Skill
Analyze symbolic meaning.

Advanced Skill
Analyze climax and denouement.

As students explore **symbolic meaning, climax,** and **denouement,** remind them not to look at these elements in isolation but to consider how they contribute to our understanding of **character, tone,** and **theme.**

Related Works

Consider teaching one of the works below from *Elements of Literature* with "Through the Tunnel."

Analyzing symbolic meaning:
"Everyday Use" by Alice Walker

Analyzing climax and denouement:
"The Cold Equations" by Tom Godwin

Collection Resources

Resources

For information on **ladders of questions** and other metacognitive strategies, see page 16 of this book.

Close Reading

Metacognitive Strategy: Ladder of Questions

Direct students to use the ladder-of-questions strategy to analyze the **symbolic meaning** of Jerry's actions in the story. Have students answer literal, interpretive, and experiential questions about the first six paragraphs of the story, beginning with "Going to the shore" and ending with "to her beach."

- Literal: What is the difference between the beach Jerry's mother visits and the bay he sees? *[The beach is a familiar place that his mother enjoys. The bay is a "wild" place that Jerry has not investigated.]*

- Interpretive: Why is the bay inviting to Jerry? *[The bay is exciting and is not associated with his mother or her oversight.]* What do the bay and the beach symbolize to Jerry? *[The beach is a comfortable place symbolizing childhood. The bay is an unknown, teen-filled location symbolizing independence.]*

- Experiential: What places do you associate with childhood? How do you know when you have outgrown childhood places? *[Students may associate playgrounds and wading pools with childhood. They may say that they physically outgrow them or that peer pressure or emotional and intellectual maturation demand new environments.]*

Close-Reading Practice: Climax and Denouement

Close Reading

The close-reading passage is on pages 482–484 of the Student Edition.

Have students re-read the passage from "A hundred" to the end of the story, and discuss these questions to explore climax and denouement:

- What effect does Jerry's counting have on the story's climactic scene? *[Jerry's counting builds extraordinary tension; by the time he reaches 115, he has also reached his physical limits. His repetition of the number implies that he has lost clarity of thought and is drifting out of consciousness, perhaps beginning to drown.]*

- How does the author's description of Jerry's condition after he finishes his swim support the story's denouement? *[The swim has taken all of Jerry's strength and stamina, leaving him unable to "swim the few feet back to the rock," feeling as if his eyes have "burst," and wanting "nothing but to get back home and lie down." His success has come at great cost, teaching him that his victory is personal and that he no longer needs the boys' approval.]*

Vocabulary: Words That Reveal Character

Vocabulary

Before assigning this activity, make sure your students have mastered the Vocabulary words on page 476 of the Student Edition.

At the story's **climax,** Jerry accomplishes a dangerous act that marks a personal transition. Focusing on the words used to describe Jerry and his actions can help students trace his growing maturity.

Activity. In her description of Jerry's experience, Lessing uses the words in the margin. Have students discuss what each word reveals about Jerry's growth. Finally, have students write sentences explaining how each word contributes to the story's climax and denouement.

*[Jerry gives the older boys a **pleading** grin. The word shows how much Jerry wants to be accepted by them. When Jerry tells his mother he wants goggles, he is **beseeching**. The word shows Jerry's powerlessness; he must beg his mother for what he wants. As he plans his swim through the tunnel, Jerry shows **persistence**. This positive word shows Jerry's ability to set a goal. Jerry is **panicky** when he thinks there might be entangling weeds in the tunnel. Here, he tests himself, not yet knowing his abilities. Near the end of the tunnel, Jerry can move only **feebly**. His strength and energy have been expended. Although he is exhausted, he has accomplished his goal.]*

Words for the Activity

pleading, p. 479
beseeching, p. 480
persistence, p. 481
panicky, p. 482
feebly, p. 483

Postreading

Discussion Method: Reading Conference

Have students discuss the story's **climax** and **denouement** in a reading conference. Ask students to prepare for the conference by creating story maps that chart the rising action in the story, the climax, and the falling action. In groups, have students finalize their story maps and discuss how Lessing makes the climax so exciting. Use the following questions to prompt students' thinking:

- How does Jerry prepare for swimming through the tunnel? What events hinder his preparation? Use your story map to help you answer. *[Jerry practices holding his breath underwater to strengthen his lung capacity. Nosebleeds and his mother's insistence that he stay home one day hinder him. He also faces a deadline: He must swim the tunnel before the vacation ends.]*

- Once he enters the tunnel, what challenges does Jerry face? *[Jerry might become entangled in weeds; he is swimming in darkness; the roof of the tunnel is sharp; and Jerry does not know whether he has enough air in his lungs to complete the journey.]* How do descriptions of Jerry's journey hint that he will fail or provide clues that he will succeed? *[Words such as* panicky, convulsive, *and* feebly *indicate that Jerry might drown in the tunnel, but the light from the surface gives hope that he will succeed.]*

- How does the story show that Jerry's experience has changed him? *[His attitude about the local boys and his behavior toward his mother change, and he no longer needs to swim in the bay.]*

Writing

Have students write an essay that responds to the prompt below.

> The climax of Lessing's story involves a passage from one place to another. Consider the importance of the tunnel on both its literal and symbolic levels. Then, write an essay in which you analyze how Lessing creates **symbolic meaning** in her story. Use details from the story to support your points.

Resources

For information on **reading conferences** and other discussion methods, see page 20 of this book.

Collection Resources

Criteria for Success

A successful response
- analyzes Lessing's techniques for creating symbolic meaning
- uses appropriate textual details to support the analysis
- shows insight into theme, character, and tone
- uses language effectively

Elements of Literature selection

The Masque of the Red Death
by Edgar Allan Poe

SKILLS FOCUS

Literary Skill
Analyze characteristics of allegory.

Advanced Skill
Analyze historical setting.

As students explore **characteristics of allegory** and **historical setting,** remind them not to look at these elements in isolation but to consider how they contribute to our understanding of **character, tone,** and **theme.**

Collection Resources

Related Works

Consider teaching one of the works below from *Elements of Literature* with "The Masque of the Red Death."

Analyzing allegory:
"The Tale of Sir Launcelot du Lake" by Sir Thomas Malory

Analyzing historical setting:
"Where Have You Gone, Charming Billy?" by Tim O'Brien

Resources

For information on **annotating text** and other metacognitive strategies, see page 16 of this book.

Literary Focus

The coverage of **allegory** below builds on the instruction in the Student Edition. You may want to introduce the additional skill of analyzing **historical setting** when teaching this story to advanced students.

Allegory

In "The Masque of the Red Death," Edgar Allan Poe creates an **allegory,** a narrative that is both literal and symbolic. Literally, the story is of Prince Prospero, who has retreated to the countryside to escape the Red Death. Prospero gives a fabulous party that ends disastrously. Allegorically, Poe's story depicts the foolhardiness of attempting to deny one's mortality and fate. Prince Prospero, whose name suggests prosperity and wealth, believes his power and influence make him invulnerable. The allegory emphasizes that neither fortress nor social station can save a person: Death finds us all.

Historical Setting

Poe's tale refers generally to the time of medieval plagues. The story's plague shares similarities with the bubonic plague. As James Cross Giblin notes in "The Black Death," people who fled to the countryside, as Prince Prospero does, often met the same fate as those who remained in cities. Prospero welds shut the gates to his abbey; however, the quarantine is not entirely effective.

Author Focus

Poe's writing is striking for its contrasts. Poems such as "Annabel Lee" and "To Helen" are sensitive celebrations of feminine beauty. However, stories such as "The Fall of the House of Usher" and "The Premature Burial" are grisly, macabre examinations of death. Poe's preoccupation with fictional mortality may have grown from personal experience: In his short life, Poe endured the deaths of his mother, his foster mother, and his young wife.

Close Reading

Metacognitive Strategy: Annotating Text

As students read, have them annotate the story, focusing on details that convey the **allegory.** To help students consider the importance of the allegory as they annotate, encourage them to remember that characters can personify abstract qualities and meanings independent of narrative. Have students note details related to the following:

- Prince Prospero and his reasons for retiring to the abbey
- the significance of Prospero's different-colored rooms
- the ebony clock and its effect on the partygoers
- the stranger and his effect on Prospero's masque

Close-Reading Practice: Allegory

Close Reading

The close-reading passage is on pages 497–498 of the Student Edition.

Have students re-read the passage beginning "It was in this apartment" and ending with "meditation as before," and discuss these questions to explore Poe's use of allegory:

- What is the literal significance of the ebony clock? *[The clock's chime is so loud and unusual that it interrupts the musicians, causing dancing to cease momentarily.]*

- How does Poe suggest that the clock has allegorical meaning? *[Poe chooses descriptive words and phrases that create an ominous tone, exaggerate the clock's effects, and imply that its value is more than literal. The clock's pendulum swings with a "heavy, monotonous clang," its chime comes from "brazen lungs," the hours "lapse," and the clock's sound makes people grow "pale," disconcerted, and "tremulous."]*

- How does the clock function on an allegorical level? *[The clock is black, a color that represents death, and its sound disturbingly marks the passage of time, causing hearers to engage in "meditation" as if they are remembering that they, too, will one day pass away.]*

Vocabulary: Word Analysis

Vocabulary

Before assigning this activity, make sure your students have mastered the Vocabulary words on page 494 of the Student Edition.

Words for the Activity
pestilence, p. 496
voluptuous, p. 496
grotesque, p. 499
phantasm, p. 499
revel, p. 500

Poe's tale contains many words derived from French and Italian—words that sometimes have elevated connotations. Looking at the origins of these words can give students deeper insight into Poe's allegory about earthly wealth and death's supremacy.

Activity. In his descriptions of Prospero's masque, Poe uses the words in the margin. Have students read the descriptions of the words below and then write synonyms with less elevated connotations. Have each student then write a sentence describing how the synonym would affect the story's allegorical meaning.

- **pestilence:** from French *pestilence;* the word means "a fatal epidemic." *[Possible response: plague—People may believe they can escape a pestilence, but plague sounds unavoidable and deadly.]*

- **voluptuous:** from French *voluptueux;* the word means "luxurious." *[Possible response: rich—Voluptuous carries the connotation of sensuality and refinement; rich might imply that Prospero spends money on sensual pleasures but may lack taste.]*

- **grotesque:** from Old Italian *grottesca;* the word means "fanciful or distorted images." *[Possible response: distorted—Distorted has a connotation of being physically misshapen but does not imply the same level of monstrosity or fanciful appearance.]*

- **phantasm:** from French *fantasm;* the word means "apparition or illusion." *[Possible response: illusion—Illusion is a narrower category; phantasm refers generally to ghostly illusions and sounds more intriguingly mysterious.]*
- **revel:** from Old French *revel;* the word means "noisy festivity." *[Possible response: party—Party is less elevated, with connotations of an event that common people might attend.]*

Postreading
Discussion Method: Reading Conference

Have students discuss the story's **allegory** in a reading conference. Ask them to prepare for the conference by jotting down important events in the story, describing their possible allegorical meanings. In groups, have students finish their descriptions and discuss why Poe might use a medieval masque for his allegory. Use these questions to prompt students' thinking:

- What is Prospero's purpose in going to the abbey? *[He wants to get away from the Red Death.]* In what way is his action allegorical? *[Many people fear and run from death. They may think that they can distance themselves from death through wealth or power.]*
- What is the significance of the series of different-colored rooms in Prospero's abbey? *[The intricately decorated rooms show Prospero's cleverness and wealth. They are additional evidence of his wealth and power. They are important to the allegory because they show a transition from east to west and from life to death. Significantly, his guests avoid the final, black room that represents death.]*
- Describe the figure of the masque's uninvited stranger. In what way is his entrance and behavior allegorical? *[The stranger is thin and silent. He does not explain his reason for attending the masque. Like death, the figure is unexpected and cannot be overcome.]*

Writing

Have students write an essay that responds to the prompt below.

James Cross Giblin describes the bubonic plague as a deadly disease that annihilated the populations of Sicily and Italy. Consider the reaction of the characters in "The Masque of the Red Death," who, in the face of death, attend an elaborate, indulgent party. Then, write an essay in which you explain why people facing a merciless, unexplained death might desire entertainment and indulgence.

Resources

For information on **reading conferences** and other discussion methods, see page 20 of this book.

Collection Resources

Criteria for Success

A successful response
- analyzes reasons that humans might desire entertainment when facing death
- supports the analysis with appropriate textual details from both the story and the article
- shows insight into theme, character, and tone
- uses language effectively

After Apple-Picking
by Robert Frost

Literary Focus

The coverage of **symbols** below builds on the instruction in the Student Edition. You may want to introduce the additional skill of analyzing **sensory imagery** when teaching this poem to advanced students.

Symbols

Robert Frost is famous for using potent symbols that elicit strong emotions and suggest layers of meaning. Even the subject of this poem, apple picking, has symbolic associations: The Genesis account holds that Eve and Adam, after picking (and eating) fruit, were driven into a world of regrets, toil, and death. Similarly, the poem's speaker descends, after acquiring countless apples, from a ladder pointing "toward heaven." Remind students that a symbol is a person, place, or thing that stands both for itself and for something beyond itself. Then, have students analyze the poem's symbolic meaning by discussing possible interpretations of the following: harvest time, the "long two-pointed" ladder, the barrels, the unpicked apples, the ice sheet, the speaker's dream, the cider-apple heap, sleep, and hibernation.

Author Focus. A number of Frost's poems focus on his interest in the biblical story of Adam's fall from grace. Frost develops this theme in "After Apple-Picking" by concentrating on the human awareness of death: The poem's speaker seems doomed to live a life of endless, Sisyphean toil, haunted by unpicked and dropped apples even during sleep.

Sensory Imagery

Frost is a master of sensory imagery, and he carefully addresses all but one of the five senses in this poem. Visual images, such as "two-pointed ladder," are abundant. The speaker cannot escape the "scent of apples." He hears the "rumbling sound" of the fruit entering the cellar. His hands "cherish" the red globes they touch. Significantly, Frost does not incorporate the *taste* of apples. An extraordinarily deliberate poet, Frost may have omitted the sense of taste to indicate that a symbolic apple, in the poem's present, has already been tasted or that the speaker is unable to share in the fruits of his own labors. With students, make a list of the poem's sensory images. Then, have students analyze the effects of Frost's appeal to each of the four senses included in the poem.

SKILLS FOCUS

Literary Skill
Analyze symbolic meaning.

Advanced Skill
Analyze sensory imagery.

As students explore **symbolic meaning** and **sensory imagery**, remind them not to look at these elements in isolation but to consider how they contribute to our understanding of **character**, **tone**, and **theme**.

Related Works

Consider teaching one of the works below from *Elements of Literature* with "After Apple-Picking."

Analyzing symbolic meaning:
"Eating Together" by Li-Young Lee

Analyzing metaphors:
"I Am Offering This Poem" by Jimmy Santiago Baca

Collection Resources

For information on **ladders of questions** and other metacognitive strategies, see page 16 of this book.

Collection Resources

The close-reading passage is on page 511 of the Student Edition.

Words for the Activity

essence, line 7

hoary, line 12

russet, line 20

spiked, line 34

stubble, line 34

Metacognitive Strategy: Ladders of Questions

Have students work as a class or in groups to paraphrase the poem. Then, have them explore the poem's **symbols** by answering the following questions:

Literal Questions

1. What does "great harvest" mean?

2. What will "trouble" the speaker as he slumbers?

Interpretive Questions

1. What similarities are there between the speaker's sleep and death?

2. What does the cellar symbolize? How does it support the theme?

Experiential Questions

1. What other Frost poems have you read? Do those poems use symbols? How are their symbols similar to or different from the ones in this poem?

2. Have you ever longed to begin work on a task, yet later, when work ended, felt that you had worked too long or had had enough?

Close-Reading Practice: Sensory Imagery

Have students re-read lines 7 through 13, and then discuss the following questions to explore Frost's sensory imagery:

- What is the "Essence of winter sleep"? To which sense does this essence appeal, and why is the appeal significant? *[The "essence" is the scent of the apples, which appeals to the sense of smell. The speaker associates this sweetly pleasing scent with winter and overwhelming drowsiness (symbols of approaching death), suggesting that winter's onset does not necessarily detract from the joys and beauties of life.]*

- What images invoke the sense of touch? How do these images of touch support the theme? *[Possible response: The speaker experiences the sensations of touching ice that has formed in the "drinking trough," his hands rubbing his eyes after looking through the sheet of ice. Just as a growing awareness of mortality may affect a person's view of life, the speaker's painful sensation of viewing the world through a "pane" of ice affects his perception, hinting that he now realizes that the onset of winter is but a preamble to an inevitable "harvest" (death).]*

Vocabulary: Context Clues

The poem's **symbols** are rendered in rich sensory vocabulary that evokes the theme. For instance, the speaker's description of his aching insteps implies that human beings cannot easily ignore or forget their physical conditions. A lover of simple words, Frost usually uses everyday terms that can easily be understood in context.

Activity. In his descriptions of the poem's symbols, Frost uses the words in the margin. Have students write down an explanation of how context clues can be used to define each word. Then, have students write sentences analyzing how each word supports one of the poem's themes.

*[Here, **essence** means "distillation" or "intrinsic nature." Lines 7 and 8 equate "Essence of winter sleep" with "The scent of apples" and make the association between the harvest and the wintry sleep of death. **Hoary** means both "covered with frost" and "ancient"; the ground is frosty. The word supports the idea that a pleasant harvest still leads to winter and old age. **Russet** means "deep red," the color of the ripe apples. The adjective, because it suggests the vibrant color of life, supports the contrast between life and death, fall and winter. **Spiked** means "having sharp points," as the fallen apples have been pierced by crop stubble. The word may refer to the thorned crown of Christ, or it may refer to life's pains and injuries. The word implies that harvested apples have one value, while others have another use, yet an end comes to all. **Stubble** refers to stumps of plants left after a harvest and reinforces the harvest imagery. This symbol supports the theme by suggesting that winter, age, and death come to all living things.]*

Postreading

Discussion Method: Reading Conference

Have students discuss the poem's **symbols** in a reading conference. Ask them to prepare for the conference by creating a list of the symbols and their meanings. Group students, and have them share, discuss, and finalize their symbol lists. Use the following questions to prompt students' thinking:

- Do the symbols create a hopeful or a resigned tone? Explain the reasons for your answer. *[Possible response: The symbols create a resigned tone; many represent the waning or ending of life.]*

- Frost's symbols often have multiple meanings. Why do you think he chooses complex symbols? *[Possible response: Frost writes deceptively simple poems; complex symbols compress layers of meaning into a few lines.]*

Writing

Have students write an essay that responds to the prompt below.

> The apples that "appear and disappear" may be a **symbol** of life. How is this symbol developed as the poem progresses, and how does the symbol provide a foundation for the poem's tone and theme? How are the apples similar to the speaker? Consider **sensory imagery**, character, tone, and theme as you write an essay answering those questions. Use details and examples to support your points.

Resources

For information on **reading conferences** and other discussion methods, see page 20 of this book.

Criteria for Success

A successful response

- thoroughly and perceptively analyzes the poem's use of the symbol
- supports the analysis with appropriate details from the poem
- shows insight into sensory imagery, theme, character, and tone
- uses language effectively

Collection Resources

Writing Workshop: Analyzing a Short Story

Writing Skill
Analyze a short story.

As students **analyze a short story**, remind them that literary analysis, like all forms of writing, gains power from attention to literary elements, such as **diction, figurative language, tone,** and **voice.**

Resources

For more information on **generalizations,** see the Handbook of Rhetorical Concepts in this book.

Prewriting
Advanced Prewriting Strategy

Formulating a Thesis. Students often have difficulty creating a meaningful **thesis** that can serve as the basis for an entire essay. Explain that the ideal thesis is not a factual statement or, at the other extreme, a statement of unsupported opinion. Instead, the thesis is an essay in miniature: A thesis contains both an insight *and* a general reference to supporting evidence from the story. Before students settle on a particular thesis, have them answer the following questions:

- Does the thesis contain a unique insight about the story?
- Does the thesis apply to the majority of the story or at least to a large part of it?
- Does the story contain enough support for the thesis to warrant a full-length (approximately 1,500-word) essay?
- Does the thesis lend itself to *analysis, evaluation,* and *interpretation* of the story?
- Does the thesis seem like a "boiled down" literary-analysis essay?

Writing
Advanced Writing Skills

Using Generalizations and Inferences. Remind students that their essays will contain both generalizations and inferences. **Generalizations** are broad conclusions drawn after evaluating multiple aspects of the story. **Inferences,** however, are educated guesses based not only on the story but also on other reading and prior experience. Successful literary generalizations and inferences are always supported by evidence from the selection.

Activity. To help students make generalizations and inferences, instruct them to write their thesis statements and to list the main idea for each supporting paragraph. Then, ask students to complete the following checklist for each statement while drafting their papers:

- This statement connects my observations to a larger understanding.
- This statement can be supported by the story's literary elements, such as character, tone, theme, mood, plot, and figurative language.
- This statement is clear, coherent, and easily understandable.

Collection Resources

SKILLS FOCUS

Grammar Solutions. Explain to students that in most cases, simple sentences do not effectively communicate a thesis or main idea. Compound or complex sentences are often sufficient, but **compound-complex sentences** are usually ideal. Use of compound-complex sentences helps writers more fully express complex ideas. Discuss the following examples with students:

COMPOUND THESIS SENTENCE

Ernest Hemingway's Death in the Afternoon *explores bullfighting; the story portrays the event as a tragic ceremony.*

COMPLEX THESIS SENTENCE

In Ernest Hemingway's Death in the Afternoon, *bullfighting is a tragic ceremony that features important rituals and gestures.*

COMPOUND-COMPLEX THESIS SENTENCE

In Ernest Hemingway's Death in the Afternoon, *bullfighting is more than a sport; it is a tragic ceremony that features important rituals and gestures.*

As students draft their essays, encourage them to use compound-complex sentences for their theses and main ideas.

Evaluating and Revising

Revising for Style

Adding Quotations. Students' analyses will be more authoritative if their ideas are supported by direct quotations. Review different methods of adding quotations, such as incorporating a few quoted words into an analytic sentence, using colons or semicolons to add quotations to analysis, and copying several quoted sentences into an offset, indented section.

Activity. Ask students to read through their essays and to locate sections that will benefit from adding quotations. As students revise, have them focus on using appropriate methods of quotation.

Publishing and Reflecting

Exchanging Ideas. To help students learn to present their ideas to an audience, have them adapt their analyses for oral presentation. After each student speaks, have other students ask questions or make comments that will help speakers better develop their analyses.

Self-Evaluation. Have students reflect on what they have written by writing responses to the following questions:

- What **thesis** did you use? Did the thesis sustain the entire essay? Was the thesis fully supported by evidence from the story?

- What **generalizations** and **inferences** did you make? Were they effective? Why or why not?

- How successful was your use of **quotations?** What are the best uses of quotation in your essay? Why?

Resources

For more information on **compound-complex sentences,** see the Handbook of Grammatical Concepts in this book.

Collection Resources

Literature Link

Before students begin revising to add quotations, encourage them to re-read Barbara Sande Dimmitt's "The Education of Frank McCourt" or Phyllis Goldenberg's "Brutus's Funeral Speech" to evaluate how these authors use quotations in different ways.

Resources

For more information on **Presenting a Literary Response,** see pages 524–525 of the Student Edition.

Section I: Multiple-Choice Questions

Directions: Carefully read the following excerpt from Stephen Crane's novel *The Red Badge of Courage*. Then, choose the *best* answer to each question.

from The Red Badge of Courage

The youth was in a little trance of astonishment. So they were at last going to fight. On the morrow perhaps there would be a battle and he would be in it. For a time, he was
5 obliged to labor to make himself believe. He could not accept with assurance an omen that he was about to mingle in one of those great affairs of the earth.

He had of course dreamed of battles all
10 of his life—of vague and bloody conflicts that had thrilled him with their sweep and fire. In visions, he had seen himself in many struggles. He had imagined peoples secure in the shadow of his eagle-eyed prowess. But
15 awake he had regarded battles as crimson blotches on the pages of the past. He had put them as things of the bygone with his thought-images of heavy crowns and high castles. There was a portion of the world's
20 history which he had regarded as the time of wars, but, it, he thought, had been long gone over the horizon and had disappeared forever.

From his home his youthful eyes had
25 looked upon the war in his own country with distrust. It must be some sort of a play affair. He had long despaired of witnessing a Greek-like struggle. Such would be no more, he had said. Men were better, or, more
30 timid. Secular and religious education had effaced the throat-grappling instinct, or, else, firm finance held in check the passions.

He had burned several times to enlist. Tales of great movements shook the land.
35 They might not be distinctly Homeric, but there seemed to be much glory in them. He had read of marches, sieges, conflicts, and he had longed to see it all. His busy mind had drawn for him large pictures, extravagant in
40 color, lurid with breathless deeds.

But his mother had discouraged him. She had affected to look with some contempt upon the quality of his war-ardor and patriotism. She could calmly seat herself and
45 with no apparent difficulty give him many hundreds of reasons why he was of vastly more importance on the farm than on the field of battle. She had had certain ways of expression that told that her statements on
50 the subject came from a deep conviction. Besides, on her side, was his belief that her ethical motive in the argument was impregnable.

At last, however, he had made firm rebel-
55 lion against this yellow light thrown upon the color of his ambitions. The newspapers, the gossip of the village, his own picturings, had aroused him to an uncheckable degree. They were in truth fighting finely down
60 there. Almost every day, the newspapers printed accounts of a decisive victory.

One night, as he lay in bed, the winds had carried to him the clangoring of the church-bell as some enthusiast jerked the
65 rope frantically to tell the twisted news of a great battle. This voice of the people, rejoicing in the night, had made him shiver in a prolonged ecstasy of excitement. Later, he had gone down to his mother's room and
70 had spoken thus: "Ma, I'm goin' t' enlist."

"Henry, don't you be a fool," his mother had replied. She had then covered her face with the quilt. There was an end to the matter for that night.

75 Nevertheless, the next morning, he had gone to a considerable town that was near his mother's farm and had enlisted in a company that was forming there. When he had returned home, his mother was milking
80 the brindle cow. Four others stood waiting.

"Ma, I've enlisted," he had said to her diffidently.

There was a short silence. "Th' Lord's will be done, Henry," she had finally replied and
85 had then continued to milk the brindle cow.

When he had stood in the door-way with his soldier's clothes on his back and with the light of excitement and expectancy in his eyes almost defeating the glow of regret for
90 the home bonds, he had seen two tears leaving their hot trails on his mother's scarred cheeks.

Still, she had disappointed him by saying nothing whatever about returning with his
95 shield or on it.[1] He had privately primed himself for a beautiful scene. He had prepared certain sentences which he thought could be used with touching effect. But her words destroyed his plans. She had doggedly
100 peeled potatoes and addressed him as follows: "You watch out, Henry, an' take good keer of yerself in this here fightin' business—you watch out an' take good keer of yerself. Don't go a-thinkin' yeh kin lick th'
105 hull rebel army at th' start, b'cause yeh can't. Yer jest one little feller 'mongst a hull lot 'a others an' yeh've got t' keep quiet an' do what they tell yeh. I know how you are, Henry."

[1] **returning with his shield or on it:** an allusion to the traditional parting words of a mother of Sparta, an ancient Greek city-state, to her son when he went to war. Spartan warriors were famous for their training, military skills, and courage.

1. "Greek-like struggle" (line 28), "distinctly Homeric" (line 35), and the allusion to Spartan mothers (lines 93–95)
   (A) give the passage a formal tone
   (B) indicate Ma's opinion about war
   (C) show Henry's view of war as epic and heroic
   (D) contrast ancient Greek wars with the Civil War
   (E) reveal the author's familiarity with Greek myths and history

2. The "yellow light" in line 55 is a
   (A) simile comparing a lamp to the sun
   (B) symbol of an inspiring holy vision
   (C) metaphor for the mother's doubt
   (D) reference to Henry's cowardice
   (E) moral allegory about war

3. The first four sentences of the last paragraph (lines 93–99) reinforce the overall tone of the passage, which is
   (A) fanciful and sentimental
   (B) reflective and bemused
   (C) optimistic and witty
   (D) harsh and judgmental
   (E) bitter and pessimistic

4. The passage is told from the point of view of a
   (A) first-person narrator
   (B) second-person narrator
   (C) third-person limited narrator
   (D) third-person omniscient narrator
   (E) two different narrators, Henry and his mother

5. Which of the following statements best represents an ironic tone?
   (A) He had imagined peoples secure in the shadow of his eagle-eyed prowess. (lines 13–14)
   (B) She could calmly seat herself. (line 44)
   (C) At last, however, he had made firm rebellion. (lines 54–55)
   (D) Later, he had gone down to his mother's room. (lines 68–69)
   (E) He had stood in the door-way with his soldier's clothes on his back. (lines 86–87)

6. The climax of the passage occurs when
   (A) Henry thinks he could be a war hero
   (B) Henry's mother tells him that he is needed on the farm
   (C) Henry hears the church-bell announcing another battle
   (D) Henry announces that he is going to enlist
   (E) Henry's mother tells Henry to be careful

7. Ma's dialect (lines 71, 83–84, and 101–109) contrasts her lack of sophistication with the
   (A) heroic expectations Henry maintains
   (B) educational level of the story's audience
   (C) optimism of gathering Northern troops
   (D) common-sense advice she gives
   (E) stories appearing in the newspapers

8. The character of the mother can be described as all of the following EXCEPT
   (A) enthusiastic
   (B) religious
   (C) sorrowful
   (D) skeptical
   (E) hardworking

9. The *most* important conflict implied in the passage is between
   (A) Henry's religious education and his mother's beliefs
   (B) the mother's chores and Henry's work responsibilities
   (C) Henry's desire for excitement and the occasional monotony of farm life
   (D) the mother's concern for animals and Henry's neglect of them
   (E) Henry's romantic view of battle and the harsh reality of war

10. From information provided in the passage, readers can tell that Henry
   (A) will lose his life during battle
   (B) plans to later finish high school
   (C) feels no regrets over leaving home
   (D) ignores news stories concerning the war
   (E) has joined a company of Union forces

Section II: Essay

Directions: Carefully read the following prompt. Then, present your response in a well-developed essay.

> Henry's mother acts as a foil, or contrasting character, to her son. Her presence therefore may lead readers to examine Henry's personality and choices more critically. Write an essay in which you compare and contrast Henry and Ma. Use examples from your reading, observation, or experience to develop a carefully reasoned comparison-and-contrast essay.

Resources

For information about how to analyze a **writing prompt** and other strategies for timed writing, see page 45 of this book.

Scoring Guidelines

9–8 These essays fully compare and contrast Henry and Ma. They present coherent, well-reasoned comparisons supported by comprehensive evidence. The students exhibit a sophisticated control of language.

7–6 These essays adequately compare and contrast Henry and Ma. They present sound comparisons using appropriate evidence. The students' prose is clear but may contain a few errors in diction or syntax.

5 These essays make clear comparisons between Henry and Ma, but their arguments may be unevenly developed or they may contain limited evidence. The students' control of language is adequate.

4–3 These essays present an inadequate response to the prompt. The students might make incorrect comparisons between Henry and Ma or use inappropriate or insufficient evidence. The students demonstrate an inconsistent control over such elements of writing as diction and syntax.

2–1 These essays do not successfully respond to the prompt. The students may fail to understand the prompt, respond tangentially, or substitute a simpler task, such as merely describing the characters. The students' prose reveals consistent weaknesses in such elements of writing as organization, grammar, and diction.

0 These essays present a response that receives no credit. They may simply paraphrase the prompt, for example.

Sample Response

The following essay represents a high-scoring response to the writing prompt.

By contrasting the two characters, Henry and Ma, Stephen Crane enables readers to understand both characters more fully. Henry is young, inexperienced, unaware of the costs of his actions, and perhaps irresponsible. In contrast, his mother is mature, careful, aware of consequences, and attentive to her responsibilities. Her actions serve as commentary on the follies and dangers of war, and her carefully reasoned concerns contrast with Henry's romantic view of war. The two characters are contrasted by age and experience, foresight, and sense of responsibility.

Henry's youth and inexperience are contrasted with Ma's maturity and experience. Henry is introduced as a "youth," emphasizing his lack of experience. He is in a "trance of astonishment," so thrilled at the prospect of battle that he does not consider the dangers. He looks forward to the coming battle and the chance "to mingle in one of those great affairs of the earth." Ma, however, "look[s] with some contempt upon the quality of his war-ardor and patriotism." With a mature perspective, she calmly gives him "many hundreds of reasons why he was of vastly more importance on the farm than on the field of battle." Henry, however, has been comparing the war to the epic battles of the Greek city-states. These allusions indicate that Henry wants to play the role of an epic hero. Ma holds no such romantic naiveté about battle.

When Henry tells his mother that he is going to enlist, she says, "Henry, don't you be a fool." This comment foreshadows something ominous—Henry is likely to take foolish risks in pursuit of "glory." On the eve of battle, Henry is excited about "at last going to fight." There is no hint that he has gained realistic foresight since leaving the farm. When Henry tells his mother that he actually has enlisted, Ma pauses before saying, "Th' Lord's will be done, Henry." She knows that it is useless to try to reason with Henry now that he has enlisted. Clearly, she fears that he will not return. Henry's continuing enthusiasm shows that he has no such misgivings. Before he leaves the farm, Ma gives him sensible advice that might help save his life. Unfortunately, nothing in the passage indicates that Henry will follow her advice.

Though eager to play a heroic role in the war, Henry does not consider the responsibilities he abandons by enlisting in the army. On the eve of battle he "had imagined peoples secure in the shadow of his eagle-eyed prowess." To gain glory and play the role of hero, Henry is prepared to ignore his mother's argument that he is needed on the farm. When Henry leaves, Ma will be left alone, with all the hard work to do by herself. Instead of recognizing his duty to his mother, Henry focuses on the glory and fame that he might gain as a war hero. Significantly, in two major scenes, Ma continues to work while talking to her son about his decision. She has no time for idle chitchat, and her son never considers how exhausted she probably is. In the barn scene, she milks one cow while four others wait their turn—and Henry makes no attempt to help. In the kitchen scene, she "doggedly peel[s] potatoes" while talking. Henry is eager to take on the responsibilities of a soldier—or, at least, his romantic idea of those responsibilities—but even while still on the farm he neglects farm work. He doesn't notice his mother's heavy burden. His irresponsibility is contrasted with his mother's attention to work, a contrast that gains emphasis because the work involves caring for animals—work that cannot be postponed without causing suffering, injury, or death for the animals.

Ma is a critical foil to Henry. Her presence emphasizes Henry's youth and inexperience, his lack of foresight about the consequences of war, and his neglect of his current duties in his eagerness to become a soldier. Ma helps develop a sense of foreboding in the passage, reinforcing the title's ill omen and inviting readers to anticipate injury, emotional trauma, or even death for Henry.

Elements of Literature selection

Grape Sherbet
by Rita Dove

Literary Focus

The coverage of a poem's **speaker** below builds on the instruction in the Student Edition. You may want to introduce the additional skill of analyzing **ambiguity** when teaching this poem to advanced students.

Speaker

A poem's **speaker** is the voice that talks to readers, whether the voice is that of the poet or of the poet's persona. Each poem's speaker has a unique voice—a mixture of personal characteristics, emotions, and attitudes. Because the concepts of poet, speaker, and voice are so closely interrelated, students may have difficulty distinguishing between them, especially when the line between poet and persona is blurred, as is the case in "Grape Sherbet." To help decrease confusion, remind students that the "I" of the poem's speaker—although vibrant, authoritative, and very real—is not necessarily the "I" of Rita Dove. Have students analyze subtle shifts in the speaker's tone.

Ambiguity

Dove's poems often include questions, describe unresolved emotions, and betray a keen sense of longing. Her use of ambiguity enriches and strengthens her work. Readers are drawn into her poems, in part, because the emotions at issue are complex and mysterious, not simple and comprehensible. Dove's speakers, like the one in "Grape Sherbet," frequently change to serve a poem's purpose. Speakers may move back and forth in time; learn and mature; or alter attitudes, feelings, and desires. To get and keep their bearings, readers must constantly engage with each poem, embracing its sometimes disconcerting ambiguities.

Author Focus. Ambiguous characters and situations have intrigued Dove throughout her career. She has written about many famous Western heroes, artists, and saints, but she focuses on their mysterious quirks as well as their achievements. Her book of poetry *Mother Love,* for example, uses sonnets based on the Demeter/Persephone myth to explore enigmatic, real-life mother-daughter connections.

Close Reading
Metacognitive Strategy: Think-Aloud

As you read the poem aloud, pause after each stanza and ask the following questions to help students understand the poem's speaker:

SKILLS FOCUS

Literary Skill
Analyze a poem's speaker.

Advanced Skill
Analyze ambiguity.

As students explore the poem's **speaker** and **ambiguity**, remind them not to look at these elements in isolation but to consider how they contribute to our understanding of **character, tone,** and **theme.**

Collection Resources

Related Works

Consider teaching one of the works below from *Elements of Literature* with "Grape Sherbet."
Analyzing speaker:
"The Taxi" by Amy Lowell
Analyzing ambiguity:
"Simile" by N. Scott Momaday

Resources

For information on **think-alouds** and other metacognitive strategies, see page 16 of this book.

First stanza: What have we learned about the speaker? *[She describes the sherbet as if it were a magical concoction. The humorous description of her father reveals that she loves him deeply. The speaker's tone is affectionate. She is probably a loving person.]*

Second stanza: What does this stanza add to our view of the speaker? *[The speaker describes events that took place earlier in the day, when the children played on graves. Later, they delight in the sherbet. The descriptions reveal that the speaker thinks that she was once innocent and unaware of death. The speaker's tone is simple and nostalgic.]*

Third stanza: How does the tone shift in this stanza? *[Although the speaker is enthusiastic and lavender is a pleasant scent, the tone becomes ominous and worrisome, especially when the speaker introduces the grandmother: She sits apart, staring, untouched by the sherbet's effects.]*

Fourth stanza: How has the speaker changed? *[In retrospect, the speaker realizes the significance of the graves. Her tone is mournful and filled with longing. Like the taste of his sherbet, her father is gone.]*

Close-Reading Practice: Ambiguity

Have students re-read the second stanza, and discuss these questions to explore Dove's use of ambiguity:

- What do the ambiguous descriptions in the first four lines indicate about the speaker's tone? *[Because the speaker does not disclose that the "grassed-over mounds" are graves or that "each stone" is a headstone, the descriptions are ambiguous. The ambiguity enables the speaker to adopt a child's playful perspective, foregrounding that tone over the darker, literal meaning of the lines.]*

- The children's naming of the headstones is mysterious. What does this action reveal about the speaker? *[Because the children, including the speaker, name the stones after their lost milk teeth, we may infer that they are very young and in the process of losing their first teeth. They probably assign names to the stones because they cannot read the inscribed words; apparently, the children do not yet associate graves with specific individuals. The speaker is older, aware of the significance of death, and able to recognize the irony underlying this childhood play.]*

Vocabulary: Synonyms

The **speaker** uses magical, mythical words to describe the setting and the pivotal sherbet. By exploring synonyms of these terms, students can better understand how each contributes to our understanding of the speaker. Thinking critically about Dove's word choices can give students insight into the depth and breadth of the speaker's emotions.

Activity. In her description of a Memorial Day gathering, Dove uses the words in the margin. Ask students to discuss or to write down a synonym for each word and consider the context in which the word appears. Finally, have students write sentences explaining how each word affects their impression of the speaker and her tone.

Close Reading

The close-reading passage is on page 548 of the Student Edition.

Vocabulary

Words for the Activity
memorial, line 1
masterpiece, line 3
gelled, line 4
dollop, line 12
torch, line 20

[**Memorial** *is a synonym for* remembrance. *The day is set aside for remembrance of people who have died. The tone is slightly sorrowful.* **Masterpiece** *is a synonym for* masterwork *or* treasure. *The speaker communicates admiration for her father. The tone is appreciative.* **Gelled** *is a synonym for* jellied *and* thickened. *The speaker describes the dessert as thickened light. The tone is one of awe.* **Dollop** *is a synonym for* dab. *The speaker implies that the sherbet is so precious that each person receives only a bite or two. The tone is reverential and grateful.* **Torch** *is a synonym for* beacon *or* flambeau. *The speaker's grandmother has insight into the meaning of the setting and the day. The tone is stern and resigned.]*

Postreading

Discussion Method: Fishbowl Discussion

Have students discuss the poem's **speaker** in a fishbowl discussion. Arrange students in inner and outer circles, and then ask the students in the inner circle the first question below. After students change seats, ask them to respond to the second question.

- How does the speaker's changing perspective on the graveyard create contrast between her childhood and her present? *[As a child, the speaker regards the graveyard as a field in which to gallop. As an adult, she realizes that the graves are not "a joke." Like her grandmother, she is wiser and cannot ignore death's somber reality.]*

- How does the speaker's tone change in the course of the poem? *[At first, the speaker's tone is joyful; she describes events positively: "swirled snow, gelled light"; a cap's bill that looks like a duck's bill; children who "galloped"; and sherbet that is "a miracle." Her tone then shifts; her grandmother is "diabetic" and "stares from the porch," refusing to join the others. Finally, the tone is reflective; the speaker recognizes that the dead were lying underfoot, that death is not a "joke," and that her father's actions had life-affirming value.]*

Writing

Have students write an essay that responds to the prompt below.

> The grape sherbet is described in sacramental terms: It is made of grapes (like holy wine), consists of "gelled light," and is "secret" and "a miracle." How does Dove's description of the sherbet help develop the poem's theme? Consider **speaker, ambiguity,** character, tone, and theme as you write an essay answering this question. Use details and examples from the poem to support your points.

Resources

For information on **fishbowl discussions** and other discussion methods, see page 20 of this book.

Collection Resources

Criteria for Success

A successful response
- analyzes the use of grape sherbet to develop the theme of the poem
- supports the analysis with apt examples and details from the poem
- shows insight into speaker, ambiguity, theme, character, and tone
- uses language effectively

The Legend
by Garrett Hongo

Literary Skill
Analyze tone.

Advanced Skill
Analyze allusion.

As students explore **tone** and **allusion**, remind them not to look at these elements in isolation but to consider how they contribute to our understanding of **character, tone,** and **theme.**

Collection Resources

Related Works

Consider teaching one of the works below from *Elements of Literature* with "The Legend."
Analyzing tone and diction:
"I Am Offering This Poem" by Jimmy Santiago Baca
Analyzing allusion:
"Sonnet for Heaven Below" by Jack Agüeros

Literary Focus

The coverage of **tone** below builds on the instruction in the Student Edition. You may want to introduce the additional skill of analyzing **allusion** when teaching this poem to advanced students.

Tone

At first glance, the tone, or attitude, of "The Legend" may seem somewhat journalistic—descriptively objective, like the tone of a radio news story. However, Hongo uses emotionally charged **diction,** or word choices, as he describes the man. The description's tone is lovingly poignant, conveyed by words and phrases such as "wrinkled shopping bag," "neatly folded clothes," "flannellike," "gloveless," "rumpled suit pants," "dingy and too large," and "dumbfounded." Hongo subtly manipulates tone and diction to communicate his perspective on his subject. You might use the poem to show students how tone is established through precise, evocative diction. Ask students to analyze and then to evaluate how the tone supports the poem's theme.

Author Focus. In his collection *The River of Heaven,* which contains "The Legend," Hongo attempts to resurrect role models and elders by vividly memorializing them. As the critic Suzanne K. Arakawa remarks, "He records their lives so that they may continue to live." Point out to students that Hongo's poem helps a man—who otherwise might have remained unknown—to continue living through literature.

Allusion

In the poem's final two stanzas, the speaker makes two allusions, one to the Western philosopher René Descartes and a second to the Asian creation story described in "Hongo Reflects on 'The Legend.'" Hongo frequently uses allusions—references to historical or fictional characters, places, events, or works—to extend meaning in his poems. Though Hongo's poems are often straightforward, simple narratives, his allusions provide depth, complexity, and connections to larger subjects or passions. Hongo understands that the power of allusions lies in connotation and suggestion and that allusions can introduce and enhance a host of poetic elements, ranging from mood to setting to meaning. In "The Legend," an understanding of the allusions of the final two stanzas is pivotal to a reader's comprehension of the poem.

Close Reading

Metacognitive Strategy: Annotating Text

While students read "The Legend," have them make annotations. Request that they concentrate on **diction** that reveals **tone**. To help students identify important terms, encourage them to note words with strong connotations. You might have them focus on diction that

- provides details about the setting
- establishes elements of character
- discloses the speaker's feelings and attitudes

Explain that most of a poem's diction, even though it has a variety of purposes, also helps to establish tone.

Close-Reading Practice: Allusion

Have students re-read the last two stanzas of the poem, and then discuss these questions to explore Hongo's use of allusion. Make certain that students have read both the poem's marginal notes and "Hongo Reflects on 'The Legend'" before the discussion.

- How does Hongo's allusion to Descartes support the tone of lines 30–37? *[The allusion points to the loneliness that will result from doubting the existence of anything or anyone other than oneself. The poem's lines express a similarly pained and lonely attitude: The man is "babbling," with no one able to understand him; people are "bewildered" by his speech; his words are "nothing" to others; and the boy is "lost." Although people are nearby, the man is alone.]*

- What is the effect of the allusion in the poem's final two lines? *[The allusion reflects the speaker's desire for "mercy and requital" and helps support the poem's theme. If the weaver girl crosses the bridge to take up the man's "cold hands," he will no longer be isolated, as he had been in death. Instead, he will be woven into the "web and warp of Being." The allusion also contrasts with the allusion to Descartes; the speaker's longing for the weaver girl's intervention suggests that an isolated existence is as tragic and deserving of pity as is the suffering of the two heavenly "lovers."]*

Vocabulary: Etymology

Hongo's **diction** helps create the poem's tender, regretful **tone**. Many of these words have long histories, or **etymologies,** that further contribute to the poem's layers of meaning. By analyzing Hongo's word choices, students can better understand the tone of the poem.

Activity. Hongo uses the words in the margin in "The Legend." Have students look up each word's etymology and consider its context. Then, have students write sentences explaining how each word contributes to the poem's tone.

*[**Rumpled** comes from the Middle Low German* rumpen, *meaning "to wrinkle." By describing the man's clothing as wrinkled, the speaker endears him to readers (he is poor and vulnerable) and creates a sympa-*

Resources

For information on **annotating text** and other metacognitive strategies, see page 16 of this book.

Close Reading

The close-reading passage is on page 553 of the Student Edition.

Collection Resources

Vocabulary

Words for the Activity
rumpled, line 15
dingy, line 16
dumbfounded, line 27
babbling, line 31
bewildered, line 33

thetic tone. The origin of **dingy** *is unclear, but the word has been used since the 1700s to mean "dirty." In this context, the word means "grimy." The word creates pity for the man, establishing a compassionate tone.* **Dumbfounded** *combines the Old English word* dumb *meaning "mute" and* (con)found *from a Latin word meaning "to pour." Together, the words mean "to confuse." In this context, dumbfounded means "baffled," and it creates a shocked tone. The origin of* **babbling** *is unclear, but the word* babelen *appears in Middle English. In this context, babbling means "to speak incoherently." Because no one speaks the man's language, the word suggests a sorrowful tone.* **Bewildered** *adds the prefix* be–, *which means "thoroughly," to the archaic* wilder, *which means "to lead astray" or "to wander." In this context, the word refers to the observers' reactions. Bewildered creates a puzzled, pitying tone.]*

Postreading

Discussion Method: Timed Discussion

Organize students into groups of five. Then, have groups discuss Hongo's **allusion** to the Asian creation legend. Tell students to focus on ways in which both "legends" are similar. Afterward, have one student from each group provide timed responses to the following questions:

- How are the poem and the myth parallel? *[In the poem, the man is essentially separated from other people, including the speaker. Similarly, the Weaver Maid and the Herd Boy are kept apart, dwelling on opposite sides of the Milky Way. The man's death brings together the poem's people, including the speaker, who pities the man and memorializes him in a poem. Likewise, the myth's lovers are united and memorialized when the universe takes pity on them.]*

- In what ways do these similarities help our understanding of the poem's theme? *[The similarities emphasize the poem's theme that compassion unites us with one another and with the universe. The tone of both the poem and the myth is contemplative and sorrowful.]*

Writing

Have students respond to the prompt below in an essay.

How is the speaker's worldview revealed in "The Legend" and its **allusions**? Consider theme, character, **tone,** and **diction** as you analyze the poem. Then, write an essay evaluating Hongo's use of literary elements to present a philosophy of life in the poem. Use details and examples from the poem to support your evaluation.

Resources

For information on **timed discussions** and other discussion methods, see page 20 of this book.

Criteria for Success

A successful response
- evaluates the use of allusion and other literary elements to reveal the speaker's worldview
- supports the evaluation with appropriate textual details and examples
- shows insight into allusion, theme, character, tone, and diction
- uses language effectively

Collection Resources

since feeling is first
by E. E. Cummings

Literary Focus

The coverage of **metaphor** below builds on the instruction found in the Student Edition. You may want to introduce the additional skill of analyzing **sound devices** when teaching this poem to advanced students.

Metaphor

E. E. Cummings uses both direct and indirect metaphors in the poem. There are only two direct metaphors: "life's not a paragraph" and "death . . . is no parenthesis" (the final two lines). However, there are many indirect metaphors, ranging from equating an orderly life with syntax to pairing eyelids and voices. These indirect metaphors are so subtle and unusual that even experienced readers may have difficulty identifying them. You might help students analyze indirect metaphors by making a list of every noun in the poem. Then, encourage students to identify whether each noun is indirectly compared with something else.

Author Focus. Cummings specializes in resurrecting dying metaphors. Like "since feeling is first," many of his poems feature metaphors comprised of tired symbols such as spring and flowers (see, for example, "in Just-"). Yet Cummings makes these shopworn metaphors come alive by creating unexpected juxtapositions; by playing with grammar, usage, and syntax; and by adding sound devices.

Sound Devices

Cummings consistently uses sound devices to unify his poems. In "since feeling is first," sound devices include alliteration (repeated initial consonant sounds, such as "laugh" and "leaning"), repetition (duplicated words or phrases, such as "wholly"), caesura (a pause, such as "—the best gesture"), euphony (melodious sounds, such as "your eyelids' flutter"), and slant rhymes (approximate rhymes, such as "you" and "fool"). These auditory effects not only help the poem cohere, but also give it a unique and engaging music.

Close Reading

Metacognitive Strategy: Thinking Notes

As students read, have them annotate the poem, focusing on identifying every instance of **metaphor.** Explain that Cummings uses four

SKILLS FOCUS

Literary Skill
Analyze metaphor.

Advanced Skill
Analyze sound devices.

As students analyze **metaphor** and **sound devices,** remind them not to look at these elements in isolation but to consider how they contribute to our understanding of **character, tone,** and **theme.**

Related Works

Consider teaching one of the works below from *Elements of Literature* with "since feeling is first."

Analyzing metaphors:
"Shall I Compare Thee to a Summer's Day" by William Shakespeare

Analyzing sound devices:
"Ode to My Socks" by Pablo Neruda

Resources

For information on **thinking notes** and other metacognitive strategies, see page 16 of this book.

Collection Resources

Collection Resources 137

categories of metaphors in the poem: metaphors of life ("Spring," "kiss," "blood"), metaphors of language ("syntax," "paragraph"), metaphors of emotion ("feeling," "fool"), and metaphors of knowledge ("pay attention," "wisdom"). All of the metaphors support the lyric's tone and theme. To help students analyze the metaphors, have them annotate each line with thinking notes to indicate the following:

- This is confusing.
- This metaphor supports the theme.
- This is surprising.
- This metaphor supports the tone.
- This is important.
- This is an indirect metaphor.
- This is a direct metaphor.

Close-Reading Practice: Metaphor

Have students re-read the poem and note where Cummings uses vivid, present-tense verbs in indirect metaphors. Then, ask them to analyze how those words are integrated with tone or theme. Discuss the following questions to assist students in understanding Cummings's use of verbs:

- How do the present-tense verbs "swear," "cry," and "laugh" relate to the poem's tone and theme? [*These present-tense verbs create an emotional, active tone. They imply life lived to its fullest, in keeping with the* carpe diem *theme.*]
- Which word appears as both a verb and a plural noun? Why does Cummings emphasize this word? [*The verb "kiss" in line four and the noun "kisses" in line eight. Cummings emphasizes this word because the poem is about love and union; "kisses are a better fate" than an excessively ordered, barren life.*]

Vocabulary: Antonyms

By exploring antonyms of important words in the poem, students may gain insight into the entwined **metaphors,** tone, and theme.

Activity. Cummings uses the words in the margin in the poem's indirect metaphors. Have students discuss or write down an antonym for each word and consider the context in which the word appears. Finally, have students write a sentence explaining how each word contributes to the poem's tone or theme.

[*Sample responses:* **Feeling** *has the antonym "apathy." In this context,* feeling *means "emotion"; the word supports the poem's passionate tone and life-embracing theme.* **Fool** *has the antonym "sage." In this context,* fool *means "a person who is reckless or passionate"; it contributes to the ardent tone.* **Spring** *has the antonym "fall," a time when things are slowly dying, not being born. In this context,* Spring *means "rejuvenation"; it contributes to the joyful tone and connotes fertility.* **Approves** *has the antonym "rejects." In this context,* approves *means "affirms"; it helps create a positive tone.* **Wisdom** *has the antonym "stupidity." In this context,* wisdom *connotes something safe but only modestly satisfying; the contrast contributes to the* carpe diem *theme.*]

Collection Resources

Resources

For information on **sentence structure,** see the Handbook of Grammatical Concepts in this book.

Vocabulary

Words for the Activity

feeling, line 1
fool, line 5
Spring, line 6
approves, line 7
wisdom, line 9

Postreading

Discussion Method: Fishbowl Discussion

Have students discuss the poem's **sound devices** in a fishbowl discussion. Arrange students in inner and outer circles; then, ask the students in the inner circle one of the following questions:

- Where does Cummings use alliteration? How do alliterative words contribute to the poem's tone and theme? *[Alliteration includes "feeling" and "first," and "will," "while," and "world." These words contribute to the rapturous, passionate tone. They also provide a foundation for the poem's* carpe diem *theme and establish a religious, ecstatic mood.]*

- Why does Cummings repeat the word "wholly"? *[Cummings is making a pun through the implicit comparison to the word "holy." The phrase "wholly kiss you" implies that Cummings thinks kissing not only involves all of one's body, mind, and soul, but also reflects a sacramental act. The phrase "wholly to be a fool" refers not only to being a complete fool, but also to his idea that foolishness can be holy.]*

- How does Cummings use harmonious sounds in the second line of the second stanza? What effect do those sounds have on readers? *[Cummings makes the line euphonic by repeating long and short* i *sounds, by repeating the "in" sound, and by linking tones in "while" and "world." These sounds have a soothing effect on readers.]*

After students trade seats, ask a question suggested by responses to the initial question, or ask a different question from the list above.

Writing

Have students write an essay that responds to the prompt below.

> This poem is famous for its complex **metaphors** comparing syntax, paragraphs, and parenthesis to different aspects of human existence. How do these comparisons establish the theme of the poem? How does Cummings emphasize them by using unusual spacing, punctuation, and capitalization? Consider **sound devices,** character, tone, and theme as you re-read the poem to formulate your ideas and gather evidence. Then, write an essay in which you explain the poem's theme and analyze how it is emphasized. Use details and examples to support your points.

Resources

For information on **fishbowl discussions** and other discussion methods, see page 20 of this book.

Collection Resources

Criteria for Success

A successful response
- explains the poem's theme and analyzes how that theme is emphasized
- supports the analysis with evidence from the poem
- shows insight into sound devices, character, tone, and theme
- uses language effectively

Elements of Literature selection

Shall I Compare Thee to a Summer's Day?
by William Shakespeare

Literary Skill
Analyze characteristics of the English **sonnet**.

Advanced Skill
Analyze figures of speech.

As students analyze characteristics of the English **sonnet** and **figures of speech,** remind them not to look at these elements in isolation but to consider how they contribute to our understanding of **character, tone,** and **theme.**

Related Works

Consider teaching one of the works below from *Elements of Literature* with "Shall I Compare Thee to a Summer's Day?"
Analyzing the sonnet:
"Sonnet for Heaven Below" by Jack Agüeros
Analyzing figures of speech:
"Waiting for *E. gularis*" by Linda Pastan

Literary Focus

Coverage of the English **sonnet** below builds on the instruction found in the Student Edition. You may want to introduce the additional skill of analyzing **figures of speech** when teaching this poem to advanced students.

Sonnet

"Shall I Compare Thee to a Summer's Day?" is a classic example of the English, or Shakespearean, sonnet. The poem is perhaps the most quoted, beloved, and admired of the 154 verse poems collected in Shakespeare's *Sonnets*. This type of sonnet features an *abab cdcd efef gg* rhyme scheme, three quatrains of alternating end rhymes, and one final couplet. In English sonnets, each quatrain usually focuses on one idea, and the concluding couplet generally has an optimistic tone. Like all but one of Shakespeare's sonnets, "Shall I Compare Thee to a Summer's Day?" is written in iambic pentameter. It also is similar to most of Shakespeare's other sonnets in that it contains a *volta,* or turn, in the ninth line. Use the poem to show students the distinct ideas presented in each quatrain, the shift that occurs in the ninth line, and the mood of the final couplet. You might then discuss how those elements contribute to the poem's tone and theme.

Author Focus. The initial 126 sonnets in Shakespeare's collection constitute a cycle, or sequence. They contain consistent characters, have similar themes, and serve as beads on a narrative thread. "Shall I Compare Thee to a Summer's Day" is the eighteenth sonnet in this cycle. The previous seventeen poems convey the speaker's unconditional, devoted love for an attractive youth. Beginning with Sonnet 18, however, the speaker begins to explore the ways that time ravages physical beauty and asserts that only art (verse) can make the youth immortal. Many of the next twenty or so poems imply that the youth has rejected the speaker.

Figures of Speech

Shakespeare's poems contain a wide variety of figures of speech. Figurative language makes associations or comparisons open to imaginative interpretation. In this poem, figures of speech include metaphor (direct comparison), hyperbole (exaggeration to express powerful emotion or to introduce comedy), and personification (presenting a non-human thing or quality as if it were human). Interestingly, this sonnet does not employ the use of similes (comparisons that use a connective word, such as *like*). Instead, the poem uses the more compressed language inherent in metaphors, personification, and hyperbole.

Close Reading

Metacognitive Strategy: Reading Journals

Because Shakespeare's poems contain such extravagant and rich figurative language, students often have difficulty teasing out the meanings inherent in each **figure of speech.** To help students identify and interpret the sonnet's figures of speech, have them copy its figurative language into the left-hand column of their reader's logs. Ask students to explain each figure of speech and to write a sentence describing their responses and interpretations. Remind students to look for instances of metaphor, hyperbole, and personification.

Close-Reading Practice: Sonnet

Ask students to re-read lines 9–14, and then discuss these questions to explore Shakespeare's use of the **sonnet** form:

- How does the tone change in the ninth line? *[Possible response: Until the ninth line, the poem's tone is jubilant and adoring. The speaker clearly loves his subject deeply. However, the ninth line, with its pivotal "but," alters the tone by referring to the "fade" of old age and, ultimately, death.]*

- How do the final five lines support the sonnet's theme? *[Possible response: Before the last five lines, the theme focuses on the mysterious nature of pure, powerful, sun-like, and eternal beauty. The final section of the poem reminds the subject that his beauty will perish, yet the theme persists: The speaker's love will achieve immortality in the speaker's verse.]*

Vocabulary: Analogies

If Shakespeare's **figures of speech** are presented as analogies, students may better understand their associations. Thinking critically about Shakespeare's word choices can help students to discern the multiple meanings in Shakespeare's figurative language.

Activity. Shakespeare uses the words in the margin in the sonnet's figures of speech. Have students complete the analogy for each word. Reassure them that there are several correct answers for each analogy. Then, ask students to write a sentence or two explaining the word's meaning in context and its relationship to theme or tone.

- *temperate* is to *unrestrained* as *brief* is to _____.
- *face* is to *complexion* as _____ is to *strength*.

Resources

For information on **reading journals** and other metacognitive strategies, see page 16 of this book.

Collection Resources

Vocabulary

Words for the Activity
temperate, line 2
complexion, line 6
declines, line 7
untrimmed, line 8
eternal, line 12

- *declines* is to _____ as *grows* is to *waxes*.
- *untrimmed* is to _____ as *lively* is to *energetic*.
- *eternal* is to *life* as *delicate* is to _____.

[Sample responses: **Temperate:** *"long" is suitably analogous. In this context,* temperate *means "mild" and contributes to the bucolic tone.* **Complexion:** *"muscle" is suitably analogous. In this context,* complexion *means "appearance of skin" and supports the theme involving ephemeral physical beauty.* **Declines:** *"wanes" is suitably analogous. In this context,* declines *means "decays" and foreshadows the thematic turn in line nine.* **Untrimmed:** *"plain" is suitably analogous. In this context,* untrimmed *means "undecorated" and alludes to the thematic shift in the last third of the poem.* **Eternal:** *"flower" is suitably analogous. In this context,* eternal *means "immortal" and supports the theme of art's deathlessness.]*

Postreading

Discussion Method: Literature Circle

Give students the choice of discussing in a literature circle either "Shall I Compare Thee to a Summer's Day?" or "Sonnet for Heaven Below" by Jack Agüeros (in Collection 8 of *Elements of Literature*). Ask students to concentrate on the **sonnet** form. To facilitate discussion, you might have students focus on

- advantages and disadvantages of using the sonnet form
- questions about the sonnet form
- possible reasons Shakespeare uses the sonnet form
- personal reactions to the sonnet form

Writing

Have students write an essay responding to the prompt below.

> The speaker in this poem passionately believes that his **sonnet** will make its subject immortal. Do you agree or disagree? Is a sonnet better suited to such intense emotions than other types of poems? Consider the **sonnet, figurative language,** character, tone, and theme as you re-read the poem to collect evidence for your opinions. Then, write an essay in which you state your beliefs. Use details and examples to support your points.

Elements of Literature selection

We Real Cool
by Gwendolyn Brooks

Literary Focus

The coverage of **alliteration** below builds on the instruction found in the Student Edition. You may want to introduce the additional skill of analyzing **rhythm** and **diction** when teaching this poem to advanced students.

Alliteration

Alliteration is the primary sound device used to unify "We Real Cool." Repeated consonant sounds may be said to mimic the brief "pop" sounds of a game of pool. Alliteration also links words—such as *gin*, *Jazz*, and *June*—stressing their interlocked meanings. In general, the alliterative action words overshadow the speakers' identities (except for the initial *We*, all the speakers' repetitions of *We* are at the ends of lines). You might tell students that the poem is deceptively simple; alliteration is just one of the many elaborate codes that Gwendolyn Brooks employs to add meaning to the poem. Use the poem to show students how alliterative pairs contribute to the poem's meaning.

Rhythm and Diction

The rhythm of "We Real Cool" reflects the strong rhythms of jukebox music. Each sentence contains three beats. Every repeated initial *We* acts as the first muted beat of a waltz rhythm (for example, "We / Strike straight.") According to Brooks, *We* lacks emphasis because she wanted the word to express the youths' "basic uncertainty, which they don't bother to question every day. . . ." The youths are indeed self-confident, and their diction, or word choices, emphasizes this swagger. The young speakers have no need for conventional diction, and the poem includes no articles. The poem's compressed and abrupt language mimics asides from pool players during a game or shorthand dialogue between old friends. The brief, gunfire-like words also evoke shots, alluding to the context and to the brevity of the youth's lives.

Author Focus. "We Real Cool" is included in Brooks's collection *The Bean Eaters.* The book's title poem explores how an old couple dines mostly on beans. Like "We Real Cool," it is a brief lyric unified by alliteration. Its diction is simple and stripped. The poem, however, contains pearl-like layers of meaning; the elderly couple's ordinary meal is contrasted with memories of their rich and vibrant past. Other poems in *The Bean Eaters* also focus on the everyday lives of ordinary people—but in tender and surprising ways.

SKILLS FOCUS

Literary Skill
Analyze alliteration.

Advanced Skill
Analyze rhythm and diction.

As students analyze **alliteration**, **rhythm,** and **diction,** remind them not to look at these elements in isolation but to consider how they contribute to our understanding of **character, tone,** and **theme.**

Related Works

Consider teaching one of the works below from *Elements of Literature* with "We Real Cool."

Analyzing alliteration:
"Sea Fever" by John Masefield

Analyzing rhythm and diction:
"Jazz Fantasia" by Carl Sandburg

Collection Resources

Collection Resources

Close Reading

Metacognitive Strategy: Think-Aloud

While reading the poem aloud, use the following commentary to help students understand how **alliteration** helps emphasize and connect terms.

- Stanza 1: *Left* begins with the same letter as *Lurk* and *late* in the next stanza. These words all have negative connotations.

- Stanza 2: "Strike straight" refers to pool but also suggests advice about striking with a weapon.

- Stanza 3: *Sing* and *sin* is an odd pairing; *sin* is *sing* with a *g* added. The *g* may remind readers of *gin*, which rhymes with *sin*. When the youths drink gin, perhaps they drunkenly "Sing sin."

- Stanza 4: "Jazz June" may have several meanings. The speakers may think that their wild behavior "jazzes up," or brings excitement to, the summer. Or perhaps they believe that their lives are like jazz music, open to the spontaneity of improvisation.

Close-Reading Practice: Rhythm and Diction

Have students re-read the poem and then discuss these questions to explore its **rhythm** and **diction**.

- Brooks has said she intended *We* to be spoken softly. How does the three-beat rhythm of each sentence reflect the poem's subject? What effect does Brooks's use of this rhythm have on our impression of the speakers? [*The soft* We *that introduces each sentence sounds like the swoosh, or slide, of a pool cue. The following stressed words echo the tap on the ball and the sound of balls clicking together. The waltz-like rhythm emphasizes the speakers' game-like attitude toward life.*]

- Why is the phrase "We real cool" unusual? What emotion does the phrase evoke? [*The phrase is missing the verb* are; *its syntax resembles that of some urban dialects. The phrase evokes a feeling of calm over-confidence and braggadocio, a sense of "cool."*]

- Except for the epigraph, every word in the poem contains one syllable. What effect do the monosyllabic words have? How is the tone of the epigraph different from that of the body of the poem? [*The monosyllabic words contribute to the cocky tone of the poem and allude to the brief life the youths will experience if they continue their behavior. Longer words are appropriate for the epigraph because it reads like an epitaph—as if the boys were already gone.*]

Vocabulary: Connotation

When Brooks uses alliteration in the poem, she draws readers' attention to words they otherwise might not have noticed. Thinking critically about Brooks's word choices can give students insight into the speakers and tone of her poem.

Activity. To establish tone in the poem, Brooks uses the words in the margin. Ask students to discuss or to write down the connotations of each word and to consider the context in which the word appears. Finally, have students write a sentence or two explaining how each word influences their perception of the tone.

*[***Left*** *connotes a departure or absence. In this context, it means "dropped out of" and contributes to the dark tone.* ***Lurk*** *carries connotations of sneaking and stalking. In this context, it means "lie in wait" and creates a malevolent tone.* ***Strike*** *connotes violence. In this context, the word means "hit" and establishes a violent tone.* ***Sing*** *may connote celebration. In this context, the pool players "sing" sin, which might mean that they perform sinful acts as one might perform music or that what they sing is sinful or harmful. The word helps establish a cool, jazzy tone. When the poem was written, the word* ***jazz*** *connoted improvisation and musical experimentation. In this context, the word is used as a verb and means "invigorate." Jazz suggests a hip, confident tone.]*

Postreading

Discussion Method: Reading Conference

Have students discuss the poem's epigraph in a reading conference. Ask them to prepare for the conference by listing and analyzing alliteration, rhythm, and diction in the epigraph. In groups, have students share their lists and analyses. Ask students to discuss their conclusions about the epigraph. Use the following questions to prompt students' thinking.

- What does the alliteration in the first line of the epigraph accomplish? *["Pool Players," which receives alliterative emphasis, instantly establishes the speakers' identities and the poem's setting. The boys are unnamed, anonymous youths.]*

- What is the significance of the diction in the epigraph's second line? *["Seven" and "shovel" start with the same letter. Seven is a lucky number in gambling, but the shovel may ironically allude to gravedigging and death. Brooks may want readers to understand that the boys believe they are so cool that they are invincible—but death inevitably waits for them.]*

Writing

Have students respond to the prompt below in an essay.

> The poem's unique **diction** is especially evident in its internal rhyme pairs, such as *gin* and *sin*. How do these pairs and the poem's underlying rhythm establish the mood? Why is that mood ominous? Consider **alliteration,** character, tone, and theme as you skim the poem to gather evidence. Then, write an essay in which you answer these questions. Use details and examples to support your points.

Vocabulary

Words for the Activity

left, line 2

lurk, line 3

strike, line 4

sing, line 5

jazz, line 7

Resources

For information on **reading conferences** and other discussion methods, see page 20 of this book.

Criteria for Success

A successful response

- analyzes the poem's diction, rhythm, and mood

- supports the analysis with apt examples

- shows insight into diction, rhythm, mood, alliteration, character, tone, and theme

- uses language effectively

Section I: Multiple-Choice Questions

Directions: Carefully read the following poem, "Cloud Painter," by Jane Flanders. This poem concerns the life and career of John Constable (1776–1837), a British artist famous for his landscapes. Then, choose the *best* answer to each question.

Cloud Painter

Suggested by the life and art of John Constable

At first, as you know, the sky is
    incidental—
a drape, a backdrop for trees and steeples.
Here an oak clutches a rock (already he
    works outdoors);
a wall buckles but does not break,
5 water pearls through a lock, a haywain[1]
    trembles.

The pleasures of landscape are endless.
    What we see
around us should be enough.
Horizons are typically high and far away.

Still, clouds let us drift and remember. He
    is, after all,
10 a miller's son, used to trying
to read the future in the sky, seeing
    instead
ships, horses, instruments of flight.
Is that his mother's wash flapping on the
    line?
His schoolbook, smudged, illegible?

15 In this period the sky becomes
    significant.
Cloud forms are technically correct—
    mares' tails,
sheep-in-the-meadow, thunderheads.
You can almost tell which scenes have been
    interrupted
by summer showers.

20 Now his young wife dies.
His landscapes achieve belated success.
He is invited to join the Academy.[2] I
    forget
whether he accepts or not.

In any case, the literal forms give way
25 to something spectral, nameless. His
    palette shrinks
to gray, blue, white—the colors of charity.
Horizons sink and fade,
trees draw back till they are little more
    than frames,
then they too disappear.

30 Finally the canvas itself begins to vibrate
with waning light,
as if the wind could paint.
And we too, at last, stare into a space
which tells us nothing,
35 except that the world can vanish along
    with our need for it.

[1] **haywain** *n.*: horse-drawn hay wagon.
[2] **the Academy** *n.*: the Royal Academy of Arts. Membership in the Academy, founded in 1768, is limited. Membership is a sign of an artist's success. Constable was not elected to full membership until 1829, the year after his wife died.

1. Which of the following sound devices is used in line 2?
   (A) Onomatopoeia
   (B) Alliteration
   (C) Assonance
   (D) End rhyme
   (E) Repetition

2. The sibilant "s" sounds and the vowels accompanying them in lines 6–7 have the effect of
   (A) establishing a strong metrical beat
   (B) increasing the pace of the poem
   (C) evoking a vivid visual image
   (D) creating a leisurely metrical pattern
   (E) foreshadowing sad events in the poem

3. In lines 13 and 14, "wash flapping on the line" and "His schoolbook, smudged, illegible" create
   (A) an active, forceful tone
   (B) a sense of unease and foreboding
   (C) a regular, unvarying metrical pattern
   (D) bitter memories of childhood
   (E) images of specific, individual clouds

4. What is the implication of lines 22–23, "He is invited to join the Academy. I forget / whether he accepts or not"?
   (A) The speaker does not consider that part of Constable's life important.
   (B) Constable was such a respected artist that honors were irrelevant.
   (C) Constable may have quarreled with some members of the Academy.
   (D) The speaker considers the honor insignificant.
   (E) The Academy's influence was waning, and many artists no longer sought membership.

5. The poem's tone shifts significantly at the beginning of the
   (A) second stanza (line 6)
   (B) third stanza (line 9)
   (C) fourth stanza (line 15)
   (D) fifth stanza (line 20)
   (E) seventh stanza (line 30)

6. Which rhetorical concept is evident in the last two stanzas?
   (A) Extended example
   (B) Logical appeal
   (C) Objection
   (D) Euphemism
   (E) Argument by analogy

7. Beginning in line 24, the speaker describes Constable's later paintings as
   (A) becoming more and more detailed
   (B) using more varied colors
   (C) including more people and animals
   (D) becoming more abstract and less colorful
   (E) demonstrating a greater interest in daily life

8. The personification in "trees draw back till they are little more than frames" (line 28) has the effect of
   (A) demonstrating the poet's skill with images
   (B) showing that Constable painted many trees
   (C) reminding the reader of a blank canvas
   (D) creating doubt about the speaker's description of Constable's colors
   (E) giving the trees an active role in Constable's paintings

9. The speaker's attitude toward the painter is
   (A) clinical and objective
   (B) lighthearted and enthusiastic
   (C) analytical and judgmental
   (D) harsh and moralistic
   (E) admiring and reflective

10. In the final stanza, it becomes clear that the speaker is using Constable's life and art to
    (A) comment upon painting in general
    (B) describe some of the typical problems of an artist
    (C) reveal truths about the nature of life
    (D) show that enjoying nature helps people remain cheerful
    (E) raise questions about the goals people pursue

Section II: Essay

Directions: Carefully read the following prompt. Then, present your response in a well-developed essay.

Resources

For information about how to analyze a **writing prompt** and other strategies for timed writing, see page 45 of this book.

> One of the most significant symbols in "Cloud Painter" is the sky. What is the sky's role in the poem? Write a carefully reasoned essay in which you analyze this symbol's meaning. Use details and examples from the poem to develop a carefully reasoned analysis.

Scoring Guidelines

9–8 These essays fully explore the meaning of the symbol of the sky in the poem. They present coherent, well-reasoned analyses supported by comprehensive evidence. The students exhibit a sophisticated control of language.

7–6 These essays adequately evaluate the symbolism of the sky. They present sound analyses using appropriate evidence. The students' prose is clear but may contain a few errors in diction or syntax.

5 These essays acknowledge the symbolism of the sky and make clear claims, but their analyses may be unevenly developed or may contain limited evidence. The students' control of language is adequate.

4–3 These essays present an inadequate response to the prompt. The students may misunderstand the symbolism of the sky or may have difficulty establishing their own position and use inappropriate or insufficient evidence. The students demonstrate inconsistent control over such elements of writing as diction and syntax.

2–1 These essays do not successfully respond to the prompt. The students may fail to understand the prompt, respond tangentially, or substitute a simpler task, such as merely paraphrasing the poem. The students' prose reveals consistent weaknesses in such elements of writing as organization, grammar, and diction.

0 These essays present a response that receives no credit. They may simply paraphrase the prompt, for example.

Sample Response

The following essay represents a high-scoring response to the writing prompt.

In Jane Flanders's "Cloud Painter," images and the speaker's commentary show the sky's symbolic value and illustrate John Constable's growth as a painter. For the poem's speaker, Constable's sky and clouds progress from unimportance into a complicated symbol for spiritual thought. Ultimately, the sky comes to represent an unchanging and spiritually satisfying life.

The imagery of the poem's first two stanzas places little emphasis on the sky or clouds. They have yet to gain value in Constable's work. Instead, "the sky is incidental— / a drape," a mere "backdrop" upon which detailed images—an oak, a wall, water, and a wagon—appear. The speaker says that Constable focuses on everyday objects and finds "endless" pleasures in landscapes. "Horizons are typically high and far away," so the sky is small. It is just a background for Constable's subjects.

By the third stanza, however, the speaker points out a change in Constable's work and starts to develop the sky's symbolic significance. Far from serving as a "backdrop," the sky and clouds now symbolize reflective thought and memory. "Clouds," readers are told, "let us drift and remember," becoming vehicles for contemplation. Constable's clouds reflect earth-bound shapes from his childhood—"ships, horses, instruments of flight"—but these images invite consideration, curiosity, and wonder. As if to emphasize this invitation, the speaker sneaks two images into questions: "Is that his mother's wash flapping on the line?" and "His schoolbook, smudged, illegible?" The clouds seem to be asking viewers to reflect on, interpret, and understand them.

Once the images have revealed the sky's symbolic, reflective purpose, the speaker's comments make the fact clear. He or she announces that "the sky becomes significant." The paintings' clouds no longer openly invite interpretation; they are concrete and certain, "technically correct." However, the speaker still views them as invitations to think. Subtle metaphors invite comparisons: The clouds are "mares' tails" and "sheep-in-the-meadow," abstract versions of objects found in landscapes. The speaker still views the images imaginatively, saying, "You can almost tell which scenes have been interrupted / by summer showers." Constable's attention has been on creating clouds that look like clouds, but the speaker sees something more profound.

The fifth and sixth stanzas mark a change in Constable's work, but the speaker keeps the sky's symbolic meaning. The poem's tone becomes somber, showing the painter's pain through words like "shrinks," "sink," "fade," and "disappear." Yet the poem's symbolic sky has an uplifting quality. Constable's "horizons sink and fade," showing that the sky is growing more important than a world marked by death. His palette is no longer bright, but the "literal forms give way / to something spectral, nameless." The image of the sky is so distanced from common experience that the speaker feels as if language can no longer describe it. Symbolically, for the speaker, Constable's sky has broken away from an impermanent world.

The final stanza puts the finishing touches on the sky's meaning. Constable's late-stage paintings are vibrant and "vibrate / with waning light," and the painter himself seems to disappear, "as if the wind could paint." Even the artist is less important than the sky. The last three lines summarize the poet's point: "we, too, at last, stare into a space / which tells us nothing, / except that the world can vanish along with our need for it." These lines show that the sky, as symbol, has inspired reflection, offered no answers, yet provided comfort.

Constable's sky, in the eyes of the speaker in "Cloud Painter," grows from relative inconsequence into a symbol for permanence and satisfaction. The poem's images and narrative descriptions reveal this symbolic meaning and trace its growth.

Elements of Literature selection

Night Calls
by Lisa Fugard

Literary Skill
Analyze mood.

Advanced Skill
Analyze pace.

As students analyze **mood** and **pace**, remind them not to look at these elements in isolation but to consider how they contribute to our understanding of **character, tone,** and **theme.**

Related Works

Consider teaching one of the works below from *Elements of Literature* with "Night Calls."
Analyzing mood:
"A Very Old Man with Enormous Wings" by Gabriel García Márquez
Analyzing pace:
"Where Have You Gone, Charming Billy?" by Tim O'Brien

Literary Focus

The coverage of **mood** below builds on the instruction found in the Student Edition. You may want to introduce the additional skill of analyzing **pace** when teaching this story to advanced students.

Setting

Lisa Fugard meticulously and incrementally creates the **mood**, or atmosphere, of her story "Night Calls." Early in the story, the narrator establishes a mournful mood in a flashback to her mother's untimely and tragic death. Subsequent paragraphs reinforce that dark mood with melancholic sensory images, or images that appeal to the five senses. In addition, memorable, dolorous figures of speech (simile, metaphor, hyperbole, and personification) describe grieving characters and establish the bleak setting.

The mood of "Night Calls" permeates the story so thoroughly that students may have trouble distinguishing between mood and tone. You might explain that mood evokes a feeling in readers, whereas tone reveals an author's attitude toward a subject, a character, or a reader. Use "Night Calls" in a discussion of the distinction between mood and tone. Show students how the story uses flashback, sensory images, and figures of speech to create its atmosphere and evoke emotions.

Pace

Pace, or tempo, and plot are interdependent. A streamlined plot invariably seems to be fast-paced, while an interrupted, meandering plot has a slow pace. The pace of "Night Calls" is languorous. Lisa Fugard creates this sluggish pace deliberately, using lengthy flashbacks, digressions, and descriptions to check the plot's momentum. Although the story takes place during a brief period of time, these devices may make the plot seem to stretch out over a period of years. Fugard especially uses involved descriptions of the story's setting to establish its relatively slow pace.

Author Focus. Formerly an actress, Fugard is exquisitely attuned to pace and suspense in her work. After years of stage experience, she understands that strategic acceleration or deceleration of plot can enhance readers' emotional involvement in a story. Her fiction, including "Night Calls," involves the slow-paced disclosure of secrets from the past. For example, her first novel, *Skinner's Drift,* concerns a young girl

Collection Resources

who knows incriminating secrets about her father and must confront them anew after a ten-year absence.

Close Reading

Metacognitive Strategy: Ladder of Questions

Have students work in groups to paraphrase the story. Then, have them answer the following questions to analyze the effects of flashback, sensory images, and figures of speech on the story's **mood:**

Literal Questions

1. What happens during the flashback? How do the characters react to events in the flashback?

2. How are the behaviors of the heron and the narrator's father similar?

Interpretive Questions

1. How do sensory images help create the story's mood? Support your ideas with examples. Why do you think the mood is appropriate to the story's theme?

2. Which figures of speech contribute to the story's mood? How do these figures of speech support the story's tone and theme?

Experiential Questions

1. Is the father's long grief believable? Why or why not?

2. Have you ever wanted to protect someone who is grieving? Describe.

Close-Reading Practice: Pace

Have students re-read from "Walking back down" to "where he slept." Then, discuss the following questions to explore Fugard's use of pace:

- How does the author's use of details describing the narrator's walk along the veranda affect the pace of the story? *[By using details about the rooms as well as about the past, such as "rooms we'd stopped using," "the dining room with its yellow wood table," and "the living room where my mother's desk was still piled high with the field guides and books she'd used to identify unknown plants," the author slows the pace, momentarily delaying the plot's action.]*

- How do details about dinner help emphasize the narrator's longing for morning? How do the details affect the pace of the passage? *[The narrator's desire to "go racing through the veld with the dogs" contrasts with the slow, monotonous pace of the evening, which is described in brief, summary details: heating up a tin, eating in silence, reading and listening to the radio, the generator being switched off, and sleep.]*

- How does the pace in this passage contribute to the story's theme? *[The passage's slow pace emphasizes the unchanging routine that results from the father's grief and helps support the story's theme that it is best to make peace with grief and move on in life.]*

Resources

For information on **ladder of questions** and other metacognitive strategies, see page 16 of this book.

Collection Resources

Close Reading

The close-reading passage is on page 661 of the Student Edition.

Before assigning this activity, make sure your students have mastered the Vocabulary words on page 656 of the Student Edition.

Words for the Activity

blotted, p. 658
shabby, p. 659
slithery, p. 661
tremulous, p. 662
dismantle, p. 662

For information on **fishbowl discussions** and other discussion methods, see page 20 of this book.

A successful response

- analyzes similarities in the roles of the heron and the father in the story
- supports the analysis with apt examples
- shows insight into sensory images, figures of speech, flashback, mood, pace, theme, and character
- uses language effectively

Vocabulary: Synonyms

When the narrator describes her father's hands as "slablike," she evokes a funereal, cold image. Thinking critically about Fugard's word choices can give students insight into the story's mood.

Activity. To establish the story's mood, Fugard uses the words in the margin. Have students discuss or write a synonym for each word and consider the context in which each word appears. Finally, have students explain how each word contributes to the story's mood.

[**Blotted** *means "erased" or "blurred." Because the girl's father no longer smiles,* blotted *evokes a doleful mood.* **Shabby** *means "dilapidated." Because the once-beautiful compound is decaying,* shabby *establishes a despondent mood.* **Slithery** *means "slippery." Drawing attention to the narrator's disturbed reaction to the heron,* slithery *creates a repugnant mood.* **Tremulous** *means "quivering" or "fearful." Because the girl's wail is frightened and shaky,* tremulous *evokes a mournful mood.* **Dismantle** *means "take apart or strip away." Because the father's reason for staying at the sanctuary is being stripped away,* dismantle *evokes a sad mood.]*

Postreading

Discussion Method: Fishbowl Discussion

Have students discuss the poem's use of **pace** in a fishbowl discussion. Arrange students in inner and outer circles; then, ask students in the inner circle one of the following questions:

- How does the pace accelerate after the heron is released? Why does the pace increase? *[Fugard uses fewer flashbacks, digressions, and descriptions once the heron is released. The increased pace reflects a change in the pace of the father's life.]*

- Why is the narrator happier when the story's pace increases? *[She is tired of her father's mourning and is ready to release the past.]*

After students trade seats, ask a question suggested by student responses to the first query or ask another question from those above.

Writing

Have students respond to the prompt below in an essay.

How are the roles of the heron and the father similar in the story? How do sensory images, figures of speech, and flashbacks convey these roles? Consider **mood, pace,** character, and theme. Then, write an essay in which you explain how the roles of the bird and the father are similar. Use details and examples from the story.

Elements of Literature selection

Waiting for *E. gularis*
by Linda Pastan

Literary Focus

This selection lends itself to the teaching of two skills: the core skill of analyzing **figurative language** and the advanced skill of analyzing **speaker's tone.**

Figurative Language

Use of figurative language allows a writer to express ideas beyond the literal meanings of words. By drawing imaginative comparisons between seemingly unlike things, writers invite readers to examine ideas, images, and events from new perspectives, often adding new depths of meaning and nuance to a work. **Similes,** a common form of figurative language, use a connective word such as *like* or *as* to form direct comparisons. **Metaphors,** also commonly used, are subtler, sometimes only implying their comparisons. Linda Pastan's similes not only provide arresting images but also direct attention to connections and ideas beyond those readily apparent in her poem.

Author Focus. Linda Pastan's poetry is economical. Her deployment of similes and metaphors allows for spare use of language and enables Pastan to reveal complex ideas in only a few well-chosen words.

Speaker's Attitude

A poem's speaker is not always its author. Instead, the speaker may be a persona, or adopted voice. When a poem uses the first-person pronoun, readers may wrongfully assume that the speaker and the poet are identical. Given this fact, students may need to be reminded that a speaker's identity is sometimes less important than what is revealed by his or her voice and tone. In "Waiting for *E. gularis*," for example, the speaker expresses an attitude toward everything he or she encounters. Point out to students that they can tell much about the poem's speaker through the author's diction and use of figurative language.

Close Reading

Close-Reading Practice: Figurative Language

Have students re-read lines 22 through 45 and discuss these questions to explore Pastan's use of figurative language:

• What are the passage's similes and metaphors? *[Metaphors: "crucible of breath"; "stockaded with eel grass"; "fans waiting for their*

SKILLS FOCUS

Literary Skill
Analyze figurative language.

Advanced Skill
Analyze speaker's tone.

As students analyze **figurative language** and **speaker's tone,** remind them not to look at these elements in isolation but to consider how they contribute to our understanding of **character** and **theme.**

Related Works

Consider teaching one of the works below from *Elements of Literature* with "Waiting for *E. gularis.*"

Analyzing figurative language:
"I Am Offering This Poem" by Jimmy Santiago Baca

Analyzing speaker's tone:
"By the Waters of Babylon" by Stephen Vincent Benét

Close Reading

The close-reading passage is on pages 665–666 of the Student Edition.

Collection Resources

rock star"; "dark side of a mirror." Similes: "like rumors of his appearance"; "as at those childhood puzzles."]

- What does the figurative language reveal about the speaker's attitude? *[The figurative language reveals that the speaker may have a harsh attitude toward people: Joggers love pain, and the bird-watchers lounge idly as if waiting for tickets to a show. The speaker is more respectful toward nature. The language suggests beautiful, transient, or hidden images: The grass guards the pond's secrets; a breeze is like a whispered rumor; the pond is like both a mirror and a puzzle.]*

Vocabulary: Tone

"Waiting for *E. gularis*," a poem of surprisingly few words, evokes a clear tone. Thinking critically about the poet's word choices can give students deeper insight into the speaker's attitude.

Activity. To create the poem's setting and to hint at the speaker's attitude, Pastan uses the words in the margin. Ask students to discuss or to write down the meanings and connotations of each word. Then, have students explain what each word reveals about the speaker's tone.

*[**Exile** means "someone barred from his or her native country" and has a negative connotation, suggesting that the speaker feels pity for the lost bird. **Inexplicable** means "unable to be explained" and has a neutral connotation. Inexplicable suggests that the speaker finds the bird's presence enigmatic and marvelous. **Crucible,** here, means "test" and suggests noble hardship; however, crucible suggests that the speaker has an ironically superior attitude toward the joggers who "worship in pain." **Stockaded** means "enclosed" and connotes protection. Stockaded may hint at the speaker's dark frame of mind about the invaded pond. **Incantation** means "words chanted as a magic spell" and may have an association with primitive magic. Incantation suggests that the speaker responds negatively to the waiting crowd and its failure to feel sympathy for the bird.]*

Postreading
Writing

Have students write an essay responding to the prompt below.

> Linda Pastan may be considered an elegiac poet: Her poetry is often reflective and mournful in content and tone. Write an essay in which you use "Waiting for *E. gularis*" to agree or disagree with this evaluation of Pastan's poetry. Consider the **figurative language, speaker's tone** and **diction,** and theme in "Waiting for *E. gularis*." Use details and examples to support your points.

Vocabulary

Words for the Activity

exile, line 1
inexplicable, line 15
crucible, line 24
stockaded, line 26
incantation, line 36

Criteria for Success

A successful response
- makes an evaluation of the poet's content and tone
- supports the statement of evaluation with apt examples
- shows insight into figurative language, speaker's tone, diction, and theme
- uses language effectively

A Very Old Man with Enormous Wings
by Gabriel García Márquez

Literary Focus

The coverage of **magic realism** below builds on the instruction found in the Student Edition. You may want to introduce the additional skill of analyzing **paradox** when teaching this story to advanced students.

Magic Realism

First-time readers of **magic realism** may be surprised by the narrator's tone. The mixture of fantasy and reality may not startle modern readers who have grown accustomed to movies such as *Freaky Friday;* however, a narrator's evenhanded treatment of the fantastic and the mundane may surprise or frustrate students. They may expect magical moments to be narrated in an awe-filled voice, but Gabriel García Márquez's speaker seems to see no real difference between an ordinary event and a supernatural one. Point out to students that the deadpan or ironic tone of "A Very Old Man with Enormous Wings" is a hallmark of García Márquez's work.

Author Focus. Gabriel García Márquez, long considered magic realism's leading writer, has inspired other writers to use the form in their stories and novels. García Márquez and many of the writers he has influenced have used magic realism to comment indirectly on political, religious, and social developments in Latin America since the 1970s.

Paradox

A **paradox** is a statement or situation that seems to express a contradiction yet reveals a truth. A paradox prompts readers to think more carefully about ideas or concepts, especially those that have been assumed to be true or understood. García Márquez's mixture of fantasy and reality provides readers with a broader sense of paradox—the situation is characterized by contradiction. The story is rife with paradoxes, from the narrator's treatment of the fantastic as if it were mundane, to the depiction of the angel as a decrepit old man, to the villagers' hostility and then indifference to the angel in their midst. Use "A Very Old Man with Enormous Wings" as an illustration of the power of paradox to make readers examine an idea or concept in a new light.

SKILLS FOCUS

Collection Resources

Literary Skill
Analyze characteristics of magic realism.

Advanced Skill
Analyze paradox.

As students explore **magic realism** and **paradox,** remind them not to look at these elements in isolation but to consider how they contribute to our understanding of **character, tone,** and **theme.**

Related Works

Consider teaching one of the works below from *Elements of Literature* with "A Very Old Man with Enormous Wings."

Analyzing magic realism:
"Sonnet for Heaven Below" by Jack Agüeros

Analyzing paradox:
"The Man in the Water" by Roger Rosenblatt

Resources

For information on **thinking notes** and other metacognitive strategies, see page 16 of this book.

Close Reading

The close-reading passage is on pages 683–684 of the Student Edition.

Vocabulary

Before assigning this activity, make sure your students have mastered the Vocabulary words on page 678 of the Student Edition.

Words for the Activity

celestial, p. 680

terrestrial, p. 683

sidereal, p. 683

stellar, p. 683

lunar, p. 684

Close Reading

Metacognitive Strategy: Thinking Notes

As students read, have them use thinking notes to document their reactions to the story. Provide students with sticky notes and common symbols for annotation. Then, have students focus on details about the characters, their motivations, and their reactions to events. Especially encourage students to consider details related to

- the old man with enormous wings

- the reactions of Pelayo, Elisenda, the priest, and the villagers

- the woman who was turned into a spider

Close-Reading Practice: Magic Realism

Have students re-read the passage from "The angel was the only one" to "cataclysm in repose" and discuss these questions to explore García Márquez's use of magic realism:

- Identify details from the passage that mix the fantastic and the ordinary. How does this mixture affect the passage's tone? *[The angel "spent his time trying to get comfortable" in the chicken coop. He is "befuddled" by the symbols of religion, the oil lamps and sacramental candles. People try to feed him mothballs, but he eats only eggplant paste. The hens peck at his wings, "looking for stellar parasites." People torment him: "The cripples pulled out feathers"; "even the most merciful threw stones at him." When he is burned by the branding iron, his giant wings throw up dung and lunar dust. This mixture of details creates a darkly humorous, ironic tone.]*

- How does the passage's mixture of fantastic and ordinary elements create an unexpected mood? *[The mood in the passage is everyday and mundane, not at all religious or exalted. Most readers would expect an angel to be glorious and strong. This angel ignores people except when they hurt him. Most readers would also expect people to treat an angel with respect and awe. Here, people show no respect, torment the angel, and treat him as a sideshow attraction. They are fascinated by him and somewhat cautious of his latent power.]*

Vocabulary: Magic Realism

In describing the angel and the world, the narrator mixes words for earthy, everyday things with words describing things heavenly or divine. Thinking critically about the vocabulary of the story can help students understand how the word choices help create magic realism.

Activity. In his descriptions of the angel and the villagers, García Márquez uses the words in the margin. Ask students to discuss the meanings and context of each word. Then, have students write sentences explaining how each word helps create magic realism.

*[**Celestial** means "of heaven"; the wise woman knows enough to associate this "dirty," "pitiful" creature with the celestial angels of religious tradition. **Terrestrial** means "of earth." The word contrasts with* celestial

and reinforces the irony that the angel is subject to ordinary things like weather. **Sidereal** *means "of the stars." The word, like* celestial *and* terrestrial, *helps reinforce the story's mixing of things from the earth with things from the heavens.* **Stellar** *also means "of the stars" and has the further connotation of "excellence." The word is used to describe parasites feeding on the angel's wings and so ironically mixes the divine with the very earthy. The parasites may be "of the stars," literally, as well as delectably "divine" to the chickens that eat them.* **Lunar** *means "of the moon" and refers to the dust kicked up in the angel's agitation. "Lunar dust" exemplifies the story's magical pairing of the heavenly with the mundane. All the words help create the story's magic realism by establishing a realm blending details both natural and supernatural.]*

Postreading

Discussion Method: Reading Conference

Have students discuss the story's paradoxes in a reading conference. Ask students to prepare by reviewing the story for unexpected details about how characters appear or act. In groups, students may share the contradictions they have identified and use them to discuss the story's theme. Use the following questions to prompt students' thinking:

- What is paradoxical about the angel's appearance and his arrival on earth? *[The angel does not arrive in a burst of glory, the way one might expect, nor does he look or act like an angel. He is not strong or glorious, but old and decrepit. He does not convey any message from God or offer divine insight. Even the healings that people claim he is responsible for "showed a certain mental disorder." For example, a blind man grows teeth but does not recover his sight.]*

- What question or questions does García Márquez raise through the use of paradox? *[Students may suggest that García Márquez uses paradox to raise questions about the nature of common beliefs, whether people are blind to divinity, and whether divine creatures are more like us than we think.]*

Writing

Have students write an essay that responds to the prompt below.

The critic Tom Faulkner suggests that "The Very Old Man with Enormous Wings" is a parody of a fairy tale. Do you agree? Consider the story's use of **magic realism, paradoxes,** and character, tone, and theme as you write an essay explaining whether or not the story is a parody of a fairy tale. Use details and examples to support your points.

Resources

For information on **reading conferences** and other discussion methods, see page 20 of this book.

Criteria for Success

A successful response

- takes a position on whether the story parodies a fairy tale

- supports the thesis with apt analysis and examples

- shows insight into magic realism, paradox, setting, plot, narrative voice, character, tone, and theme

- uses language effectively

Collection Resources

Section I: Multiple-Choice Questions

Directions: Carefully read the following passage by Annie Dillard. Then, choose the *best* answer to each question.

from Heaven and Earth in Jest

A couple of summers ago I was walking along the edge of the island to see what I could see in the water, and mainly to scare frogs. Frogs have an inelegant way of taking
5 off from invisible positions on the bank just ahead of your feet, in dire panic, emitting a froggy "Yike!" and splashing into the water. Incredibly, this amused me, and, incredibly, it amuses me still. As I walked along the
10 grassy edge of the island, I got better and better at seeing frogs both in and out of the water. I learned to recognize, slowing down, the difference in texture of the light reflected from mudbank, water, grass, or frog. Frogs
15 were flying all around me. At the end of the island I noticed a small green frog. He was exactly half in and half out of the water, looking like a schematic[1] diagram of an amphibian, and he didn't jump.

20 He didn't jump; I crept closer. At last I knelt on the island's winter-killed grass, lost, dumbstruck, staring at the frog in the creek just four feet away. He was a very small frog with wide, dull eyes. And just as I looked at
25 him, he slowly crumpled and began to sag. The spirit vanished from his eyes as if snuffed. His skin emptied and drooped; his very skull seemed to collapse and settle like a kicked tent. He was shrinking before my
30 eyes like a deflating football. I watched the taut, glistening skin on his shoulders ruck,[2] and rumple, and fall. Soon, part of his skin, formless as a pricked balloon, lay in floating folds like bright scum on the top of the

35 water: it was a monstrous and terrifying thing. I gaped bewildered, appalled. An oval shadow hung in the water behind the drained frog; then the shadow glided away. The frog skin bag started to sink.

40 I had read about the giant water bug, but never seen one. "Giant water bug" is really the name of the creature, which is an enormous, heavy-bodied, brown insect. It eats other insects, tadpoles, fish, and frogs. Its
45 grasping forelegs are mighty and hooked inward. It seizes a victim with these legs, hugs it tight, and paralyzes it with enzymes injected during a vicious bite. That one bite is the only bite it ever takes. Through the
50 puncture shoot the poisons that dissolve the victim's muscles and bones and organs—all but the skin—and through it the giant water bug sucks out the victim's body, reduced to a juice. This event is quite common in warm
55 fresh water. The frog I saw was being sucked by a giant water bug. I had been kneeling on the island grass; when the unrecognizable flap of frog skin settled on the creek bottom, swaying, I stood up and brushed the knees
60 of my pants. I couldn't catch my breath.

Of course, many carnivorous animals devour their prey alive. The usual method seems to be to subdue the victim by drowning or grasping it so it can't flee, then eating
65 it whole or in a series of bloody bites. Frogs eat everything whole, stuffing prey into their mouths with their thumbs. People have seen frogs with their wide jaws so full of live

[1]**schematic** *adj.:* having the characteristics of a diagram or detailed, outlined plan.
[2]**ruck** *v:* crease, fold, or pucker.

dragonflies they couldn't close them. Ants
70 don't even have to catch their prey; in the
spring they swarm over newly hatched,
featherless birds in the nest and eat them
tiny bite by bite.

That it's rough out there and chancy is
75 no surprise. Every live thing is a survivor on
a kind of extended emergency bivouac.[3] But
at the same time we are also created. In the
Koran, Allah asks, "The heaven and the
earth and all in between, thinkest thou I
80 made them in *jest*?" It's a good question.
What do we think of the created universe,
spanning an unthinkable void with an unthinkable profusion of forms? Or what do
we think of nothingness, those sickening
90 reaches of time in either direction? If the
giant water bug was not made in jest, was it
then made in earnest? Pascal[4] uses a nice
term to describe the notion of the creator's,
once having called forth the universe, turn-
95 ing his back to it: *Deus Absconditus.*[5] Is this
what we think happened? Was the sense of

it there, and God absconded[6] with it, ate it,
like a wolf who disappears round the edge
of the house with the Thanksgiving turkey?
100 "God is subtle," Einstein said, "but not mali-
cious." Again, Einstein said that "nature con-
ceals her mystery by means of her essential
grandeur, not by her cunning." It could be
that God has not absconded but spread, as
105 our vision and understanding of the universe have spread, to a fabric of spirit and
sense so grand and subtle, so powerful in a
new way, that we can only feel blindly of its
hem. In making the thick darkness a swad-
110 dling band for the sea, God "set bars and
doors" and said, "Hitherto[7] shalt thou come,
but no further." But have we come even that
far? Have we rowed out to the thick darkness, or are we all playing pinochle[8] in the
115 bottom of the boat?

From "Heaven and Earth in Jest" from *Pilgrim at Tinker Creek* by Annie Dillard. Copyright © 1974 by Annie Dillard. Reproduced by permission of **HarperCollins Publishers.**

---

[3]**bivouac** *n:* temporary encampment of soldiers in the field.
[4]**Pascal:** Blaise Pascal (1623–1662), French philosopher and mathematician.
[5]***Deus Absconditus:*** Latin for "the vanished God."
[6]**absconded** *v:* sneaked away or ran away in secret.
[7]**hitherto** *adv:* to here.
[8]**pinochle** *n:* a card game.

1. In the first paragraph the phrase "emitting a froggy 'Yike!'" (lines 6–7) is an example of
   (A) sarcasm
   (B) imagery
   (C) personification
   (D) euphemism
   (E) metonymy

2. The sentence "Frogs were flying all around me" (lines 14–15) serves to
   (A) illustrate the meaning of "inelegant way of taking off" (lines 4–5)
   (B) explain why "it amuses me still" (line 9)
   (C) show how the speaker "got better and better at seeing frogs" (lines 10–11)
   (D) help define the meaning of "texture of the light" (line 13)
   (E) introduce the simile "like a schematic diagram of an amphibian (lines 18–19)

3. Which of the following words is grammatically and thematically parallel to "skin" (line 27)?
   (A) "emptied" (line 27)
   (B) "skull" (line 28)
   (C) "tent" (line 29)
   (D) "shoulders" (line 31)
   (E) "formless" (line 33)

4. In the second paragraph (lines 20–39) the speaker uses all of the following EXCEPT
   (A) simile
   (B) parallelism
   (C) repetition
   (D) understatement
   (E) alliteration

5. The mood in the second paragraph (lines 20–39) is best described as
   (A) eerily tense
   (B) deeply threatening
   (C) ironically mysterious
   (D) utterly quizzical
   (E) openly reproachful

6. The *main* effect of the reference to Pascal and his philosophy (lines 92–95) is to
   (A) give readers a clearly objective way to understand the frog's death
   (B) appeal to people with strongly held beliefs
   (C) offer an explanation for seemingly non-sensical events
   (D) establish Dillard's mysterious tone
   (E) contrast Pascal's opinion with that of Einstein

7. Throughout the passage the author employs
   (A) objectivity
   (B) circular reasoning
   (C) euphemistic phrasing
   (D) pathos
   (E) appeal to authority

8. The function of the last paragraph (lines 74–115) of the passage is to
   (A) refute counterarguments
   (B) restate points raised earlier
   (C) raise rhetorical questions
   (D) reestablish the writer's connection to the audience
   (E) make a call to action

9. The reader can infer from the conclusion of the passage that the author
   (A) has the answer to the questions she raises
   (B) will continue to study the behavior of frogs
   (C) wishes that she had not witnessed the death of the frog
   (D) thinks that scientists can provide the answers to the meaning of life
   (E) believes that we have little understanding of the universe

10. The *main* idea of the passage is that
    (A) all creatures must fight to survive
    (B) humans have a natural advantage over animals
    (C) the ethos of the natural world is "eat or be eaten"
    (D) there are no winners in the game of life
    (E) life is a great but inexplicable mystery

Section II: Essay

Directions: Carefully read the following prompt. Then, present your response in a well-developed essay.

In "Heaven and Earth in Jest," Annie Dillard considers the beauty and horror of the natural world as she observes and interprets a gruesome yet fascinating event in nature. As you re-read the essay, notice the author's use of rhetorical strategies, including repetition, rhetorical questions, figurative language, parallelism, and restatement. Also, think about the essay's theme. Then, write an essay in which you analyze three of Dillard's rhetorical strategies and explain how they support her theme.

Resources

For information about how to analyze a **writing prompt** and other strategies for timed writing, see page 45 of this book.

Scoring Guidelines

9–8 These essays fully explore the relationship between Dillard's use of rhetorical strategies and the theme. They present coherent, well-written analyses supported by comprehensive evidence. They show insight into the author's use of rhetorical strategies. The students exhibit a sophisticated control of language.

7–6 These essays adequately explore the relationship between Dillard's use of specific rhetorical strategies and her theme. They offer insights into the reason Dillard uses specific strategies, but the analyses may be less thorough, perceptive, or specific than essays in the 9–8 range. The students' prose is clear but may contain a few errors in diction or syntax.

5 These essays acknowledge the relationship between Dillard's use of rhetorical devices and her theme and make clear claims, but their analyses may be unevenly developed or contain limited evidence. The students' control of language is adequate.

4–3 These essays present an inadequate response to the prompt. The students may misidentify the rhetorical strategies or misinterpret the theme. They may have difficulty establishing a clear position or use inappropriate or insufficient evidence. The students demonstrate an inconsistent control over such elements of writing as diction and syntax.

2–1 These essays do not successfully respond to the prompt. The students may fail to understand the prompt, respond tangentially, or substitute a simpler task, such as merely summarizing Dillard's ideas. The students' prose reveals consistent weaknesses in such elements of writing as organization, grammar, and diction.

0 These essays present a response that receives no credit. They may simply paraphrase the prompt, for example.

Sample Response

The following essay represents a high-scoring response to the writing prompt.

In the essay "Heaven and Earth in Jest," writer Annie Dillard explains how she witnesses the sudden but completely natural death of a frog and how that death led her to raise age-old questions about our place in the universe. Dillard's writing style reflects her theme—that the world is at once a dangerous, mystifying, and beautiful place that we humans may never fully comprehend. Her use of figurative language (simile and metaphor) and rhetorical questions reflects her struggle to make connections, question assumptions, and search for answers, and her rhetorical strategies invite readers to join in the same struggle.

By associating the unfamiliar experience of the frog's death with everyday objects, Dillard uses figurative language to reflect her struggle to understand an extraordinary event. Most of her similes appear in the second paragraph, where Dillard describes the appearance of the frog as it dies. For example, "The spirit vanished from his eyes as if snuffed," "his very skull seemed to collapse and settle like a kicked tent," and "He was shrinking before my eyes like a deflating football" indicate that Dillard seeks to understand the frog's death in terms of the familiar. Similarly, she describes the frog's skin as "formless as a pricked balloon" and says that it lies in "floating folds like bright scum." Later in the essay, she associates a runaway God with another easily understood image, "a wolf who disappears round the edge of the house with the Thanksgiving turkey." This use of figurative language provides readers with vivid imagery and helps Dillard make some sense of what she has witnessed. By drawing connections between a confusing new experience and ordinary objects such as tents, balloons, and footballs, Dillard tries to make the experience familiar and more comprehensible, indicating that she is struggling to understand the meaning of the frog's death.

Likewise, the rhetorical devices Dillard uses in the last paragraph of the essay—rhetorical questioning and repetition—indicate that she is trying to understand the meaning of life and the place of living things in the universe. In this paragraph, Dillard asks <u>seven</u> rhetorical questions, all of which address the meaning of life. Ironically, those questions will not prompt realistic answers: Why was the universe formed? Was the universe created by a kind or a cruel creator? Will we ever be able to figure out the meaning of the universe? The repetition does not clarify Dillard's position; instead, the rhetoric points to her confusion. Answers are not her goal. Her questions are intended to challenge readers to begin "working" the problem. Dillard's devices are designed to bring readers into the same confusing realm that she has entered—a philosophical and religious world that inspires inhabitants to join the struggle to make sense of a universe that sometimes does not make sense.

In her essay, Dillard recalls a small creature's death and then uses figurative language and rhetorical questions to share her confusion with readers. These devices are meant to prompt readers to consider the greater questions of existence. As a writer, Dillard appears quite disturbed by the scene she has witnessed, and she is clearly uncertain about its meaning for the rest of us. Her use of rhetorical strategies—figurative language, questions, and repetition— reflect this struggle to make meaning of a world that we all share.

Where Have You Gone, Charming Billy?

by Tim O'Brien

Literary Focus

The coverage of **historical context** below builds on the instruction found in the Student Edition. You may want to introduce the additional skill of analyzing a **hero** or **protagonist** when teaching this story to advanced students.

Historical Context

Historical context describes the time, place, and circumstances that inform a work of literature. All writing is shaped in some way by the time and place in which the author lived or lives and which influence the author's beliefs, attitudes, and language. The story "Where Have You Gone, Charming Billy?" is based on the author's direct experiences as a soldier in Vietnam. The story was written eight years after the author's return, so its historical context includes both the conflict in Vietnam and the period of disillusionment that followed the conflict's end. Use the story to illustrate how historical context influences a writer's work.

Hero or Protagonist

Although the terms *hero* and *protagonist* are often used interchangeably, the connotations of the words differ. A **protagonist** is the main character of a work of literature, and the word has a somewhat neutral connotation. The word **hero,** however, suggests that the character is noble and courageous, a role model for readers. Heroes appear in myths and epics, and although sometimes flawed, heroes demonstrate admirable qualities. The protagonist of O'Brien's story is not a noble, brave, or charismatic hero. In fact, Paul Berlin demonstrates qualities associated with an antihero: He is ordinary and capable of no more than what average human beings might do and feel.

Author Focus. Tim O'Brien has returned again and again to the conflict in Vietnam as the setting for his stories and novels. His characters are American soldiers whose decency and bravery are tested by the horrors of war. Often, his characters are ordinary young men trying to make sense of war and its aftermath.

SKILLS FOCUS

Literary Skill
Analyze historical context.

Advanced Skill
Analyze a hero or protagonist.

As students analyze **historical context, hero,** and **protagonist,** remind them not to look at these elements in isolation but to consider how they contribute to our understanding of **character, tone,** and **theme.**

Related Works

Consider teaching one of the works below from *Elements of Literature* with "Where Have You Gone, Charming Billy?"

Analyzing historical context:
"Typhoid Fever" by Frank McCourt

Analyzing a hero or protagonist:
"By the Waters of Babylon" by Stephen Vincent Benét

Collection Resources

Close Reading

Metacognitive Strategy: Ladder of Questions

As students read, encourage them to formulate and answer ladders of questions that address the different levels of meaning in the text. Provide students with the following questions to help get them started:

- **Literal:** What event has upset the main character of the story? [*The main character has watched Billy Boy Watkins die of a heart attack.*]

- **Interpretive:** Why does Paul Berlin imagine he is a boy camping with his father? [*He is a new, frightened soldier, so he recalls a time when he felt safe.*]

- **Experiential:** Can you describe a time when fear or anger made you respond inappropriately to a situation? [*Responses will vary.*]

Close-Reading Practice: Hero or Protagonist

Have students re-read the passage from "The grass along the path" to "Yeah" and discuss the following questions to explore O'Brien's protagonist:

- What does the protagonist, Paul Berlin, dream of telling his father? What does this dream indicate about Berlin? [*Berlin dreams of telling his father that he (Paul) is not afraid. Paul is young, and this may be his first time away from home. Unconsciously, he wants to impress his father by remaining heroically unafraid, but he is frightened and unsure of himself. His fear of disappointing his father haunts him even as he sleeps.*]

- Should Paul Berlin be considered a hero? an antihero? Why? Use details from the story to explain your answer. [*Responses will vary. Berlin's fear and his average, ordinary responses to the situation might mark him as an antihero. As might be expected of anyone, Berlin uses tricks to help himself "forget the war," for example, embracing simple experiences from his past such as sleeping and licking dew from the grass. He also tries to hide his inexperience from others, denying that he has been asleep and withholding a response to the soldier's invitation to talk, "Bad day, today, buddy."*]

Vocabulary: Historical Context

Authors usually use language suited to the historical context of a story or novel. Thinking critically about O'Brien's use of language can give students deeper insight into the story's historical context.

Activity. To communicate the story's historical context, O'Brien uses the words in the margin. Have students consult a dictionary to identify the meaning of each word. Then, ask students to discuss the context of the words. Finally, have students write a few sentences explaining how each word helps define the story's historical context.

[**Platoon** *is a military term used to describe two or more squads of soldiers. Here, the word introduces the unit in which Berlin serves. A* **rice**

Resources

For information on **ladders of questions** and other metacognitive strategies, see page 16 of this book.

Close Reading

The close-reading passage is on page 735 of the Student Edition.

Collection Resources

Vocabulary

Before assigning this activity, make sure your students have mastered the Vocabulary words on page 730 of the Student Edition.

Words for the Activity

platoon, p. 732
rice paddy, p. 732
breech, p. 733
muzzle, p. 733
medevac, p. 737

paddy is an irrigated or flooded field where rice is grown. Much of the Vietnam War was fought in rural areas with many rice paddies; the detail helps signal that the story is set in Vietnam. **Breech,** here, means "the back end of the barrel of a rifle"; the use of the word indicates that Berlin is familiar with the weapon. Similarly, **muzzle** refers to the open end of Berlin's weapon. **Medevac** is the shortened form of the words medical evacuation, referring to the evacuation by helicopter of wounded combat soldiers. Each word creates a sense of historical context by reflecting the experiences and language of soldiers serving in Vietnam. The terms all refer to the conflict: sites of battle, weapons, and medical-emergency procedures.]

Postreading

Discussion Method: Literature Circle

Have students discuss the story's **historical context** in a literature circle. Ask students to form groups and select roles. Then, use the following questions to prompt students' thinking:

- What details about the setting and the characters reflect the historical context of the story? *[The characters are soldiers, and the setting includes the jungles and rice paddies of Vietnam. Details about the activities, appearances, and emotions of the soldiers, as well as descriptions of the warm, muggy climate and the sights and smells of the setting, help establish the story's historical context.]*

- How does the story's language reflect the historical period in which it takes place? *[The characters use language that seems distinctive yet realistic. The author seems to have direct knowledge of what soldiers in Vietnam would do and say.]*

- How would you describe the story's tone? What does the tone suggest about the author's feelings about serving in Vietnam? *[The tone is fearful, anxious, and grimly humorous. The story focuses on Paul Berlin's attempts to keep his fear and panic at bay, including moments of near hysteria, suggesting that the author has a very deep sympathy for soldiers who served in Vietnam.]*

Writing

Have students write an essay responding to the prompt below.

In the story, Tim O'Brien re-creates a scene from a particular war in a particular time and place. Consider other depictions of war you have read or seen in films or on television. Then, write an essay in which you compare the depiction of war in O'Brien's story with at least one other depiction. Consider setting, **historical context, protagonist (hero** or **antihero),** tone, and theme in your comparison. Use details and examples to support your points.

Resources

For information on **literature circles** and other discussion methods, see page 20 of this book.

Collection Resources

Criteria for Success

A successful response
- compares the story's depiction of war with other depictions in literature or other media
- supports the comparison with apt examples
- shows insight into setting, historical context, protagonist (hero or antihero), tone, and theme
- uses language effectively

Declaration of Independence from the War in Vietnam
by Martin Luther King, Jr.

SKILLS FOCUS

Collection Resources

Literary Skill
Analyze primary sources.

Advanced Skill
Analyze repetition, parallelism, and juxtaposition of ideas.

As students analyze **primary sources, repetition, parallelism,** and **juxtaposition of ideas,** remind them not to look at these elements in isolation but to consider how they contribute to our understanding of **character, tone,** and **theme.**

Related Works

Consider teaching one of the works below from *Elements of Literature* with "Declaration of Independence from the War in Vietnam."

Analyzing primary sources:
from "The Vietnam War: An Eyewitness History," edited by Sanford Wexler

Analyzing repetition and parallelism:
"Sea Fever" by John Masefield

Literary Focus

This selection lends itself to the teaching of two skills: the core skill of analyzing **primary sources** and the advanced skills of analyzing **repetition, parallelism,** and **juxtaposition of ideas.**

Primary Sources

Martin Luther King, Jr., is perhaps best remembered as a proponent of civil rights and a Nobel Prize winner who captivated the nation with his famous "I Have a Dream" speech. In his final years, however, King shifted his focus to the conflict in Vietnam. On April 4, 1967, King spoke at Riverside Church in New York City, openly opposing the use of U.S. troops in Southeast Asia. "Declaration of Independence from the War in Vietnam" is a primary-source document in which King argues that the injustices endured by African Americans at home were further perpetuated by their recruitment into the military, where they served in much greater proportion than white Americans.

Author Focus. King's speech "Declaration of Independence from the War in Vietnam" was delivered at a time when his leadership was being challenged. A middle-class minister who argued for patience and moderation, King was criticized by younger activists who questioned King's ideas about nonviolence. One year after King presented his antiwar speech, he was assassinated in Memphis, Tennessee.

Repetition, Parallelism, and Juxtaposition of Ideas

King declares that he is "a preacher by trade." As a preacher, he crafted sermons and speeches designed to be spoken aloud. His use of repetition and parallelism grew from this oral emphasis. Both techniques are found in King's denunciation of those who "possess power *without* compassion, might *without* morality, and strength *without* sight"—a powerful rhythmic statement that listeners find both memorable and moving. Listeners also find King's use of juxtaposition of ideas striking. He declares that he is "a child of God and a brother of the suffering poor of Vietnam," a statement that helps his immediate audience connect with fellow sufferers on the other side of the world.

Close Reading

Metacognitive Strategy: Reading Journals

As students read, have them make notes about elements of this speech that appeal to listeners: **repetition, parallelism,** and **juxtaposition of ideas.** Ask students to consider the following ideas:

- what the effect of hearing the speech might have been

- why parallel structures such as "Shall we say the odds are too great? Shall we tell them the struggle is too hard?" effectively convey emotional content

- why the juxtaposition of Southeast Asia with "southwest Georgia" might make an audience reconsider its attitude about both places

Close-Reading Practice: Primary Sources

Have students re-read the passage from "My third reason" to "my own government" and discuss these questions to evaluate the ideas presented in King's speech:

- After talking with young men from the urban North, King says "their questions hit home." What happened in these conversations, and how did they influence King's thoughts about nonviolence? *[King spoke against "Molotov cocktails and rifles" and in favor of nonviolent action. The men responded by asking him about Vietnam. King realized that he would have to address the war and the violence of the U.S. government if he wanted to continue to advocate nonviolence, to "raise my voice against the violence of the oppressed."]*

- What is King's assessment of the U.S. policy in Vietnam? *[King believes that the United States is using violence in Vietnam to "bring about the changes it wanted" and that his own government is "the greatest purveyor of violence in the world today."]*

- King was known as a civil rights leader; in this speech, however, he addresses foreign policy. What is his purpose in presenting the part of his argument found in this passage? *[King is explaining that in order to uphold his "conviction that social change comes most meaningfully through nonviolent action" and to argue against the "violence of the oppressed in the ghettos," he must respond to the conflict in Vietnam and the role of his own government, "the greatest purveyor of violence in the world."]*

Vocabulary: Word Parts

In his speech, Martin Luther King, Jr., uses many nouns that have been formed from verbs by adding the suffix *–tion.* The repetition of this form allows him to use nouns that connote action. Thinking about King's word choices can help students analyze the effectiveness of his speech, which presents a call for change and action.

Activity. In his descriptions of the war in Vietnam and of inequality in the United States, King uses the words in the margin. Have students identify the verb contained in each noun and describe how the action relates to the theme of King's speech.

Resources

For information on **reading journals** and other metacognitive strategies, see page 16 of this book.

Close Reading

The close-reading passage is on pages 750–751 of the Student Edition.

Collection Resources

Vocabulary

Words for the Activity

connection, p. 749

rehabilitation, p. 749

recognition, p. 750

manipulation, p. 750

corruption, p. 751

*[**Connection** contains the verb connect. King connects the idea that African Americans are being neglected at home with the U.S. military buildup. **Rehabilitation** contains the verb rehabilitate. King says the Vietnam War prevents government from implementing programs to rehabilitate the poor. **Recognition** contains the verb recognize. King recognizes that the war impacts African Americans. **Manipulation** contains the verb manipulate. The government, King argues, manipulates African Americans, allowing discrimination at home while asking them to fight in Vietnam. **Corruption** contains the verb corrupt. King argues that that the poor of the United States are corrupted by fighting in Vietnam.]*

Postreading

Discussion Method: Bulletin-Board or Threaded Discussion

Determine whether you will use the bulletin board or an electronic forum for posting questions for student discussion. Then, post the following questions to initiate a **bulletin-board** or **threaded discussion.** Invite students to research unfamiliar historical references.

- What connection does King see between the conflict in Vietnam and the struggle for civil rights? between African Americans and the people of Vietnam? *[King sees that the war is using money that otherwise would be spent on domestic poverty programs. He sees that large numbers of African Americans are asked to fight even though their civil rights are not guaranteed at home. Both African Americans and the Vietnamese are victims of poverty and violence.]*

- Why might King's speech have invited criticism? Which of his ideas might have been controversial? *[King calls his country's actions "violent" and calls for an end to the war, positions that ran counter to government policy. He also may have been criticized for changing his focus from domestic to foreign affairs.]*

Writing

Have students write an essay responding to the prompt below.

> After years of fighting for civil rights, Martin Luther King, Jr., made a public speech about the conflict in Vietnam. Consider how this **primary-source document** reflects King's experience as a minister who has fought for social change. Then, write an essay in which you analyze how King's arguments for ending the war reflect his personal experiences as a civil rights leader.

Elements of Literature selection

"The Magic Happened"
by John Steinbeck

Literary Focus

This selection lends itself to the teaching of two skills: the core skill of analyzing **author's tone** and the advanced skill of analyzing **author's purpose.**

Author's Tone

Authors with a deft touch can bring whimsy, irony, even poignancy to topics that initially seem inaccessible. John Steinbeck does just that in "The Magic Happened" as he describes his introduction to the world of reading. The tone he brings to this potentially sober tale is a bantering one. He exaggerates, describing books as "tongs and thumbscrews." Yet he also shows the gravity of his entrance into the world of books: He returns to *Le Morte d'Arthur* in times of "pain or sorrow or confusion." In other hands, a reflection about literacy could be ponderous; with Steinbeck, however, it is joyous.

Author's Purpose

Authors' memoirs may instruct, persuade, or entertain. Steinbeck's purpose in recalling this childhood event may be a bit of each. His tale revels in the sounds of archaic English, luxuriating in words such as *yclept* and *hyght.* His example, though, is instructive. To teach children to love reading, he suggests, give them books they can love. Although his story makes no claims about the proper approach to reading instruction, his example is persuasive: With his magical book, the child who hated books grew up to win the Nobel Prize in literature.

Author Focus

In novels such as *The Grapes of Wrath,* John Steinbeck depicts Depression-era poverty in heartbreaking detail. His work is known both for its social conscience and for its ability to describe images with remarkable clarity. He revisited his childhood fascination with Arthurian legend in *Tortilla Flat,* his first novel set in the Salinas Valley. In this novel, Steinbeck retells a chivalrous tale by using a "Round Table" of Mexican American workers who band together to form a brotherhood.

Close Reading

Metacognitive Strategy: Ladder of Questions

Direct students to use the ladder of questions strategy to understand the levels of meaning in Steinbeck's tone. To help students consider

SKILLS FOCUS

Literary Skill
Analyze author's tone.

Advanced Skill
Analyze author's purpose.

As students analyze **author's tone** and **author's purpose,** remind them not to look at these elements in isolation but to consider how they contribute to our understanding of **character, tone,** and **theme.**

Collection Resources

Related Works

Consider teaching one of the works below from *Elements of Literature* with "The Magic Happened."

Analyzing tone:
"Typhoid Fever" by Frank McCourt

Analyzing author's purpose:
"The Day the Clowns Cried" by R. J. Brown

Resources

For information on **ladders of questions** and other metacognitive strategies, see page 16 of this book.

the thematic importance of tone, direct them to answer the following literal, interpretive, and experiential questions:

- **Literal:** What is the "outrageous persecution" that Steinbeck describes? *[Being made to read is the "persecution."]*

- **Interpretive:** Why do you think Steinbeck uses words and phrases such as *printed demons, persecution,* and *hatred* to describe his relationship with books? *[Steinbeck may have been forced to read books he did not like or understand. Because he does not enjoy the activity, books are "demons."]*

- **Experiential:** Think of activities that you learned to enjoy after first resisting them. What does Steinbeck's tone reveal about how this resistance can be overcome? *[Students may say that they learned to enjoy an activity after gaining more skill or information. Steinbeck's change in attitude shows that overcoming this resistance can be almost instantaneous—books change from "demons" to the givers of "glorious and secret words."]*

Close Reading

The close-reading passage is on page 758 of the Student Edition.

Close-Reading Practice: Tone

Have students re-read from "And in that scene" to the end of the passage and discuss these questions to explore Steinbeck's use of tone:

- Steinbeck declares that his secret book contained "all the vices that ever were." What is the tone of this statement, and how does Steinbeck expect readers to respond? *["All the vices that ever were" is Steinbeck's hyperbole. He shows that "vices" add to the book's richness, showing humanity's flaws as well as its virtues. He expects readers to see his subtle humor while acknowledging that children must learn to understand both evil and good.]*

- What is the tone of Steinbeck's statement that he returned to his "magic book" in times of "pain or sorrow or confusion"? What does the tone of this statement reveal about Steinbeck? *[This statement is poignant, revealing that Steinbeck's childhood contained difficult experiences. It also shows the power of reading and imagination, since the "magic book" helped the writer overcome these difficult times.]*

Vocabulary: Synonyms

When Steinbeck says his aunt "fatuously" ignored his hatred of books, his elevated **tone** shows the degree of his early dislike of reading. Examining Steinbeck's vocabulary can show students how individual word choices help set a story's tone.

Activity. In describing his relationship with his "magic book," Steinbeck uses the words in the margin. Ask students to write down each word's connotations. Then, have students note a synonym for each word and discuss how use of the synonym might affect tone.

*[Sample responses: **Fatuously** connotes unconscious stupidity. Foolishly is a less elevated word that would not show the degree to which Steinbeck considered his aunt's present misguided. **Glorious** connotes majesty.*

Vocabulary

Words for the Activity

fatuously, p. 758

glorious, p. 758

vaulted, p. 758

gallantry, p. 758

virtue, p. 758

Wonderful *is a more common word that would not indicate the intensity of Steinbeck's love of archaic language.* **Vaulted** *is an archaic word. Steinbeck would once again lose the archaic tone if he were to use a more modern word such as* jumped. **Gallantry** *has connotations of chivalry and knighthood.* Courage *would not have this historical connotation.* **Virtue** *connotes morality. A word such as* goodness *would not carry the same weight.]*

Postreading

Discussion Method: Timed Discussion

Discuss the author's purpose in a timed discussion. Begin the discussion with broad questions about Steinbeck's recollections, allowing students about thirty seconds to answer. Subsequent speakers should respond to the previous speaker, adhering to the same time limit. Use the following questions to begin a timed discussion:

- Describe Steinbeck's initial reaction to Le Morte d'Arthur. How did his response change? *[Steinbeck originally did not want the book; as he read it, however, he fell in love with the story.]* Why do you think Steinbeck retold this story? *[Steinbeck may have wanted people to know how he became interested in writing. He may have wanted people to see how children can become interested in books.]*

- Why do you think Steinbeck stresses the archaic language of his "magic book"? Could these unfamiliar words be off-putting to some readers? *[Students may say that the puzzle of the archaic language is part of the fun for Steinbeck. If readers don't get his wordplay, that's fun, too. He revels in the idea that his book is secret and exclusive.]*

- Steinbeck's passage concludes with a discussion of morality—right and wrong, sin and virtue. Why do you think he includes this discussion in his description of books for children? *[Steinbeck may be trying to convey that books are important not only to children's education but also to their moral growth. He also may be trying to impress on readers that children are sophisticated thinkers, even though they may not be avid readers.]*

Writing

Have students write an essay in response to the prompt below.

> For John Steinbeck, the introduction to *Le Morte d'Arthur* was a magical experience that he long remembered. Consider his **purpose** in writing this recollection. Then, write an essay in which you analyze how books can or cannot work "magic" in the lives of children. Think about what Steinbeck's example might say to teachers, librarians, and parents, as well as to young readers.

Resources

For information on **timed discussion** and other discussion methods, see page 20 of this book.

Collection Resources

Criteria for Success

A successful response
- analyzes the role of books in the lives of children
- supports the analysis with apt examples
- shows insight into purpose and tone
- uses language effectively

Writing Workshop: Writing a Research Paper

Writing Skill
Write a research paper.

As students explore **research writing,** remind them that research writing, like all forms of writing, gains power from attention to literary elements such as **diction, figurative language, tone,** and **voice.**

Collection Resources

Resources

For more information on **types of evidence,** see the Handbook of Rhetorical Concepts in this book.

Resources

For more information on **appeals to authority,** see the Handbook of Rhetorical Concepts in this book.

Prewriting
Advanced Prewriting Strategy

Finding Reliable Sources. Students who conduct Internet research may find enormous amounts of historical and biographical information. They can begin to evaluate the sources of their data by reading each Web site's URL (uniform resource locator). Direct students to look at the three-letter extension at the end of the files they find online. Useful sources often will have the following extensions:

- **.gov** State, local, and federal government sites use this extension. Government agencies often provide archived historical information.

- **.edu** Files with this extension are usually maintained by schools and universities, which often provide online access to their collections.

- **.org** Nonprofit organizations use this extension. Cultural heritage societies and groups devoted to historical preservation often have Web sites with ".org" extensions.

Advise students to use information from ".com" sites with caution. These commercial sites may not be as reliable as those listed above.

Writing
Advanced Writing Skills

Choosing Quotations. Tell students that their research papers are only as strong as the sources they use to support their arguments. Interesting, colorful quotations may keep readers interested while providing evidence to support a thesis. Have students critically evaluate quotations to make sure that they are apt and effective.

Activity. To help students choose their quotations, have them answer the following questions about each quotation they choose:

- Is my quotation an appropriate length? Does it support my idea adequately? Is it too long?

- Is the language of my quotation appropriate? If it contains jargon, would a paraphrase be more effective?

- What is my purpose in including the quotation? To show the idea of a leading authority? To include analysis or data? Or to state something in a particularly salient manner?

Revising

Revising for Voice

Maintaining Continuity of Tone. Historical and biographical sources may contain a particular kind of language or even jargon specific to a historical period. After reading dozens of sources using a specific jargon, students may unwittingly adopt that voice in their essays. Remind students that their voice should not necessarily be like that of their most learned source or of a reference source. Students should monitor their diction to ensure that their reports reflect a cohesive personal style.

Activity. Ask students to read their reports aloud to themselves and to compare the tone and voice of their quotations with that of their own writing and analysis. As students revise their papers, have them focus on diction, revising for consistency of tone.

Grammar Solutions. As students read for authorial voice, tell them that they can establish voice by choosing appropriate modifiers. Specific modifiers can also display the depth of students' research and understanding. Discuss the following examples with students:

USE OF GENERAL MODIFIERS	*The Romans brought Britain the **important** improvements of roads and aqueducts and established a **significant** legal system.*
USE OF SPECIFIC MODIFIERS	*The Romans brought Britain the **technical** improvements of roads and aqueducts and established an **enduring** legal system.*

The specific modifiers in the second sentence add important information and give weight to the analysis.

Publishing

Build a Web Log. Have students read one another's research and respond on a class Web log. If possible, set up an online site to allow students to ask each other questions about their findings. Students may also want to create a "For Further Reading" by including links to the online sources in their *Works Cited* lists.

Self-Evaluation. Finally, have students reflect on what they have written by responding to the following questions:

- How does my research reveal something new about a historical period? Do I now know a historical figure or time period in depth?

- Did I handle my sources well? Does each quotation offer interesting information in an articulate fashion?

- After reading my analysis, would readers want to read more about my historical period? Does my *Works Cited* list offer a good place to start?

Literature Link

Before students begin reading to revise for authorial voice, encourage them to re-read Karen Watson's "An Ancient Enemy Gets Tougher" to see how a writer uses different types of data while maintaining continuity of tone.

Resources

For more information on **modifiers,** see the Handbook of Grammatical Concepts in this book.

Resources

For more information on **bulletin boards** and other discussion methods, see page 20 of this book.

Collection Resources

Section I: Multiple-Choice Questions

In his farewell address of January 14, 1981, U.S. President Jimmy Carter reviewed the roles and responsibilities of U.S. presidents and citizens, challenges facing the United States, and issues facing the world in general. In the following excerpt from that address, Carter discusses American individualism, his beliefs about fundamental human rights, and his faith in the strength and resilience of American democracy.

Directions: Carefully read the following excerpt from President Jimmy Carter's farewell address. Then, choose the *best* answer to each question.

from Jimmy Carter's Farewell Address

America did not invent human rights. In a very real sense, it is the other way round. Human rights invented America.

5 Ours was the first nation in the history of the world to be founded explicitly on such an idea. Our social and political progress has been based on one fundamental principle—the value and importance of the individual. The fundamental force that unites us

10 is not kinship or place of origin or religious preference. The love of liberty is a common blood that flows in our American veins.

The battle for human rights—at home and abroad—is far from over. We should

15 never be surprised nor discouraged because the impact of our efforts has had, and will always have, varied results. Rather, we should take pride that the ideals which gave birth to our nation still inspire the hopes of

20 oppressed people around the world. We have no cause for self-righteousness or complacency. But we have every reason to persevere, both within our own country and beyond our borders.

25 If we are to serve as a beacon for human rights, we must continue to perfect here at home the rights and values which we espouse around the world: a decent education for our children, adequate medical care for

30 all Americans, an end to discrimination against minorities and women, a job for all those able to work, and freedom from injustice and religious intolerance.

We live in a time of transition, an uneasy

35 era which is likely to endure for the rest of this century. It will be a period of tensions both within nations and between nations—of competition for scarce resources, of social, political and economic stresses and

40 strains. During this period we may be tempted to abandon some of the time-honored principles and commitments which have been proven during the difficult times of past generations.

45 We must never yield to this temptation. Our American values are not luxuries but necessities—not the salt in our bread but the bread itself. Our common vision of a free and just society is our greatest source of cohesion

50 at home and strength abroad—greater even than the bounty of our material blessings.

Remember these words:
"We hold these truths to be self-evident: that all men are created equal; that they

55 are endowed by their creator with certain inalienable rights; that among these are life, liberty and the pursuit of happiness."[1]

---

[1]**We hold . . . happiness:** Lines from Declaration of Independence of 1776. The following line is "that to secure these rights, governments are instituted among men, deriving their just powers from the consent of the governed."

This vision still grips the imagination of the world. But we know that democracy is always an unfinished creation. Each generation must renew its foundations. Each generation must rediscover the meaning of this hallowed vision in the light of its own modern challenges. For this generation, ours, life is nuclear survival; liberty is human rights; the pursuit of happiness is a planet whose resources are devoted to the physical and spiritual nourishment of its inhabitants.

1. The first paragraph (lines 1–3) uses which of the following rhetorical devices?
   (A) Argument by analogy
   (B) Extended example
   (C) Emotional appeal
   (D) Euphemism
   (E) Juxtaposition of ideas

2. When the speaker says "kinship or place of origin or religious preference" (lines 10–11), he is using
   (A) sarcasm
   (B) polysyndeton
   (C) colloquial diction
   (D) understatement
   (E) synecdoche

3. The tone of the third paragraph (lines 13–24) can best be described as
   (A) candid and indignant
   (B) earnest and confident
   (C) haughty and unsympathetic
   (D) moralistic and disdainful
   (E) impartial and reflective

4. A synonym for "espouse" (lines 27–28) is
   (A) demand
   (B) recognize
   (C) neglect
   (D) support
   (E) witness

5. Readers can infer from paragraph five (lines 34–44) that the speaker believes that
   (A) global levels of freedom are in decline
   (B) problems will be solved in the following century
   (C) values of the past no longer suit modern sensibilities
   (D) numerous challenges threaten the spread of human rights
   (E) future generations will not face the same struggles as those of the past

6. The antecedent of "It" in line 36 is
   (A) "this period" (line 40)
   (B) "an uneasy era" (lines 34–35)
   (C) "this century" (line 36)
   (D) "competition" (line 38)
   (E) "difficult times" (lines 43–44)

7. The words "greater even than the bounty of our material blessings" (lines 50–51)
   (A) appeal to the audience's sense of pride
   (B) reject a commonly held misconception
   (C) restate one of the excerpt's main ideas
   (D) associate materialism and individualism
   (E) reveal the speaker's religious perspective

8. Footnote 1 clarifies the meaning of which of the following phrases?
   (A) "impact of our efforts" (line 16)
   (B) "ideals which gave birth to our nation" (lines 18–19)
   (C) "uneasy era which is likely to endure" (lines 34–35)
   (D) "bounty of our material blessings" (line 51)
   (E) "light of its own modern challenges" (lines 64–65)

9. In lines 60–61, "we know that democracy is always an unfinished creation" implies that citizens in a democracy
   (A) continually redefine and improve democracy
   (B) have not successfully defined democracy
   (C) are unsure how to proceed
   (D) desire a stable form of government
   (E) easily export ideas about human rights

10. The style of the passage can best be described as
    (A) terse and argumentative
    (B) instructive and encouraging
    (C) plain and colloquial
    (D) detached and objective
    (E) moralistic and ironic

Section II: Essay

Directions: Carefully read the following prompt. Then, re-read the passage in Section I. Next, read the following passages and view the photograph. Present your response to the prompt in a carefully developed essay.

Resources

For information about how to analyze a **writing prompt** and other strategies for timed writing, see page 45 of this book.

> In the excerpt from "Jimmy Carter's Farewell Address," President Carter says that "democracy is always an unfinished creation." Booker T. Washington speaks of the solemnity with which freed slaves faced their emancipation, saying, "freedom was a more serious thing than they had expected to find it." And E. M. Forster says that he supports democracy "because it permits criticism." The photograph accompanying these excerpts shows a student who was part of a 1989 demonstration advocating expanded individual liberties in China.
>
> All of these sources indicate that it is no simple matter to create and maintain democratic liberties. In an essay that synthesizes ideas expressed in at least three of these sources, explain what responsibilities citizens have for establishing and upholding individual liberties.

Scoring Guidelines

9–8 These essays fully explain the responsibilities of citizens for establishing and upholding individual liberties. The essays synthesize ideas from at least three of the sources. The essays present a clear thesis defining the responsibilities of citizens, and the thesis is supported by evidence from selected sources. The students exhibit a sophisticated control of language.

7–6 These essays adequately explain the responsibilities of citizens for establishing and upholding individual liberties. The essays present a sound thesis defining the responsibilities of citizens, and they offer support from at least three of the sources. Their explanations may be less thorough, perceptive, or specific than essays in the 9–8 range. The students' prose is clear but may contain a few errors in diction or syntax.

5 These essays address responsibilities and make clear claims but may be unevenly developed or may contain limited evidence from the sources. The students' control of language is adequate.

4–3 These essays do not successfully respond to the prompt. The students may fail to explain the responsibilities of citizens, synthesize ideas from at least three of the sources, or provide a clear thesis. They may fail to provide support from the excerpts or the photograph. The students demonstrate an inconsistent control over such elements of writing as diction and syntax.

2–1 These essays are unacceptably brief or may substitute a simpler task, such as merely summarizing an author's position. The students may fail to understand the prompt or may respond tangentially. The students' prose reveals consistent weaknesses in such elements of writing as organization, grammar, and diction.

0 These essays give a response with no more than a reference to the task or a repetition of the prompt.

from A Slave Among Slaves

Booker T. Washington (1856–1915), a former slave, led a successful life and founded Tuskegee Institute, a school to train African Americans for work in the trades, teaching, agriculture, and mechanics. In the following excerpt from his autobiography, *Up from Slavery,* Washington describes the days leading up to and following emancipation, including the responses of slaves to their new-found freedom.

Finally the war closed, and the day of free-dom came. It was a momentous and event-ful day to all upon our plantation. We had been expecting it. Freedom was in the air,
5 and had been for months. Deserting soldiers returning to their homes were to be seen every day. Others who had been discharged, or whose regiments had been paroled, were constantly passing near our place. The
10 "grape-vine telegraph" was kept busy night and day. The news and mutterings of great events were swiftly carried from one planta-tion to another. In the fear of "Yankee" inva-sions, the silverware and other valuables
15 were taken from the "big house," buried in the woods, and guarded by trusted slaves. Woe be to any one who would have at-tempted to disturb the buried treasure. The slaves would give the Yankee soldiers food,
20 drink, clothing—anything but that which had been specifically intrusted to their care and honor. As the great day grew nearer, there was more singing in the slave quarters than usual. It was bolder, had more ring,
25 and lasted later into the night. Most of the verses of the plantation songs had some ref-erence to freedom. True, they had sung those same verses before, but they had been careful to explain that the "freedom" in
30 these songs referred to the next world, and had no connection with life in this world. Now they gradually threw off the mask; and were not afraid to let it be known that the "freedom" in their songs meant freedom of
35 the body in this world. The night before the eventful day, word was sent to the slave quarters to the effect that something un-usual was going to take place at the "big house" the next morning. There was little, if
40 any, sleep that night. All was excitement and expectancy. Early the next morning word was sent to all the slaves, old and young, to gather at the house. In company with my mother, brother, and sister, and a large
45 number of other slaves, I went to the mas-ter's house. All of our master's family were either standing or seated on the veranda of the house, where they could see what was to take place and hear what was said. There
50 was a feeling of deep interest, or perhaps sadness, on their faces, but not bitterness. As I now recall the impression they made upon me, they did not at the moment seem to be sad because of the loss of property, but
55 rather because of parting with those whom they had reared and who were in many ways very close to them. The most distinct thing that I now recall in connection with the scene was that some man who seemed to be
60 a stranger (a United States officer, I pre-sume) made a little speech and then read a rather long paper—the Emancipation Proclamation, I think. After the reading we were told that we were all free, and could go
65 when and where we pleased. My mother, who was standing by my side, leaned over and kissed her children, while tears of joy ran down her cheeks. She explained to us what it all meant, that this was the day for
70 which she had been so long praying, but fearing that she would never live to see.

For some minutes there was great rejoic-ing, and thanksgiving, and wild scenes of ecstasy. But there was no feeling of bitter-
75 ness. In fact, there was pity among the slaves for our former owners. The wild rejoicing on the part of the emancipated colored peo-ple lasted but for a brief period, for I no-ticed that by the time they returned to their
80 cabins there was a change in their feelings. The great responsibility of being free, of

having charge of themselves, of having to think and plan for themselves and their children, seemed to take possession of them. It was very much like suddenly turning a youth of ten or twelve years out into the world to provide for himself. In a few hours the great questions with which the Anglo-Saxon race had been grappling for centuries had been thrown upon these people to be solved. These were the questions of a home, a living, the rearing of children, education, citizenship, and the establishment and support of churches. Was it any wonder that within a few hours the wild rejoicing ceased and a feeling of deep gloom seemed to pervade the slave quarters? To some it seemed that, now that they were in actual possession of it, freedom was a more serious thing than they had expected to find it.

from What I Believe

E. M. Forster (1879–1970) was a British essayist, novelist, and professor. In the following excerpt from his essay "What I Believe," Forster presents his ideas about democracy, the individual, and the importance of freedom of thought and expression.

This brings me along to democracy, "even Love, the Beloved Republic, which feeds upon freedom and lives." Democracy isn't a beloved republic really, and never will be. But it is less hateful than other contemporary forms of government, and to that extent it deserves our support. It does start from the assumption that the individual is important, and that all types are needed to make a civilization. It doesn't divide its citizens into the bossers and the bossed, as an efficiency-regime tends to do. The people I admire most are those who are sensitive and want to create something or discover something, and don't see life in terms of power, and such people get more of a chance under a democracy than elsewhere. They found religions, great or small, or they produce literature and art, or they do disinterested scientific research, or they may be what are called "ordinary people," who are creative in their private lives, bring up their children decently, for instance, or help their neighbors. All these people need to express themselves, they can't do so unless society allows them liberty to do so, and the society which allows them most liberty is a democracy.

Democracy has another merit. It allows criticism, and if there isn't public criticism there are bound to be hushed-up scandals. That is why I believe in the press, despite all its lies and vulgarity, and why I believe in Parliament. The British Parliament is often sneered at because it's a talking-shop. Well, I believe in it *because* it is a talking-shop. I believe in the Private Member who makes himself a nuisance. He gets snubbed and is told that he is cranky or ill-informed, but he exposes abuses which would otherwise never have been mentioned, and very often an abuse gets put right just by being mentioned. Occasionally, too, in my country, a well-meaning public official loses his head in the cause of efficiency, and thinks himself God Almighty. Such officials are particularly frequent in the Home Office. Well, there will be questions about them in Parliament sooner or later, and then they'll have to mend their ways. Whether Parliament is either a representative body or an efficient one is very doubtful, but I value it because it criticizes and talks, and because its chatter gets widely reported.

So two cheers for democracy: one because it admits variety and one because it
permits criticism. Two cheers are quite
enough: there is no occasion to give three.
60 Only Love, the Beloved Republic, deserves
that.

Tiananmen Square: During student-led calls for democracy and political freedom in China
(June 3–4, 1989), this unidentified man single-handedly blocked a column of approaching tanks,
climbed atop one tank, and apparently spoke to its occupants. By the time that protests had been
brought to an end, hundreds, if not thousands, of protesters had lost their lives.

AP Photo/Jeff Widener

Sample Response

The following essay represents a high-scoring response to the writing prompt.

Each of the authors—Jimmy Carter, Booker T. Washington, and E. M. Forster—offers reasons for citizens to establish and uphold individual liberties. Forster argues that freedom ensures creative expression and guards against abuses of power. Carter asserts that liberty promotes social and political progress. And Washington suggests that the idea of liberty inspires hope. These authors and the photograph suggest that citizens should prioritize freedom, struggle for liberty, set aside differences, and broaden liberty's reach.

First, the authors suggest that citizens are responsible for prioritizing individual liberty over other concerns. Jimmy Carter states simply that "kinship or place of origin or religious preference" do not unite a free people. As Forster observes, the "individual is important" and "all types are needed to make a civilization." Free nations are not predicated on families, ethnicities, or religions. Instead, they are products of a belief in human rights. Booker T. Washington hints at the same idea. After briefly engaging in "rejoicing, and thanksgiving, and wild scenes of ecstasy," former slaves quickly realized that their first concern was with liberty itself, with "the great questions with which the Anglo-Saxon race had been grappling for centuries." According to Carter, a free society is "our greatest source of cohesion at home and strength abroad." For a free and diverse people, the unifying principle must be belief in liberty itself.

Second, the authors and the photograph suggest that citizens are responsible for waging "battle" on behalf of individual liberty. Despite the dangers, a single Chinese protester stood down a column of tanks, reminding the world of how compelling the desire for freedom is—and of the power of individuals. The struggle to obtain freedom, as Carter observes, will never be easy, yet we must never give in to pessimism, ignore "the time-honored principles" of the past, nor "yield" to that "temptation." Instead, as Washington suggests, citizens must maintain hope. Throughout their ordeal the slaves sang secretly about "freedom of the body," and Washington's mother considered her first day of freedom a "day for which she had been so long praying, but fearing that she would never live to see." Citizens must persist.

Third, the authors suggest that citizens of free nations must put aside their differences. Forster points out that "all types [of people] are needed to make a civilization," hinting that citizens need to celebrate this fact— especially since "people need to express themselves" in literature, in art, in scientific research, and in their private lives. Similarly, Carter holds that citizens must put "an end to discrimination against minorities and women" and work to create "freedom from injustice and religious intolerance." Washington celebrates this same goal. He tells readers that former slaves did not turn against their oppressors or feel "bitter" toward them; they instead felt "pity." In turn, former slaveholders were saddened, not "because of the loss of property, but rather because of parting with those . . . who were in many ways very close to them." According to Washington, the two groups behaved like free individuals: They set aside their differences.

Finally, the authors suggest that citizens must keep individual liberties alive. Washington implies that oppressed people must gather information, just as slaves sang verses that "had some reference to freedom" and used the "grape-vine telegraph" to receive news of freedom's approach. Forster suggests that citizens must maintain vigilant oversight of their leaders, offering "public criticism" to expose abuses and prevent tyranny. Carter tells his hearers that they must persevere, serving as "a beacon for human rights" and perfect "here at home the rights and values which we espouse around the world," as each generation works to "rediscover" and "renew" the foundations of liberty.

Together, the authors' works and the photograph outline a set of broad responsibilities for citizens who intend to build and maintain the "unfinished creation" that is democratic liberty. Citizens are to prioritize freedom, persist in the quest for liberty, set aside their differences, and work to keep freedom alive. Acting on these four fundamental responsibilities is the job of each and every free citizen.

Elements of Literature selection

The Tragedy of Julius Caesar
by William Shakespeare

Literary Focus

The coverage of characteristics of **tragedy** (including tragic flaw, exposition, rising action, crisis or turning point, falling action, climax, and resolution or denouement) below builds on the instruction found in the Student Edition. You may want to introduce the additional skills of analyzing **rhetorical devices** when teaching this play to advanced students.

Tragedy

For centuries, literary critics have struggled with the question of which character, Julius Caesar or Brutus, is the play's hero. This debate sometimes makes analyzing the tragedy challenging. Depending on which character they deem to be the **tragic hero,** students may have radically different interpretations of the play. For example, if the hero is Caesar, the antagonists are Brutus, Cassius, and their co-conspirators. On the other hand, if Brutus is the hero, then the antagonists are Caesar and Antony.

The claim that Julius Caesar is the tragic hero can be supported in several ways. First, the tragedy is named after him, and every event in the play is connected to him. Although he appears in only three scenes (four, if his ghost is included), Caesar is pivotal. Next, as is characteristic of tragic heroes, Caesar is a figure of high rank with lofty goals. Also characteristic of tragic heroes, Caesar has a tragic flaw: He is overconfident and arrogant. This fatal weakness is revealed in the rising action of Scene 2, when Caesar refuses to respect the omens. After Caesar's tragic death, the crisis or turning point in Act III, the remaining half of the play is haunted by his presence—both literally (when he manifests as a ghost) and figuratively. Even Brutus's last words are directed to Caesar: "Caesar, now be still. / I killed not thee with half so good a will."

Yet an equally convincing case can be made that Brutus is the play's tragic hero. Like Caesar, he is introduced early, in the exposition, and at great depth. Like other tragic heroes, he is noble and has impressive plans. Also, the play's first half focuses primarily on Brutus's internal conflict: He cannot decide which he should value more—friend or country. Brutus eventually leads the conspirators, and Caesar does not collapse until he receives Brutus's stab wound. Along with Antony, Brutus is at the center of the chaotic falling action of Act IV. When

SKILLS FOCUS

Literary Skill
Analyze characteristics of tragedy.

Advanced Skill
Analyze rhetorical devices.

As students analyze **tragedy** and **rhetorical devices,** remind them not to look at these elements in isolation but to consider how they contribute to our understanding of **character, tone,** and **theme.**

Related Works

Consider teaching one of the works below from *Elements of Literature* with *The Tragedy of Julius Caesar.*

Analyzing tragedy:
"Theseus" retold by Edith Hamilton

Analyzing rhetorical devices:
"*Julius Caesar* in an Absorbing Production" by John Mason Brown

Collection Resources

Brutus dies during the tragedy's climax in Act V, the primary action comes to an end, whereas Caesar's death drives the plot forward. Importantly, during the resolution or denouement, Octavius and Antony spend more time discussing Brutus than Caesar. Antony, who had recently attacked Brutus, praises him by saying he was "the noblest Roman of them all."

You might present these conflicting analyses to students and ask them to discuss which one they prefer. Afterward, explain that some scholars believe that Shakespeare intended the tragedy to have two protagonists. Elizabethans were thoroughly familiar with the story of Caesar. Earlier, in the medieval era, most people thought that Caesar's murder was a despicable, inexcusable act. However, during the more liberal Renaissance, many people reasoned that the murder was justified because it resulted in the preservation of freedom. Perhaps Shakespeare was trying to present both sides of the issue. If so, both perspectives are correct. The play may in fact have two tragic heroes.

Rhetorical Devices

The classical Greeks considered skilled use of **rhetorical devices,** or skilled use of language, an art. When they gave speeches, orators were determined to use the most effective means of persuasion possible. Aristotle's *Rhetoric* pointed out that clarity and appropriateness were essential aspects of effective persuasion.

Each act of *The Tragedy of Julius Caesar* contains excellent examples of the high art of rhetoric. However, rhetorical devices are used to greatest effect in the famous speeches of Act III, Scene 2. This act contains the crisis, or turning point, of the play. Caesar has just been slain. Rome's fate—and the tragedy's outcome—depend on who will be able to persuade the crowd, Brutus or Antony.

Brutus is the first to speak, and he immediately attempts to soothe the crowd, affirming that he will ensure respect for Caesar's body. He makes an emotional appeal to gain their trust. He then follows with a logical appeal: "Censure me in your wisdom, and awake your sense that you may the better judge." That plea is the crux of Brutus's argument. He hopes that the crowd will understand the causal relationship: Caesar has been assassinated because he might have become a tyrant. To quell any outrage (the crowds adored Caesar) over the implied *ad hominem* argument, Brutus immediately uses pathos, claiming that he, too, loved Caesar—but not more than he loves Rome. Brutus then makes a long series of logical appeals, arguing that the crowd has not been harmed by Caesar's murder; instead, Caesar's death ensures that they will have freedom from tyranny. Finally, Brutus concludes with an emotional appeal. He offers to commit suicide if Rome needs him to (the crowd, of course, does not assent). Ultimately, Brutus's rhetoric so convinces the crowd that they demand that he be renamed Caesar.

Antony then takes the stage. Less principled than Brutus, he understands that the public is naive and fickle. He therefore uses extensive

Resources

For information on **rhetorical devices,** see the Handbook of Rhetorical Concepts in this book.

Collection Resources

emotional appeals, generalizations, and misconceptions to sway them. Antony systematically dismantles Brutus's claim that Caesar was a danger to Rome. Among other emotional appeals, he reminds the crowd that Caesar cried for and helped the poor. Most important, however, Antony states that Caesar three times refused the crown. The crowd, riled up by Antony's emotional rhetoric, is ripe for his invitation to attack the conspirators. Yet Antony digresses and fosters suspense by stirring up curiosity about Caesar's will; he says that the will proves how much Caesar loved his subjects. With a flourish, Antony suddenly reveals Caesar's gory body, which spurs the crowd to seek vengeance.

Here, Antony's art of rhetoric moves into high gear, making Brutus's logical, grounded speech seem hollow and false. Antony sarcastically reminds the crowd that the conspirators are "honorable," which only angers the crowd further. Then he puts forth an implicit ad hominem argument, claiming that when compared to Brutus, he himself is a poor orator. The claim drives the crowd to pity him and consider him one of its own. As a stunning finale, Antony reads Caesar's will, which provides money for each citizen and gives his property to the public. This emotional appeal—which may be considered an appeal to the citizens' greed—triggers rioting. Although Brutus's logic originally had persuaded the crowd, Antony relies on the one topic that truly galvanizes the Roman public: a threat to personal material well-being.

Author Focus. A real-life tragedy occurred in England while Shakespeare was writing *The Tragedy of Julius Caesar*. Like Brutus, the Earl of Essex was the dear friend of a ruler, Queen Elizabeth I. Betraying the queen, Essex revolted and attempted to remove her trusted secretary of state. He wanted to replace that key position with a gang of young, conspiratorial aristocrats. Although the plot was not successful, it horrified Elizabeth and most citizens. The throne fell under attack from all sides. Elizabeth was Protestant, but many people wanted a Catholic queen. Others wanted to replace the monarchy with a democracy. Everyone, however, was uniformly concerned because Elizabeth was ill and had no heirs; if the question of her successor remained unresolved at her death, religious and civil war seemed inevitable. Shakespeare indirectly incorporated many of these events into *The Tragedy of Julius Caesar*.

Close Reading

Metacognitive Strategy: Annotating Text

As students read, have them annotate the play, focusing on identifying important elements of **tragedy**, including tragic flaws, exposition, rising action, crisis or turning point, falling action, climax, and resolution or denouement. To help students consider elements of tragedy as they annotate, encourage them to identify the following types of details:

Resources

For information on **annotating text** and other metacognitive strategies, see page 16 of this book.

- **tragic flaws:** allusions to ambition, pride, ego, envy, dissatisfaction, or resentment

- **exposition:** introductory information about main characters, festering conflicts, ominous settings, and suspicious backgrounds

- **rising action:** descriptions of questions and internal conflicts, mistakes, disagreements between characters, and superstitions

- **crisis** or **turning point:** imagery or instances of violence, blood, rage, revenge, terror, and rioting

- **climax:** portrayals of external conflicts, battles, losses, victories, and funerals

- **falling action:** portrayals of misgivings, grief, corruption, chaos, and apparitions

- **resolution** or **denouement:** discussion of amnesty, peace, honor, forgiveness, and the common good

Close Reading

The close-reading passage is on pages 950–951 of the Student Edition.

Close-Reading Practice: Rhetorical Devices

Have students re-read portions of Antony's post-assassination speech, Act III, Scene 2, lines 73–107. Then, ask the following questions to help students analyze Shakespeare's use of rhetorical devices:

- What emotional appeal is Antony making in the first four lines? *[Antony starts his speech by immediately appealing to the crowd's empathy for Caesar.* Bury *is a far stronger word than* praise. *Antony is also implying that Caesar was a good man, as he will quickly prove that no "evil" of Caesar's has lived on after the murder.]*

- What is the effect of Antony's repeated use of *honorable*? *[Antony's repetition draws attention to the ironic meaning with which he invests the term. By juxtaposing Brutus's claims to have acted honorably with a catalog of Caesar's traits and successes, Antony uses Brutus's claim against him. The crowd becomes convinced that Brutus is dishonorable.]*

- What logical appeal is made in lines 88–89? *[Antony makes a logical appeal to the public's need for funds. In a highly stratified society such as that of Rome, the captives' ransoms were an important source of money for the state. Antony is portraying Caesar as a generous and effective leader, once again reminding his audience of why they once loved Caesar.]*

- What rhetorical device is used in lines 100–101? What is its effect? *[Antony uses emotional appeals—self-deprecation, deceit, and false modesty—to gain the public's trust. He presents himself as being above a lowly argument in which he would "disprove what Brutus spoke." He says he will, rather, "speak what I do know," although his goal is actually to refute Brutus. His deceit is an effective device in swaying the crowd.]*

- How is the art of rhetoric evident in the last four lines? What is the response that Antony wants from his audience? *[Antony indirectly compares the conspirators to beasts and implies that members of the crowd are also beasts if they support the conspirators. He draws the crowd to him with a plea for patience: "Bear with me." Then, with high drama, he says, "My heart is in the coffin there with Caesar / And I must pause till it come back to me." By communicating deep grief and associating himself with Caesar, Antony manages to transfer the crowd's sorrow and sympathy for the assassinated leader to himself.]*

Vocabulary: Tone

This tragedy is rife with bleak vocabulary that creates a grim tone. For instance, in the play's first few lines, the Cobbler mentions "bad soles." His pun on "souls" sets an unpropitious tone and prepares readers for the dire events ahead. Thinking critically about Shakespeare's word choices can give students insight into his tragedy.

Activity. In his tragedy, Shakespeare uses the words in the margin. Ask students to discuss or to write down the meaning of each word and consider the context in which it appears. Then, have students write a sentence or two explaining how each word affects their impression of the tragedy and contributes to the play's tone.

[Ingratitude means "ungratefulness." In this context, the word refers to the commoners' shallow loyalty to the defeated Pompey and foreshadows the fickleness of the crowds after Caesar's death, supporting a dark tone. **Tongue-tied** *means "speechless." In this context, the word refers to the commoners' guilty response to the criticisms of Marullus and helps establish a negative tone.* **Rabblement** *means "disorderly mob." In this context, the word indicates Casca's distrust of the crowd and creates an arrogantly pessimistic tone.* **Tyranny,** *in this context, refers to absolute, unjust rule. The word suggests that oppressive actions are imminent, and it contributes to the darkly threatening tone.* **Dismember** *means "tear off limbs." Although Brutus uses* dismember *to warn against punishing Caesar's followers, the word foreshadows a bloody end to the tragedy, contributing to the anxious tone.* **Entrails** *are inner organs, especially intestines. The augurers' use of entrails creates the impression that the play will soon be moving into a period of coldblooded mayhem, as the slain beast has entrails but no heart. Entrails establishes a tone of gruesome foreboding.* **Banished** *means "forced into exile." In this context, the word supports the impression that Caesar acts without human mercy, refusing to reconsider a life-destroying decree. The word contributes to the pessimistic tone.* **Choleric** *means "irritable" or "quick tempered." In this context,* choleric *suggests that an infectious disease is spreading among the conspirators, including Cassius. Brutus's use of the word reinforces the angry tone of disapproval.* **Covetous** *means "greedy." The word creates an angry, self-righteous tone, as the enraged Brutus disassociates himself from greedy behavior.* **Everlasting** *means "eternal" or "infinitely long." Brutus uses* everlasting *to allude to the conspirators' doom, contributing to the ominously resigned tone.]*

Collection Resources

Postreading

Discussion Method: Bulletin-Board or Threaded Discussion

Determine whether you will use the bulletin board or an electronic forum for posting questions for student discussion. Explain to students that a good writer or speaker tailors **rhetorical devices** to his or her subject, purpose, and audience. This process may require writers and speakers to deploy a wide array of rhetorical devices, even in brief communications. Have students write a one- to three-paragraph evaluation of rhetorical devices used by Portia in Act II, Scene 1, lines 237–256. Post the following questions to prompt students' thoughts and to initiate a bulletin-board or threaded discussion:

- What extended example is used in the speech? Why is it effective? *[Portia describes her husband's aberrant behavior in great detail. She thereby catches his attention and also indirectly communicates her own suffering. Her example is effective; it ignites sympathy.]*

- How does Portia use sensory images to strengthen her plea? *[Portia uses many images that appeal to our senses of hearing and sight, such as "sighing" and "ungentle looks." These images make the speech more effective and engaging.]*

- Portia describes her husband as a ghost of the night, as if he were already dead. How does Brutus respond to her description? If Portia had not used the rhetorical device of overstatement, would the speech have been as potent? Why or why not? *[Brutus responds by feebly protesting that he is ill. Her speech would not have been as compelling if she had toned it down, but it might have achieved a better response.]*

Writing

Have students write an essay that responds to the prompt below.

> It may be argued that the character Caesar has more influence in the play after death than while alive. Do you agree or disagree? Why? Write a well-organized essay that thoroughly explains your opinion. Consider characteristics of **tragedy** (tragic flaw, exposition, rising action, crisis or turning point, falling action, climax, and resolution or denouement) in your analysis. Use details and examples to support your points.

Writing Workshop: Comparing a Play and a Film

Prewriting
Advanced Prewriting Strategy

Narrative Techniques in Film. At this point in their academic careers, students have acquired a set of concepts that they can use to analyze literature on the printed page. And half of this assignment—the analysis of the text of a play—will draw on those skills. Analyzing a filmed adaptation of a play, however, will require a related but slightly different set of skills. Although many of their effects are similar (e.g., creating a mood or setting a pace), filmmakers have recourse to an entirely different set of tools. Go over the following two elements of filmmaking with students to draw attention to the way each shapes a film's narrative.

- **Long or short shots?** In film, a director decides how long the viewer looks at everything. A shot can be five minutes long, or it can last just a few seconds. Students should be sensitive to how shot length can affect the mood and pacing of a scene.

- **What point of view does the camera express?** In film, a camera quite literally expresses a point of view. It can represent the perspective of an uninvolved observer (i.e., the audience) or it can show what a specific character is looking at. Often in a scene the camera will switch back and forth between the observer's view and a character's view. This switching can provide insight into the character's thoughts and experience.

Writing
Advanced Writing Skills

Organization. Students will use two different organizational schemes in their essays: point-by-point order when comparing the play and the film, and order of importance when discussing film techniques.

Activity. To help students think more deeply about the benefits of each scheme, have them work though the following questions:

- What are the advantages of using point-by-point organization? What would be the disadvantages of discussing the play all at once and then the film all at once?

SKILLS FOCUS

Writing Skill
Write a comparison of a play and a film.

As students explore **comparing plays and films,** remind them that analytical writing, like all forms of writing, gains power from attention to literary elements such as **diction, figurative language, tone,** and **voice.**

Collection Resources

Resources

For more information on different types of **organization,** see pages 1085–1088 of the Student Edition.

For more information on **order-of-importance organization,** see page 1129 of the Student Edition.

- Why is order of importance suited to the discussion of film techniques?
- How does the model essay effectively integrate these two organizational schemes? *[by using a very clear transitional sentence]*

Revising

Revising to Strengthen an Argument

Focusing on the Thesis. In the prewriting phase, students collected information about the differences between the play and the film adaptation. Some of these differences might be very pronounced or intrinsically interesting but have little to do with the essay. Now is the time for students to weed those out.

Activity. Ask students to read through their essays and circle points of comparison between the play and the film. Tell students to evaluate each comparison. If the connection between a comparison and the essay's thesis is weak, have students elaborate on the point or delete it.

Grammar Solutions. Parallel structure is a good technique for compressing information into a compact space without overly taxing readers. By creating parallel structures, writers create order for readers.

> **NONPARALLEL** *The audience hears footsteps on the battlements. Quietly, soft notes of music play in the background. These elements and the quiet moaning of the wind add to the suspenseful atmosphere.*
>
> **PARALLEL** *Footsteps on the battlements, quiet notes of soft music, and the moaning of the wind add to the suspenseful atmosphere.*

The parallel sentence more elegantly and succinctly expresses the same information as the nonparallel example.

Publishing

Exchanging Impressions. If you have access to audio-visual equipment, you might ask student volunteers to present their film scenes, with commentary, to the entire class. Have the class study the original text of each play and then engage in a **fishbowl discussion** about the strengths and weaknesses of each version.

Self-Evaluation. Finally, have students reflect on their writing by responding to the following questions:

- Did the film adaptation of your scene improve on the play or "dumb it down" for easier viewing?
- Do you think film is less artistically sophisticated than theater? More sophisticated? Why?
- If Shakespeare were alive today, would he write plays or would he write films? Explain your answer.

Section I: Multiple-Choice Questions

Directions: Carefully read the following excerpt from *Life's a Dream* by Pedro Calderón de la Barca. Then, choose the *best* answer to each question.

from Life's a Dream

Basilio. Brave peers of Poland, vassals,
   kinsmen, friends.
You know already that for my deep
   wisdom
I am surnamed the Learned by the world,
And in defiance of Time's dusty heel
5 Painters and sculptors all around the globe
Create star-glowing images of me,
Which will outlive by tens of centuries
This fading face, these failing bones, this
   flesh:
Basilio the Learned. And the Great.
10 You know the science that I love the most:
The mathematics, by the means of which
I make a fool of Fate and cheat old Time,
Whose function is to unfold fate itself.
I am the canny duellist who so far
Has always made the winning thrust. Poor
15   Time,
His every stroke and counter-stroke is
   marked
Upon my charts ahead of him. I read him.
There are star mountains and I climb their
   peaks.
There are star forests and I know their
   paths,
And there are swamps and whirlpools
20   made of stars.
Circles of snow, bright canopies of glass,
Cut by the moon, illumined by the sun,
These crystalline, concentric necklaces
These specks, these beads, these spirals,
   whirling tear-drops:
These are my life, my study and my
25   passion,
These are my books, their diamond letter-
   ing

Printed upon bright sapphire-paper pages
By the great golden printing-press of
   Heaven.
I turn one blue page of the Universe
And, cruel or kind, there is our human
30   future,
Easy to read as a child's alphabet.
And yet I wish, before I'd understood
The universe's simplest syllable,
The stars had poured their poison-fire on
   me.
35 A learned man's the victim of his learning.
For he who has foreknowledge of his fate
Murders himself and plays the suicide
In his own story. So perhaps with me.
Be silent still and hear me out with
   wonder.

I'm old now, but when I was young and
40   fresh
I had a secret and unhappy son
At whose sad birth there was high rage in
   heaven.
Before the warm grave of his mother's
   womb
Transmitted him into the yellow daylight
45 (For birth and death are very much alike)
His mother dreamed a child monstrosity
Smeared with her life's blood, burst out of
   her entrails,
Took life and was her death. And when the
   day
Came for his birth, this omen was proved
   true:
50 In my experience, omens always are.
The sun was red as blood and fought the
   moon.

They took our planet as their wrestling-
    ground;
Silver and gold grappled and interlocked.
It was the greatest and most terrible
55 Of all the eclipses that the sun has suffered
Since it wept blood, mourning the death
    of Christ.
There was no star-fire in the firmament.
Palaces shook. And Sigismund was born.
He tore his mother's life out and so showed
60 His nature to the world as if to say,
"I repay good with evil. I'm a man."

I knew then he would grow up to be vicious.
A cruel prince and a despotic King;
That Poland would be torn by civil war
And that his wildness would debauch the
65   Kingdom
Into a foul academy of chaos.
I knew he'd strike me down and use my
    beard
As if it were a carpet for his boots.
Who'd not believe such omens? I decided
That I must cage the beast and find out
70   whether
One cunning King could overcome the stars.
I gave out that my son had died at birth.
I built a tower among night-black boulders
In a ravine beyond the reach of daylight,
75 And that is where he lives. The penalty
For trespassers is death without a trial.
He sees and talks with no one but Clotaldo
Who tutors him in science and religion
And is the only witness of his woes.

Three things must now be thought on.
80   Pray you, mark me.
One, I love Poland and I won't allow her to
    be oppressed or crushed by tyranny.
Two, Christian charity: what right have I
To keep my son from that prerogative
Which by divine and human law is his?
85 Shall I turn criminal because of crimes
Which he has not committed, though he
    may?
Three, what if I have been too credulous?
What if he's gentle? The most cruel star
Can influence the will but cannot force it
90 Because a man's will is a gift from God.

I've wavered and I've weighed this, and I
    have
Devised a remedy which will amaze you.
I mean to set my son upon my throne
And to invest him with my royal power,
95 And you must all obey him as your King.
This stratagem can lead us to three out-
    comes
Which complement the three points I have
    made.
One, if he's prudent, wise and kind and
    gentle
And gives the lie to what is prophesied,
100 Then you shall have him as your own true
    King.
Two, if he proves reckless and cruel and
    wild
My moral obligation's at an end,
And it will seem in me a kind of mercy
To reimprison him, not punishment
But justice. Three, if that should be the
105   outcome
I will ensure the Polish throne shall be
By you two occupied illustriously.
This, as I am your King, I now command
And, as I am his father, I require
110 And, as I am a wise man, I advise it,
And, as I'm told, I tell you blunt and plain.
And last, if Kings be slaves to their own
    kingdoms,
I, as your humble slave, beseech you all.
Astolfo. Justice herself could form no plan
    more fair.
Estrella. God save the Prince and let him
115   be your heir.
Astolfo. Long live Basilio.
Estrella. God save the King.
All. Long live Basilio.
                            God save the King.
(*Music. Exit all but Basilio.*)
Basilio. I thank you for listening.
120 We shall learn tomorrow
Whether my son shall be a King
Or whether he'll bring sorrow.

From *Life's a Dream* by Pedro Calderón de la Barca, trans-
lated and adapted by Adrian Mitchell and John Barton.
Copyright © 1990 by Adrian Mitchell and John Barton.
Reproduced by permission of **Oberon Books Limited**.

Collection Resources

1. Which of the following literary devices is used in lines 15–28?
   (A) Similes
   (B) Flashback
   (C) Verbal irony
   (D) Rhyme scheme
   (E) Extended metaphor

2. In line 51 the image "The sun was red as blood and fought the moon" shows that Basilio considers an eclipse to be
   (A) a wonder of nature
   (B) an event that he needs to study
   (C) a sign of impending violence
   (D) an occurrence that science can explain
   (E) the cause of earthquakes

3. Which statement provides a refutation of Basilio's beliefs about Sigismund?
   (A) "'I repay good with evil.'" (line 61)
   (B) "I decided / That I must cage the beast." (lines 69–70)
   (C) "He sees and talks with no one but Clotaldo." (line 77)
   (D) "Shall I turn criminal because of crimes / Which he has not committed?" (lines 85–86)
   (E) "A man's will is a gift from God." (line 90)

4. Which character is most likely to provide evidence contrary to Basilio's interpretation of the omens?
   (A) Estrella
   (B) Clotaldo
   (C) Sigismund
   (D) Astolfo
   (E) the queen

5. Basilio's flaw is best revealed when he says
   (A) "Painters and sculptors . . . / Create star-glowing images of me" (lines 5–6)
   (B) "This fading face, these failing bones" (line 8)
   (C) "Be silent still and hear me out" (line 39)
   (D) "I gave out that my son had died at birth" (line 72)
   (E) "I won't allow her to be oppressed" (line 81)

6. The powerful foil described in this passage is
   (A) the stars
   (B) a son
   (C) Poland
   (D) a wife and mother
   (E) the public

7. Based on lines 46–61, readers can infer that
   (A) Basilio loved his late wife deeply
   (B) Basilio holds a pessimistic view of human nature
   (C) Basilio considers nature a powerful antagonist
   (D) Sigismund will mature into a cruel adult
   (E) Sigismund hates his father and his nation

8. Basilio's rhetorical strategies in lines 81–90 include all of the following EXCEPT
   (A) assumptions
   (B) ethical appeals
   (C) emotional appeals
   (D) rhetorical questions
   (E) *ad hominem* arguments

9. The major conflict in Basilio's speech is between
   (A) science and religion
   (B) education and emotions
   (C) tyranny and democracy
   (D) fate and free will
   (E) violence and kindness

10. The king's purpose is to persuade his audience
    (A) that the stars do not determine fate
    (B) to study books about the universe
    (C) that it is wise to distrust family members
    (D) to allow his son to take the throne
    (E) that he is a wise and thoughtful king

Section II: Essay

Directions: Carefully read the following prompt. Then, present your response in a well-developed essay.

> The excerpt begins with Basilio's claim to have great wisdom and knowledge. Consider Basilio's ability to make effective decisions. What evidence does he offer for his own authority? What limitations does he admit to? Write a well-developed essay analyzing the effectiveness of Basilio's speech in convincing his listeners that his decisions have been sound. Use details and examples from the play to develop a carefully reasoned analysis.

Scoring Guidelines

9–8 These essays fully explore the effectiveness of Basilio's arguments and appeals. They present coherent, well-reasoned analyses supported by comprehensive evidence. The students exhibit a sophisticated control of language.

7–6 These essays adequately evaluate the effectiveness of Basilio's arguments and appeals. They present sound analyses using appropriate evidence. The students' prose is clear but may contain a few errors in diction or syntax.

5 These essays acknowledge limitations in the effectiveness of Basilio's arguments and appeals and make clear claims, but their analyses may be unevenly developed or may contain limited evidence. The students' control of language is adequate.

4–3 These essays present an inadequate response to the prompt. The students may misunderstand Basilio's arguments and appeals, or they may have difficulty establishing their own position and use inappropriate or insufficient evidence. The students demonstrate inconsistent control over such elements of writing as diction and syntax.

2–1 These essays do not successfully respond to the prompt. The students may fail to understand the prompt, respond tangentially, or substitute a simpler task, such as merely summarizing Basilio's assertions. The students' prose reveals consistent weaknesses in such elements of writing as organization, grammar, and diction.

0 These essays present a response that receives no credit. They may simply paraphrase the prompt, for example.

Sample Response

The following essay represents a high-scoring response to the writing prompt.

King Basilio, in his speech from Pedro Calderón de la Barca's <u>Life's a Dream</u>, indicates that his decisions have been based on his ability to control the future. However, Basilio's listeners are likely to recognize that his leadership has been limited. Because Basilio undermines his own authority, points out that he may be dangerous, and doubts his own abilities, his speech is far from effective.

Early in his speech, Basilio boasts of having great wisdom and an ability to control fate. The boasts are meant to appeal to his own authority, but Basilio manages to undermine that appeal. Claiming that he knows how to interpret celestial omens, he says he is able to "make a fool of Fate and cheat old Time." A "deep wisdom," Basilio wants his listeners to believe, allows him to read the future. Ironically, he also suggests that he has consistently <u>altered</u> foretold events. His hearers should wonder why Basilio would leave certain other events unaltered. At the very least, they should notice that Basilio's appeal includes no evidence that his fate-altering decisions are sound: He claims to decide the future yet provides no proof that these decisions are reasonable or well informed.

The second section of Basilio's speech reveals his willingness to make heartless decisions without reasonable grounds. A dream and a solar eclipse lead him to imprison his infant son—who, according to Basilio, is destined to develop a depraved character. Basilio tells his hearers that his late wife's dream revealed that "a child monstrosity" had killed her. He says that the solar eclipse and sun turning "red as blood" support his judgment: The eclipse substantiated the dream. Based on omens alone, Basilio announces that his son died at birth and deprives him of all human contact, save that of his teacher. Basilio's hearers are likely to wonder why he ignores alternative interpretations of the two "omens," or why his "knowledge" had not prompted him to alter the future—perhaps to save his wife's life. Significantly, Basilio provides no additional justification for his son's imprisonment, nor does he offer additional evidence to allow his hearers to evaluate the decision. Basilio has admitted that he can be dangerous. He is capable of unjustified and irrational cruelty.

In the final portion of his speech, Basilio indicates that his decision-making abilities have always been poor. Now that he is older he recognizes his limitations. He poses rhetorical questions such as "what right have I / To keep my son from that prerogative / Which by divine and human law is his ?" and "what if I have been too credulous?" and "What if he's gentle?" The questions are intended to justify his decision to offer his son the throne, but they have an unintended effect: The questions reveal that he feels that fate should not be altered, wonders whether he can predict fate at all, and regrets having been cruel to a child. Basilio has not bothered to talk with his son or his son's tutor, Clotaldo, and Basilio now admits to a flaw in his past leadership, "The most cruel star / Can influence the will but cannot force it / Because a man's will is a gift from God." Anyone, including Sigismund, has free will and can, by force of character, overcome fated evil. Implicitly, Basilio admits that his actions and reliance on omens have been wrongheaded.

Throughout his life, Basilio made decisions based on his professed ability to alter the future. Now he realizes that his decisions may have been ungrounded. Basilio has been a poor decision maker, as is indicated by his self-undermining appeal to his own authority, his unjustifiable cruelty, and his concession to the power of free will. As the final line indicates, he can only wait and see whether Sigismund will prove to be a king or a criminal.

Collection 1 Test Practice, Section 1 (pp. 63–67)

Answers

1. E	2. B	3. A	4. C	5. D
6. D	7. D	8. C	9. E	10. D

Annotated Answer Choices

Item 1 asks students to identify the purpose of the first three paragraphs (lines 1–23) of the excerpt.

- **A. Incorrect.** While the third paragraph (lines 16–23) includes an implied analogy between affluent college students and "rich" dumpsters, there is no extended analogy in these paragraphs.
- **B. Incorrect.** The paragraphs include generalities about the author's experience, but they do not recreate a specific moment from the author's past.
- **C. Incorrect.** The paragraphs refer to a specific dumpster; however, no clear sense of time is created. These paragraphs describe typical experiences rather than a particular place and time.
- **D. Incorrect.** The passage describes typical successes in finding food and useful items. Although the descriptions support one of the author's arguments, they do not establish that argument.
- **E. Best answer.** As implied by the title, these paragraphs describe the author's typical experiences while searching dumpsters for food and other items.

Item 6 asks students to identify the literary term that best describes the phrase "gaudy bauble."

- **A. Incorrect.** Asyndeton is the omission of conjunctions between coordinate sentence elements.
- **B. Incorrect.** An allusion is a reference to a person, place, thing, or idea in a given culture.
- **C. Incorrect.** Alliteration is the repetition of consonant sounds, usually at the beginning of nearby words. No consonant sounds are repeated in "gaudy bauble."
- **D. Best answer.** Assonance is the close repetition of similar vowel sounds, as in *gaudy bauble.*
- **E. Incorrect.** An analogy compares two or more things, but no comparison exists in the phrase "gaudy bauble."

Collection 2 Test Practice, Section 1 (pp. 74–77)

Answers

1. E	**2.** C	**3.** B	**4.** D	**5.** E
6. E	**7.** A	**8.** B	**9.** C	**10.** D

Annotated Answer Choices

Item 2 asks students to recognize details supporting the speaker's assertion that Nani serves food "instinctively."

- **A. Incorrect.** The metaphorical phrase "dribble down her mouth" describes Nani's speech.
- **B. Incorrect.** "I taste the mint" implies that Nani cooks according to her own recipes; the clause does not imply that she serves others instinctively.
- **C. Best answer.** These lines suggest unconscious behavior on Nani's part: To serve the speaker, she watches "with her skin, her hair," with every fiber of her exterior, as if she watches habitually and without volition.
- **D. Incorrect.** The lines describe Nani's actions, but they do not indicate that her actions are instinctive.
- **E. Incorrect.** The lines indicate that Nani injures herself, but they do not suggest that the injury is instinctive.

Item 9 asks students to recognize terms that describe Nani's character.

- **A. Incorrect.** Nani's behavior in both the present and the past suggests that she may be subservient, but the speaker does not directly indicate that she is meek.
- **B. Incorrect.** Readers may conclude that Nani suffers without complaint; however, the speaker does not directly describe this characteristic.
- **C. Best answer.** Nani acts out of affection for the speaker and the man in her past; she is also obliging and quick to serve. These two qualities indicate that she is loving and officious.
- **D. Incorrect.** Nothing in the poem suggests that Nani is either angry or resigned.
- **E. Incorrect.** While readers may conclude that Nani is determined and strong, the speaker's description does not directly address either characteristic.

Collection 3 Test Practice, Section 1 (pp. 86–90)

Answers

1. A	**2.** C	**3.** D	**4.** B	**5.** D
6. D	**7.** E	**8.** E	**9.** C	**10.** D

Annotated Answer Choices

Item 6 asks students to understand Tobermory's attitude toward other characters in the story.

- **A. Incorrect.** While Tobermory may lack tact, he does not speak unpleasant truths about the other characters until they press him to express his opinion. There is no indication that he is characteristically cruel.

B. Incorrect. Tobermory is confident and dignified. Though he has a sense of privacy, he is not defensive about his own actions or assertions.

C. Incorrect. There is no indication that Tobermory is nostalgic.

D. Best answer. Tobermory is comfortable and feels no need to abide by human rules. He is coolly indifferent to humans and their ideas of social decorum, though he maintains his own standards for proper behavior.

E. Incorrect. Tobermory is confident and sure of himself, not humble. His responses to inquiries indicate that he considers himself to be more intelligent than the other characters.

Item 8 asks students to identify the effect of the allusion to Sisyphus (lines 127–129). To fully understand the allusion's effect, students must synthesize information from the accompanying footnote.

A. Incorrect. The allusion, although significant, is not directly linked to the story's theme.

B. Incorrect. While the allusion naturally connects the story to mythology, the answer choice does not identify the allusion's effect.

C. Incorrect. The tone of the allusion is consistent with that of the excerpt.

D. Incorrect. Because the allusion introduces a comic image, it does not darken the scene's mood.

E. Best answer. By associating the car's owner with Sisyphus, the author introduces a comic image: Mavis may be destined to push the car up each hill, just as Sisyphus had been forced to purposely push a boulder up a mountain. The allusion implies that the car, too, will roll downhill just after it has crested each hilltop.

Collection 4 Test Practice, Section 1 (pp. 99–103)

Answers

1. B	**2.** B	**3.** A	**4.** D	**5.** A
6. E	**7.** E	**8.** C	**9.** E	**10.** C

Annotated Answer Choices

Item 4 asks students to understand the use of rhetorical questions in paragraph 5 (lines 54–58).

A. Incorrect. The speaker's attitude is contemplative, thoughtful, and insightful. The lines do not indicate that the speaker is angered or confused by her condition.

B. Incorrect. The questions may indirectly reflect an underlying sense of the speaker's desire; however, the questions are directed to sighted individuals and do not directly express her longing for sight.

C. Incorrect. The speaker does not claim to have superior understanding of human nature. She does indicate that she feels a great appreciation for the gift of sight.

D. Best answer. The questions are directed to sighted individuals and indicate that the speaker believes that they take sight for granted. The questions suggest that she thinks sighted individuals do not use sight to help them better understand the people around them.

E. Incorrect. The questions are directed to sighted individuals in general, not to the speaker's friends and acquaintances alone. She does not indicate a need for reconciliation with friends and acquaintances.

Item 7 asks students to identify the speaker's purpose for using the phrase "intimate trifles."

A. Incorrect. Use of the word "trifles" suggests that the rugs and pictures have no great significance, but they are items the speaker would like to see.

B. Incorrect. The phrase "small simple things" provides a context clue for the meaning of "trifles," rather than the reverse.

C. Incorrect. The phrase refers to household items, not to books.

D. Incorrect. "Warm colors" applies only to the rugs in the speaker's house.

E. Best answer. For the speaker, "intimate trifles" help create and define a home, distinguishing it from a house.

Collection 5 Test Practice, Section 1 (pp. 110–114)

Answers

1. B	2. C	3. E	4. C	5. D
6. D	7. C	8. E	9. B	10. A

Annotated Answer Choices

Item 4 asks students to understand the effect of Twain's suggestion that his hearers read *The Innocents Abroad*. To fully understand the effect, students must synthesize information from multiple footnotes.

A. Incorrect. The contrast between the contents of Twain's humorous travel book and that of each book of sermons reveals that he speaks ironically.

B. Incorrect. The speech does not address the topic of spiritual insight.

C. Best answer. By including his book in a list of works by respected religious figures, Twain maintains the speech's humorous tone. Twain's audience would have recognized the humorous contrast.

D. Incorrect. Twain's book, a humorously exaggerated account of his travels, is not a factual, objective travelogue.

E. Incorrect. While Twain may have wanted book sales to increase, his speech does not indicate that increased sales are an intended effect of the recommendation.

Item 7 asks students to identify the speech's tone and to recognize a quotation that best reveals that tone.

A. Incorrect. The quotation contains straightforward, commonly given advice. It does not reflect the comically ironic tone of the speech.

B. Incorrect. A paraphrase of advice from Benjamin Franklin, this statement, too, does not reflect the tone of the speech.

C. Best answer. By suggesting that poor lying skills, not lies themselves, get young people into trouble, the quotation captures the sly, comically ironic tone of the speech.

D. Incorrect. The quotation has a didactic, rather pedantic tone, not the comically ironic tone of the speech.

E. Incorrect. The quotation presents conventional advice and is not in keeping with the speech's tone.

Collection 6 Test Practice, Section 1 (pp. 126–130)

Answers

1. C	2. C	3. B	4. D	5. A
6. D	7. A	8. A	9. E	10. E

Annotated Answer Choices

Item 9 asks students to identify the most important implied conflict in the passage.

A. Incorrect. There is no direct evidence for Henry's religious education, although readers may infer information about Ma's religious beliefs. The excerpt does not indicate that there is a religious conflict between Henry and Ma.

B. Incorrect. Henry's irresponsibility is implied, but the passage does not indicate that a conflict exists between Ma's chores and Henry's farm responsibilities.

C. Incorrect. Readers may infer that a conflict exists between Henry's desire for excitement and his boredom with farm life, but this is not a significant conflict in the passage.

D. Incorrect. The conflict between Ma's concern for the animals and Henry's neglect of them is secondary, resulting from the conflict between Henry, who wants to enlist, and Ma, who wants to keep him home.

E. Best answer. The most important implied conflict in the passage is between Henry's romantic view of battle and the harsh reality of war. War's reality is revealed in both the narrator's description of Henry's thoughts and in Ma's dialogue.

Item 10 asks students to use information provided in the passage to identify a specific fact about Henry.

A. Incorrect. While students may draw inferences about Henry's future battle experiences, they cannot conclude that he will lose his life.

B. Incorrect. The excerpt does not directly treat Henry's educational level, nor does the excerpt list any of his future plans.

C. Incorrect. Although students may suspect that Henry feels no regrets over leaving home, lines 89–90 indicate that he displays a "glow of regret for the home bonds."

D. Incorrect. The passage indicates that newspapers are in part responsible for having "aroused him to an uncheckable degree" (line 58).

E. Best answer. In lines 104–105, Ma warns Henry not to think that he can "lick th' hull rebel army at th' start," indicating that he has joined a company of Union troops.

Collection 7 Test Practice, Section 1 (pp. 146–149)

Answers

1. C	2. D	3. E	4. D	5. D
6. A	7. D	8. E	9. E	10. C

Annotated Answer Choices

Item 4 asks students to understand the implication of the lines by recognizing the speaker's attitude, given the death of Constable's wife, toward honors. Students must use information in the footnote to understand the lines' implication.

A. Incorrect. On the contrary, the lines indicate an important turning point in Constable's life, style of painting, and choice of subjects.

B. Incorrect. As revealed by information in the footnote, membership in the Royal Academy is one of the highest honors a British artist can receive. The speaker does not indicate that the honor, given Constable's success, is irrelevant.

C. Incorrect. Nothing in the poem indicates that Constable had quarreled with members of the academy.

D. Best answer. The speaker of the poem indicates that he or she thinks that the honor of Royal Academy membership had little effect on Constable or his art, especially relative to the effects of Constable's wife's death.

E. Incorrect. Nothing in the poem indicates that the academy's influence was waning or that artists no longer sought membership.

Item 10 asks students to draw an inference about the speaker's use of Constable's life and art as the subject of the poem.

A. Incorrect. The speaker's use of details and examples includes information only from Constable's life and paintings; details and examples do not mention painting in general.

B. Incorrect. The speaker, who summarizes Constable's life, does not describe problems specific to artists in general.

C. Best answer. The speaker uses events in Constable's life to reveal insights about human life, maturation, and responses to mortality.

D. Incorrect. The poem does not indicate that an enjoyment of nature helped Constable remain cheerful. The speaker indicates that Constable, after the death of his wife, painted with more subdued colors and with fewer details from nature.

E. Incorrect. The speaker does not address the question of goals. Though Constable is elected to full membership in the Royal Academy, the poem does not indicate that gaining membership was one of his goals.

Collection 8 Test Practice, Section I (pp. 158–162)

Answers

1. C	2. A	3. B	4. D	5. A
6. C	7. D	8. C	9. E	10. E

Annotated Answer Choices

Item 3 asks students to identify a term grammatically parallel to "skin" (line 27).

A. Incorrect. *Emptied* is a verb, the subject of which is *skin*.

B. Best answer. *Skull*, like *skin*, is the subject of an independent clause.

C. Incorrect. *Tent* is the object of the preposition *like*.

D. Incorrect. *Shoulders* is the object of the preposition *on*.

E. Incorrect. *Formless* is an adjective modifying *skin*.

Item 6 asks students to identify the main effect of the excerpt's reference to Pascal and his philosophy. To place the reference in context, students must synthesize information from footnotes 4 and 5.

A. Incorrect. The writer's description of the frog's death is not objective, nor does the reference to Pascal offer an objective lesson about the frog's death.

B. Incorrect. The reference to Pascal and his philosophy is too vague to appeal to most people with strongly held beliefs. Only people already familiar with Pascal's philosophy are likely to understand the depth of the allusion.

C. Best answer. By alluding to Pascal's philosophy, Dillard suggests that inexplicable events may seem nonsensical because the creator of the universe has hidden their explanations from human perception.

D. Incorrect. In this section of the essay, the allusion helps establish an academic, scholarly tone.

E. Incorrect. The speaker does not provide enough information to establish a contrast between the opinions of Pascal and those of Einstein. Instead, the excerpt's information suggests similarity rather than contrast.

Collection 9 Test Practice, Section I (pp. 174–180)

Answers

1. E	2. B	3. B	4. D	5. D
6. B	7. B	8. B	9. A	10. B

Annotated Answer Choices

Item 2 asks students to identify the device used in the phrase "kinship or place of origin or religious preference" (lines 10–11).

A. Incorrect. The lines do not employ sarcasm, or a sneering or caustic remark.

B. Best answer. The lines include a list employing the conjunction *or* without the use of commas.

C. Incorrect. The lines do not include colloquial diction, or informally conversational word choices.

D. Incorrect. The lines do not employ understatement, or a statement that is weaker than is warranted.

E. Incorrect. The lines do not employ synecdoche, or a figure of speech using a part for the whole.

Item 5 asks students to draw an inference from lines 34–44.

A. Incorrect. Although the speaker refers to "an uneasy era," he does not refer to growth or decline in global levels of freedom.

B. Incorrect. The speaker refers to the problems of his own century. He does not suggest a time in which those challenges will be overcome.

C. Incorrect. The speaker regrets that people may be tempted to "abandon some of the time-honored principles" of the past, implying that past values still suit modern needs.

D. Best answer. The speaker asserts that challenges within and among nations will continue throughout the century. Given the assertion's context, the speaker implies that continued tensions will threaten to undermine or overwhelm the quest to secure human rights.

E. Incorrect. Although the statement may be supported by lines appearing later in the excerpt, here the speaker does not compare past struggles with those of the future.

Collection 10 Test Practice, Section 1 (pp. 189–193)

Answers

1. E	2. C	3. E	4. B	5. D
6. B	7. B	8. E	9. D	10. D

Annotated Answer Choices

Item 2 asks students to interpret Basilio's use of the image in line 51.

A. Incorrect. The bloody and violent associations of the image lack the pleasing details that would be expected of a wonder of nature.

B. Incorrect. Basilio claims that he already knows what the omen means; he does not suggest that he needs to study the eclipse further.

C. Best answer. Rather than describing the eclipse in objective, scientific language, Basilio describes the sun as "red as blood" and as fighting and wrestling with the moon. Basilio's description reflects his interpretation of the eclipse as a sign of Sigismund's violent character.

D. Incorrect. The description shows that the eclipse is not an ordinary occurrence, and Basilio offers no suggestion that the eclipse can be explained by science.

E. Incorrect. Line 58 indicates that "Palaces shook," a clue that an earthquake had occurred on the same day; however, there is no indication that Basilio thinks the eclipse caused the earthquake.

Item 3 asks students to identify evidence undermining Basilio's expectation about Sigismund's character.

    A. Incorrect. The lines are Basilio's, and they interpret the meaning of Sigismund's birth; they agree with Basilio's expectation.

    B. Incorrect. The lines reveal Basilio's reasoning, based on his expectation about Sigismund's character.

    C. Incorrect. Although the line suggests that Sigismund may have been influenced by Clotaldo, it does not describe the effects of Clotaldo's influence.

    D. Incorrect. The question suggests that Basilio has doubts about his own expectations, but the question does not offer direct refutation.

    E. Best answer. By associating free will with personality, the line undermines Basilio's expectation about Sigismund's fated character: The existence of Sigismund's free will proves Basilio's expectation to be baseless.

Test Practice, Section 1

Answer Sheet

1. Ⓐ Ⓑ Ⓒ Ⓓ Ⓔ
2. Ⓐ Ⓑ Ⓒ Ⓓ Ⓔ
3. Ⓐ Ⓑ Ⓒ Ⓓ Ⓔ
4. Ⓐ Ⓑ Ⓒ Ⓓ Ⓔ
5. Ⓐ Ⓑ Ⓒ Ⓓ Ⓔ
6. Ⓐ Ⓑ Ⓒ Ⓓ Ⓔ
7. Ⓐ Ⓑ Ⓒ Ⓓ Ⓔ
8. Ⓐ Ⓑ Ⓒ Ⓓ Ⓔ
9. Ⓐ Ⓑ Ⓒ Ⓓ Ⓔ
10. Ⓐ Ⓑ Ⓒ Ⓓ Ⓔ

Collection Resources

Handbook

Handbook of Literary Concepts

The following is a list of literary concepts commonly used in advanced placement tests. Knowing these concepts will help advanced students analyze the literature selections they encounter in their daily studies and become comfortable with assessment terminology.

Act A major division in a play. Most plays have between one and five acts. Most acts are divided into one or more scenes. *The Brute: A Joke in One Act* is a one-act play by Anton Chekhov. *The Tragedy of Julius Caesar* by William Shakespeare has five acts, as do many Elizabethan plays.

Allegory A narrative in which characters, settings, and events stand for abstract ideas or moral qualities. (For more on **allegory,** see the Handbook of Literary Terms in the Student Edition.)

Alliteration The repetition of the same or similar consonant sounds in words that are close together. (For more on **alliteration,** see the Handbook of Literary Terms in the Student Edition.)

Allusion A reference to a statement, a person, a place, an idea, or an event from literature, history, religion, mythology, politics, sports, science, or the arts. (For more on **allusion,** see the Handbook of Literary Terms in the Student Edition.)

Ambiguity An element of uncertainty in a text, in which something can be interpreted in a number of different ways. (For more on **ambiguity,** see the Handbook of Literary Terms in the Student Edition.)

Analogy A comparison made between two things to show their similarities or to clarify the meaning of a statement or an idea. (For more on **analogy,** see the Handbook of Literary Terms in the Student Edition.)

Anecdote A very brief account of a particular incident, frequently used to illustrate a point. (For more on **anecdote,** see the Handbook of Literary Terms in the Student Edition.)

Antagonist A character in fiction who opposes or struggles against the **protagonist.** In some cases, the antagonist can be a force in nature or a group of people. The monster Grendel serves as an antagonist in the first portion of the famous English epic *Beowulf.* The ocean serves as an antagonist in Stephen Crane's short story "The Open Boat."

Anticlimax Something less than what is expected. An author can use anticlimax for humor, lightening a serious topic by referring to something trivial. Alexander Pope often uses anticlimax in his poem *The Rape of the Lock.* In his poem, Pope describes characters and events in heroic terms and then, in anticlimax, reveals that his subject is a young woman who has lost a lock of her hair.

Antithesis A figure of speech using contrasting words, sentences, or ideas. Antitheses are usually presented in grammatically parallel structures, such as in Brutus's famous line from Shakespeare's *Julius Caesar:*

> "Not that I loved Caesar less, but that I loved Rome more."
>
> —*Act 3, Scene 2*

Archetype An old imaginative pattern that appears across cultures and is repeated through the ages. Archetypes are universal actions (such as mourning lost loved ones), characters (the hero, the traitor), and images (a garden as paradise). Sir Gawain is an archetypal hero who must undergo a quest in *Sir Gawain and the Green Knight.*

Aside In drama, words spoken by a character directly to the audience or to another character but that are not meant to be overheard by other onstage characters. (For more on **aside,** see the Handbook of Literary Terms in the Student Edition.)

Assonance The repetition of similar vowel sounds followed by different consonant sounds, especially in words that are close together. (For more on **assonance,** see the Handbook of Literary Terms in the Student Edition.)

Atmosphere The overall mood or tone of a work of literature. The atmosphere of a work can often be described in one or two adjectives, such as *joyous* or *gloomy.* In such short stories as "The Pit and the Pendulum" and "The Tell-Tale Heart," Edgar Allan Poe uses descriptions of setting, narrative voice, and characters to create a somber and horrifying atmosphere.

Attitude (of speaker) The speaker's attitude in a poem is often revealed through the poet's choice of details, images, and words. The attitude of the speaker in Robert P. Tristram Coffin's poem "Forgive My Guilt" is sorrowful and penitent.

Blank verse Poetry written in unrhymed iambic pentameter. Each line of a poem written in blank verse consists of five **iambs.** Each iamb consists of a single unaccented syllable followed by an accented syllable. (For more on **blank verse,** see the Handbook of Literary Terms in the Student Edition.)

Cadence The natural rhythm of spoken language, created by the arrangement of stressed and unstressed syllables. The American poet Walt Whitman mastered cadence as the basis of his free verse poetry.

Catharsis An emotional release said to be experienced by an audience following powerful feelings evoked by tragedy. The term was coined by the Greek philosopher Aristotle, who described tragedy's power to purge the emotions of pity and fear.

Character An individual who takes part in the action of a story, poem, or play. (For more on **character,** see the Handbook of Literary Terms in the Student Edition.)

Climax The moment of greatest emotional intensity or suspense in a plot. The climax in a story or play usually marks the moment at which the conflict is resolved. In *The Tragedy of Julius Caesar,* the climax occurs with the death of Caesar.

Colloquial Colloquial writing uses words, phrases, or sentences to reflect informal conversation. Dialogue in literature often relies on colloquial writing to convey the everyday speech of characters. In Mark Twain's "The Celebrated Jumping Frog of Calaveras County," for example, Simon Wheeler's speech is full of colloquialisms: "There was a feller here once by the name of *Jim* Smiley. . . . he was the curiousest man about always betting on anything that turned up you ever see, if he could get anybody to bet on the other side; and if he couldn't, he'd change sides."

Comedy In general, a story that ends happily. (For more on **comedy,** see the Handbook of Literary Terms in the Student Edition.)

Handbook

Comic relief A comic scene or event that relieves tension in a serious play or narrative. Comic relief allows writers to lighten the tone of a work and show the humorous side of a dramatic theme. In Shakespeare's *Romeo and Juliet,* for example, the characters of the nurse and Mercutio provide comic relief. (For more on **comic relief,** see the Handbook of Literary Terms in the Student Edition.)

Conceit An elaborate figure of speech that often includes metaphor, simile, hyperbole, or analogy. There are two main types of conceits: Petrarchan and metaphysical. Petrarchan conceits compare the subject of a poem to an object, such as the sun or a rose. Shakespeare's Sonnet 18, which begins, "Shall I compare thee to a summer's day? / Thou art more lovely and more temperate" is an example of a Petrarchan conceit. Metaphysical conceits, characteristic of the poet John Donne, include unusual analogies, such as Donne's comparison in "A Valediction Forbidding Mourning" of two souls to the legs of a compass and Richard Crashaw's description of Mary Magdalene's eyes: "Two walking baths; two weeping motions, / Portable and compendious oceans."

Conflict A struggle or clash between opposing characters or opposing forces. (For more on **conflict,** see the Handbook of Literary Terms in the Student Edition.)

Connotation All the meanings, associations, or emotions that have come to be attached to some words, in addition to their literal definitions, or **denotations.** (For more on **connotation,** see the Handbook of Literary Terms in the Student Edition.)

Consonance The close repetition of identical consonant sounds before and after differing vowel sounds: *full, fill; sleep, slip.* Consonance is used in poetry to create a musical effect, to evoke tone, and to add emphasis to given words. Some modern poets use consonance in place of rhyme.

Contradiction A person, thing, statement, or situation that is in opposition to another, or one that has opposing qualities. The selection from *Into Thin Air* by Jon Krakauer includes an example of a contradiction. The leader of an expedition to the top of Mount Everest contradicts his own rule of a firm cutoff time for reaching the summit. This contradiction has consequences for the leader and the other climbers.

Contrast The placement of dissimilar or opposed images, ideas, or both next to each other. For example, in his short story "The Things They Carried," Tim O'Brien contrasts the horror of war with the simple, sometimes everyday items carried by the soldiers, such as can openers, pocket knives, chewing gum, and photographs of loved ones.

Controlling image A dominant image or metaphor that is sustained throughout all or part of a literary work, especially with respect to structure or theme. The controlling image of William Wordsworth's "Lines Composed a Few Miles Above Tintern Abbey" is a beautiful valley.

Couplet Two consecutive end-rhymed lines of poetry. (For more on **couplets,** see the Handbook of Literary Terms in the Student Edition.)

Denotation The literal meaning of a word, without its emotional associations. For example, the words *house* and *home* have approximately the same denotation—a dwelling. However, the words have different **connotations,** or emotional or imaginative associations: The word *home* may evoke feelings of warmth and comfort not associated with the word *house.*

Dénouement The resolution of a play, short story, or novel. The dénouement usually follows the narrative's climax and includes resolution of the conflict and answers to questions raised by the plot. In *Julius Caesar,* the dénouement begins after the death of Caesar. Also called **falling action.**

Deus ex machina An unexpected force or event that suddenly appears and resolves a seemingly irresolvable problem. Examples include a last-minute witness stepping forward to solve a murder case, an unknown relative unexpectedly arriving to save a protagonist from bankruptcy, or a deity entering a scene to save a character from death. The term means "god from the machine" and refers to the ancient Greek practice of lowering an actor playing a god onto the stage to resolve a plot complication.

Dialect A way of speaking characteristic of a particular region or a particular group of people. (For more on **dialect,** see the Handbook of Literary Terms in the Student Edition.)

Dialogue A conversation between characters in a story or play. (For more on **dialogue,** see the Handbook of Literary Terms in the Student Edition.)

Diction A writer's or speaker's choice of words. Diction is an essential element of a writer's style. Some writers use simple, down-to-earth, or even slang words *(house, home, digs);* others use ornate, official-sounding, or even flowery language *(domicile, residence, abode).* The connotations of words are an important aspect of diction. (For more on **diction,** see the Handbook of Literary Terms in the Student Edition.)

Double-entendre A word or expression that can have two meanings, one of which is usually risqué. Double-entendres are common in the works of Shakespeare and Restoration dramatists.

Dramatic monologue A poem in which a speaker addresses one or more silent listeners, often reflecting on a specific problem or situation. (For more on **dramatic monologue,** see the Handbook of Literary Terms in the Student Edition.)

Elegy A poem mourning the dead or a poem with a sorrowful or reflective mood. W. H. Auden's poem "In Memory of W. B. Yeats" is an elegy marking the death of the famous Irish poet.

End-stopped line A line of poetry in which the grammar, meaning, and meter end at the end of the line. End-stopped couplets were popular in the eighteenth century. Note the use of end-stopped lines in the first stanza of Thomas Gray's "Elegy Written in a Country Churchyard":

> The curfew tolls the knell of parting day;
> The lowing herd wind slowly o'er the lea;
> The plowman homeward plods his
>   weary way,
> And leaves the world to darkness and to
>   me.

Enjambment In poetry, the continuation of a sentence from one line to another. The Romantic poets made frequent use of enjambment to write more natural-sounding sentences. The following stanza from Samuel Taylor Coleridge's "Kubla Khan" provides an example of enjambment:

> In Xanadu did Kubla Khan
> A stately pleasure-dome decree:
> Where Alph, the sacred river, ran
> Through caverns measureless to man
>   Down to a sunless sea.

Epic A long narrative poem, written in elevated language, that relates the great deeds of a larger-than-life hero who embodies the values of a particular society. (For more on **epic,** see the Handbook of Literary Terms in the Student Edition.)

Epigram A short, clever statement in poetry or prose. Samuel Taylor Coleridge defined the term in his own epigram:

> What is an epigram? A dwarfish whole,
> Its body brevity, and wit its soul.

Epilogue A brief concluding section added to a literary work. In the case of a fable, the epilogue usually provides a moral. In drama the epilogue may include a plea to the audience and critics for approval.

Epiphany A moment of profound insight into the true meaning of a situation. In James Joyce's short story "Araby," a young boy places all his hopes on a bazaar and has vivid fantasies of its being a thrilling, romantic place. Instead, he arrives at the bazaar to find it dreary and filled with cheap trinkets. The boy has a moment of epiphany when he gains insight into his own naiveté for having held such high hopes for the bazaar.

Episode An event that consists of a single action but is also part of a longer narrative. Although episodes do not always advance a plot's action, they can provide readers with information about characters or a story's background. In chapter 3 of Charles Dickens's *Bleak House,* Esther Summerson recalls sharing her secrets with her only friend, her doll, and so indicates the shyness and gentleness of her own character.

Epithet An adjective or descriptive phrase that is used regularly to characterize a person, place, or thing. We speak of "Honest Abe," for example, and "America the Beautiful." The Greek poet Homer referred to "the wine-dark sea." (For more on **epithet,** see the Handbook of Literary Terms in the Student Edition.)

Euphemism A mild or neutral expression substituted for a more blunt one. The term *downsizing,* for example, is a euphemism for *being laid off; passed away* is a euphemism for *died.*

Evocative Bringing about strong emotions through the use of images, feelings, or memories. Tim O'Brien's short story "Where Have You Gone, Charming Billy?" is evocative because it elicits a strong emotional response to the characters' experiences during the conflict in Vietnam.

Exposition A type of writing that explains, gives information, defines, or clarifies. (For more on **exposition,** see the Handbook of Literary Terms in the Student Edition.)

Fable A very brief story in prose or verse that teaches a moral, or a practical lesson about how to get along in life. (For more on **fable,** see the Handbook of Literary Terms in the Student Edition.)

Falling action The action in a literary work that follows the climax. In Shakespeare's *Romeo and Juliet,* the discovery of the dead young lovers marks the beginning of the play's falling action. Also called **dénouement.**

Farce A mostly visual comedy designed to appeal through exaggerated physical action, stereotyped characters, and ridiculous situations. Farces often have fast-paced plots and unexpected turns of event. *The Brute: A Joke in One Act* by Anton Chekhov is an example of a farce.

Figure of speech / figurative language
A word or phrase that describes one thing in terms of another and that is not meant to be understood on a literal level. (For more on **figure of speech** and **figurative language,** see the Handbook of Literary Terms in the Student Edition.)

Flashback A scene that interrupts the present action of the plot to show events that happened at an earlier time. (For more on **flashback,** see the Handbook of Literary Terms in the Student Edition.)

Foil A character who serves as a contrast to another character. (For more on **foils,** see the Handbook of Literary Terms in the Student Edition.)

Foot A group of syllables forming the basic unit of measurement in a line of poetry. Feet are categorized according to how many syllables they have and which ones are accented. A poem's meter is determined by the number and type of feet in a line. Accented syllables are marked with a ´ sign, while unaccented syllables are marked with a ˘. For example, the iambic foot consists of one unaccented syllable followed by one accented syllable.

    in·tend   be·hold   be·calm

Foreshadowing The use of clues to hint at events that will occur later in a plot. (For more on **foreshadowing,** see the Handbook of Literary Terms in the Student Edition.)

Form The structure, shape, and style of a piece of work. Form is distinguished from substance, although the two cannot be separated. Form can also refer to the genre of a piece of literature, such as a poem or a play.

Free verse Poetry that does not have a regular meter or rhyme scheme. (For more on **free verse,** see the Handbook of Literary Terms in the Student Edition.)

Genre The category under which a work of literature is classified. Major genres of literature include nonfiction, fiction, poetry, drama, and myth. (For more on **genre,** see the Handbook of Literary Terms in the Student Edition.)

Hero The central character in a literary work. In ancient times, the hero was a figure of great strength or courage. Modern heroes are generally noble, but imperfect, characters. Stephen Dedalus is the hero of James Joyce's novel *A Portrait of the Artist as a Young Man.*

Hyperbole A figure of speech that uses exaggeration to express strong emotion or to create a comic effect. (For more on **hyperbole,** see the Handbook of Literary Terms in the Student Edition.)

Iambic pentameter A line of poetry made up of five iambs. (For more on **iambic pentameter,** see the Handbook of Literary Terms in the Student Edition.)

Imagery Language that appeals to the senses. (For more on **imagery,** see the Handbook of Literary Terms in the Student Edition.)

Incongruity A lack of consistency or appropriateness, often verging on absurdity. When a character attends a formal dinner party dressed in a bathing suit, the situation is incongruous. Incongruity is often used to create irony in literature. For example, in Jonathan Swift's "A Modest Proposal," the narrator's sincere tone is incongruous with his satiric proposal—that impoverished Irish children should be sold and eaten to relieve levels of poverty. This incongruity helps create a sense of irony in the work.

Inversion The reversal of normal word order in a sentence. (For more on **inversion,** see the Handbook of Literary Terms in the Student Edition.)

Irony A contrast or discrepancy between expectation and reality or between what is said and what is meant. (For more on **irony,** see the Handbook of Literary Terms in the Student Edition.)

Handbook

Juxtaposition The placement of ideas, characters, images, or actions close together to create an effect, such as a comparison, a contrast, a rhetorical point, or a characterization. In "The Arrogance and Cruelty of Power," a speech given at the Nuremberg trials, Robert H. Jackson juxtaposes a description of the former Nazi leaders as "broken captives" with a vivid description of their horrific acts. The rhetorical effect supports his insistence that the men be punished despite their present powerlessness.

Lyric poetry Poetry that expresses a speaker's emotions or thoughts and does not tell a story. (For more on **lyric poetry,** see the Handbook of Literary Terms in the Student Edition.)

Magic realism A style of fiction, commonly associated with contemporary Latin American writers, in which fantasy and reality are casually combined, producing humorous and thought-provoking results. Gabriel García Márquez's "A Very Old Man with Enormous Wings," in which an old, winged, humanlike creature lands in a poor family's backyard, is an example of magic realism.

Measure In poetry, a metrical grouping, such as a foot. *Measure* is often used as a synonym for *meter.*

Melodramatic Indicative of a type of extravagant drama that pits excessively "good" characters against "evil" ones in a thrilling plot replete with dire events and near disasters. Melodramas are designed to appeal to an audience's emotions. One of the first English melodramas was Thomas Holcroft's *A Tale of Mystery* (1802).

Metaphor A figure of speech that makes a comparison between two unlike things without using a connective word such as *like, as, than,* or *resembles.* (For more on **metaphor,** see the Handbook of Literary Terms in the Student Edition.)

Meter A pattern of stressed and unstressed syllables in poetry. (For more on **meter,** see the Handbook of Literary Terms in the Student Edition.)

Monologue An extended speech presented by one character in a play to other characters or the audience. In *The Importance of Being Earnest* by Oscar Wilde, Lady Bracknell delivers a humorous monologue on the deception of the main character, Algernon.

Mood A literary work's atmosphere or the feeling it evokes. (For more on **mood,** see the Handbook of Literary Terms in the Student Edition.)

Motivation The justification for a character's actions, thoughts, and feelings. Providing psychological and moral reasons for a character's actions helps make the character believable. In Katherine Mansfield's short story "A Cup of Tea," the main character, Rosemary Fell, invites a penniless girl into her home and shows her kindness, only to ask her later to leave. Rosemary's motivation for suddenly getting rid of the homeless girl is jealousy: Rosemary's husband has called the girl "pretty."

Ode A long and elaborate lyric poem. Odes are usually lofty in tone, elaborate, and dignified. John Keats's "Ode on a Grecian Urn" is a famous example.

Onomatopoeia The use of a word whose sound imitates or suggests its meaning, such as *buzz, squish,* or *sizzle.* (For more on **onomatopoeia,** see the Handbook of Literary Terms in the Student Edition.)

Oxymoron A figure of speech in which two contradictory words or phrases are combined. Examples include "a wise fool," "cruel to be kind," and "bittersweet."

Pace The rate at which the action of a literary work proceeds. Authors use elements such as subplots and flashbacks to control the pace of the action in a story. They can also speed up the pace of a work through such elements as **asyndeton** (expressions without conjunctions) and slow it down with elements such as **polysyndeton** (the use of more conjunctions than is usual).

Parable A brief story that teaches a moral or religious lesson. A parable usually has human characters, and its events are drawn from the stuff of everyday life. A **fable,** in contrast, usually has animal characters and teaches a practical lesson about how to succeed in life.

Parallelism The repetition of words, phrases, or sentences that have the same grammatical structure or that state a similar idea. (For more on **parallelism,** see the Handbook of Literary Terms in the Student Edition.)

Parody A humorous imitation of a literary work. Parodies are usually designed to ridicule another work, style of work, or author. Shakespeare may be said to parody romantic love poems in Sonnet 130, which begins "My mistress' eyes are nothing like the sun; / Coral is far more red than her lips' red; / If snow be white, why then her breasts are dun; / If hairs be wires, black wires grow on her head."

Persona The mask or voice assumed by a writer. The persona is not the actual author, but a character or narrator through whom the author speaks. (For more on **persona,** see the Handbook of Literary Terms in the Student Edition.)

Personification A type of figure of speech in which nonhuman things (animals, weather) or abstract qualities (love, jealousy) are granted human characteristics. (For more on **personification,** see the Handbook of Literary Terms in the Student Edition.)

Point of view The vantage point from which a writer narrates, or tells, a story. (For more on **point of view,** see the Handbook of Literary Terms in the Student Edition.)

Prologue An introduction, usually to a play. In ancient Greek drama, an actor presented the prologue, which provided necessary background information about the play. Some prologues are written in verse. In Shakespeare's prologue to *Romeo and Juliet,* the chorus provides background information but also tells of the play's outcome, stating that the "star-crossed lovers take their life."

Prose Most writing and speech that does not have a regular rhythmic pattern. Essays, short stories, and novels are usually written in prose. Poetry, in contrast, often has regular rhythm.

Protagonist The main character in a literary work. (For more on **protagonists,** see the Handbook of Literary Terms in the Student Edition.)

Proverb A brief saying that expresses a truth about life. "A friend in need is a friend indeed" is an example of a proverb.

Pun A play on the multiple meanings of a word or on two words that sound alike but have different meanings. (For more on **puns,** see the Handbook of Literary Terms in the Student Edition.)

Quatrain A stanza or poem that is four lines long. The lines may be rhymed or unrhymed. The poem "I May, I Might, I Must" by Marianne Moore is a quatrain:

> If you will tell me why the fen
> appears impassable, I then
> will tell you why I think that I
> can get across it if I try.

Refrain A repeated sound, word, phrase, line, or group of lines in a poem, song, or speech. (For more on **refrain,** see the Handbook of Literary Terms in the Student Edition.)

Repartee A witty response or exchange. The writers Oscar Wilde and Dorothy Parker were each famous for a gift for repartee. Oscar Wilde once claimed he could converse on any subject. When asked to discuss the queen, he responded with a witty response in the form of a pun. "The queen," he responded, "is not a subject."

Repetition The recurrence of a word, sound, phrase, or idea. Repetition is used by speechmakers for emphasis and is frequently used in poetry to create rhythm. In her poem "Remember," the poet Joy Harjo starts many sentences with the word *remember,* creating rhythm and emphasizing the poem's theme.

Rhyme The repetition of accented vowel sounds and all sounds following them in words that are close together in a poem. (For more on **rhyme,** see the Handbook of Literary Terms in the Student Edition.)

Rising action The portion of the plot leading to the climax. The rising action begins with a moment that sets the conflict into action (called the exciting force or the inciting moment), moves through one or more complications, and ends with the climax. In Shakespeare's play *Romeo and Juliet,* the rising action begins when Romeo and Juliet meet and ends with the pair's joint suicide.

Romance Historically, a medieval verse narrative about the adventures of a hero who undertakes a quest for a high ideal. The tales of King Arthur are typical romances. The term *romance* later came to mean any story set in a world of wish fulfillment, with larger-than-life characters having superhuman powers. Romances usually involve a series of adventures that end with good triumphing over evil. Fairy tales and movie westerns are often built on the old romance plots and rely on characters typical of romance literature.

Sarcasm A harsh, bitter kind of irony. In sarcasm, what is said is the opposite of what is meant. In Jane Austen's novel *Pride and Prejudice,* for example, Mrs. Bennet complains to her husband that he has no compassion for her nerves. His response is both humorous and sarcastic: "You mistake me, my dear. I have a high respect for your nerves. They are my old friends. I have heard you mention them with consideration these last twenty years at least."

Satire A work that mixes humor and wit with criticism to ridicule human shortcomings. Satire tries to improve human beings by pointing out people's faults. Jonathan Swift's *Gulliver's Travels* includes satire that harshly criticizes people for abusing their reasoning skills.

Scansion The analysis of meter in lines of poetry. Scansion is accomplished by dividing lines into feet (|), counting syllables, and noting accented (´) and unaccented (˘) syllables. The following example shows the scansion of the first two lines of William Shakespeare's Sonnet 29:

> ˘   ´   ˘   ´   ˘   ´   ˘   ´
> When, in | disgrace | with For|tune and |
> ˘   ´
> men's eyes, |
> ˘   ´   ˘   ´   ˘   ´   ˘   ´   ˘   ´
> I all | alone | beweep | my out|cast state

Scene A subdivision of an act in a dramatic work. In modern plays, a scene is an uninterrupted unit. The end of a scene is indicated by the dropping of curtains or the dimming of lights. Sometimes *scene* is used to refer to an action around a single incident, such as a death scene.

Simile A figure of speech that makes a comparison between two seemingly unlike things by using a connective word such as *like, as, than,* or *resembles.* (For more on **similes,** see the Handbook of Literary Terms in the Student Edition.)

Slang Informal, colloquial language. Slang in literature is often used in dialogue. For example, in "The Treasure of Lemon Brown" by Walter Dean Myers, Greg's father uses slang when he tells his son to "hit those books," meaning to study.

Soliloquy A long speech in which a character who is alone onstage expresses private thoughts or feelings. (For more on **soliloquy,** see the Handbook of Literary Terms in the Student Edition.)

Sonnet A fourteen-line lyric poem, usually written in iambic pentameter. (For more on **sonnets,** see the Handbook of Literary Terms in the Student Edition.)

Speaker The voice that addresses the reader in a poem. (For more on **speaker,** see the Handbook of Literary Terms in the Student Edition.)

Stanza A group of consecutive lines that form a single unit in a poem. (For more on **stanza,** see the Handbook of Literary Terms in the Student Edition.)

Subplot A minor story within a fictional work; a "story within a story." In Shakespeare's *Hamlet,* the conflict between Hamlet and Laertes forms a subplot.

Symbol A person, place, thing, or event that stands both for itself and for something beyond itself. (For more on **symbol,** see the Handbook of Literary Terms in the Student Edition.)

Theme The central idea or insight about life revealed by a work of literature. (For more on **theme,** see the Handbook of Literary Terms in the Student Edition.)

Tone The attitude a writer takes toward a subject, a character, or the reader. Tone is conveyed through the writer's choice of words and details. In Stephen Crane's poem "War Is Kind," Crane takes an ironic, bitter tone toward the subject of war. (For more on **tone,** see the Handbook of Literary Terms in the Student Edition.)

Tragedy / tragic flaw A play, novel, or other narrative, usually depicting serious and important events, in which the protagonist, through a flaw in character, comes to an unhappy end. (For more on **tragedy,** see the Handbook of Literary Terms in the Student Edition.)

Understatement A statement that says less than what is meant. Understatement is often used to make an ironic point or as humor.

Verse Another term for poetry, for a single line of poetry, or for a stanza of poetry.

Voice The writer's or speaker's distinctive use of language in a text. (For more on **voice,** see the Handbook of Literary Terms in the Student Edition.)

Handbook

Handbook of Rhetorical Concepts

The following is a list of rhetorical concepts commonly used in advanced placement tests and other assessments. Knowing these concepts will help advanced students analyze texts they encounter in their daily studies and become comfortable with assessment terminology.

Ad hominem argument A faulty argument attacking the character of a person making a claim rather than the claim itself. Most arguments should address the quality of the specifics supporting a claim, rather than the person making the claim. However, in some instances, such as when questioning an expert witness, it is pertinent to critique a person's credibility.

Appeal to authority Citing an expert in a field or one's own authority during an argument. The expert's qualifications should be considered when evaluating an argument. An appeal to false authority involves citing a popular rather than a knowledgeable person. An example of an appeal to false authority is citing a soap opera star who provides testimony about a healthcare product. The star may be familiar to the audience but may not have much knowledge about medical health.

Argument by analogy Comparing parallel, or similar, instances to make an argument. In a strong analogy, there are many points in common between the two instances; in a weak analogy, there are few or no points in common.

Assertion A statement claiming that something is or is not so. The premise of an argument and the statements on which an argument is based are assertions.

Assumption A belief that may or may not be warranted or justified. Making assumptions is permitted in argument; however, readers or listeners must determine whether an assumption is unwarranted, unjustified, or naïve. Sometimes assumptions are unstated. For example, in the case of an argument calling for a law mandating bicycle helmets for children under age ten, an unstated assumption is that saving the lives of young children is desirable.

Attitude (of writer) The writer's stance toward a subject or an audience. A well-reasoned argument will often convey a fully objective attitude.

Categories Classes or concepts into which information is placed. Categorical arguments and writing often require information to be classified according to shared traits.

Causal relationship A correlation in which one event or action causes another. In sound arguments, arguers explore as many causes of a problem as possible before proposing a solution.

Circular reasoning Using the premise of an argument as evidence for the argument. The statement "It's an excellent movie because it's one of the best ones I've seen" is an instance of circular reasoning. Circular reasoning is also commonly called begging the question.

Counterargument Reasoning or argument offered in opposition to an anticipated argument. During debate and in writing, debaters and writers offer counterarguments to address specific points of disagreement.

Details In rhetoric, facts, opinions, and other information used to support an argument. In effective arguments, writers choose only those details that directly support an argument or refute a counterargument.

Digression from topic Discussing an issue outside the agreed-upon or selected topic. In argument, digression may be used to distract an audience from the argument at hand; however, digression usually indicates a loss of focus.

Emotional appeal / pathos An appeal to the feelings or imagination of the audience. Emotional appeals evoke feelings in audience members in order to convince them of a point of view or to motivate them to action.

Ethical appeal An appeal to the morality of the audience. For example, a speaker might make an argument in favor of fuel-efficient cars. He or she might make an ethical appeal by pointing out the benefits of these cars to the environment.

Euphemism A less offensive word or expression substituted for one that may be seen as unpleasant. A common euphemism for *died* is *passed on.*

Exception to a rule A case in which the generally accepted rule does not apply.

Generalization A general conclusion or opinion drawn from particulars. Valid generalizations are based on sufficient evidence, such as examples, details, or testimony. Hasty generalizations are based on insufficient evidence. (For more on **generalization,** see the Handbook of Reading and Informational Terms in the Student Edition.)

Juxtaposition of ideas The placement of ideas close together to show comparison and contrast or to create rhetorical effect. For example, a speaker might choose to describe two vastly different scenarios—a struggling family and a wealthy actor—to make a point about values. Ideas are also juxtaposed in **antitheses,** opposing phrases used close together.

Logical appeal An appeal to an audience's rational judgment by giving reasons supported by evidence, such as examples, statistics, or expert opinions.

Misconception A false or mistaken view or perception of an idea, a situation, or a communication.

Objection A challenge to the opinion stated in a persuasive speech or essay. Also, argument or reasoning that anticipates and addresses opposing opinions and points of opposition; a counterargument.

Objectivity A lack of bias. A writer seeking objectivity is more concerned with presenting facts and opposing views than with one-sided efforts to persuade. *Objective* is often used to describe the tone of a speech or piece of writing.

Persuasion The act or intent of convincing others. In rhetoric, an essay is labeled "persuasive" if it is intended to convince others, regardless of its success in doing so.

Support (for a thesis) Reasons, evidence, and other arguments used to convince an audience to agree with the writer's thesis. Facts, expert opinions, examples, personal experience, observation, and analogies may be used to support theses. (In persuasive texts and speeches, **emotional** and **ethical appeals** are also used as support.)

Syllogism A formal logical statement consisting of a conclusion formed from two or more premises. In categorical syllogisms, there are four forms that premises might take:

1) All *A* is *B*.
2) Some *A* is *B*.
3) No *A* is *B*.
4) Some *A* is not *B*.

An example of a syllogism that uses the first premise ("All *A* is *B*") follows:

All Shar-Peis are dogs.
All dogs are mammals.
Therefore, all Shar-Peis are mammals.

Voice The unique, recognizable style of a writer or speaker as conveyed through choice of words, details, and images.

Handbook

Handbook of Grammatical Concepts

The following is a list of grammatical concepts commonly used in advanced placement tests and other assessments. Knowing these concepts will help advanced students analyze texts they encounter in their daily studies and become comfortable with assessment terminology.

Antecedent An antecedent is the word or words that a pronoun stands for.

EXAMPLES	**Jay** left a **bucket** on the floor, and **his** mother kicked **it** over. [*Jay* is the antecedent of *his*. *Bucket* is the antecedent of *it*.]

Appositive An appositive is a noun or pronoun placed beside another noun or pronoun to identify or explain it. An **appositive phrase** consists of an appositive and its modifiers.

EXAMPLES	Regina loves to take her dog, **Corky,** on walks in the park.
	Regina walks her dog, a **frenetic dachshund,** twice daily.

Asyndeton Asyndeton is the omission of conjunctions. Conjunctions are normally used to connect clauses or sentences or to link words in the same clause. Omitting conjunctions can speed the pace of a sentence or give a statement an epigrammatic or memorable quality.

EXAMPLES	He woke up, washed, set out for work.
	I came, I saw, I conquered.

Capitalization Writers capitalize words to communicate specific information to readers. The most common use of capitalization is to indicate the start of a new sentence. Other common uses of capitalization are to indicate proper nouns, abbreviations, and titles of works of literature. (For more on **capitalization,** see the Language Handbook in the Student Edition.)

Clause A clause is a group of words that contains a verb and its subject. An **independent** (or **main**) **clause** expresses a complete thought and can stand by itself as a sentence.

EXAMPLE	Lakshmi opened the door. [*Lakshmi* is the subject and *opened* is the verb.]

Clauses can also be subordinate to, or dependent on, the main clause. There are three main types of **subordinate clause:** adjective, noun, and adverb clauses. Each of these labels describes how the clause functions in the sentence.

ADJECTIVE CLAUSE	The blue chair, **which is broken,** is in the hall. [This adjective clause modifies the noun *chair*.]
NOUN CLAUSE	I want to hear **what you have to say.** [This noun clause is the object of the verb *hear*.]
ADVERB CLAUSE	**While Joan was sleeping,** her dog knocked over the trash can. [This adverb clause modifies the verb *knocked over*, indicating when the dog knocked over the trash.]

Compound subject A subject tells who or what a sentence is about. A compound subject consists of two or more subjects that are joined by a conjunction and that have the same verb.

EXAMPLE	**France, Germany,** and **Spain** are members of the European Union.

Handbook

Direct object A direct object is a word or word group that receives the action of a verb or shows the result of an action. A direct object answers the question *whom?* or *what?* after a transitive verb.

EXAMPLE	Nora raised her **hand.**

Ellipsis Ellipsis is the omission of words from a sentence; a reader must infer and supply these words in order for the sentence to make complete sense.

EXAMPLES	I like apples much more than peaches. [*I like apples much more than **I like** peaches.*]
	Brent liked to read science fiction; Lisa, historical novels. [*Brent liked to read science fiction novels; Lisa **liked to read** historical novels.*]

Fragment For a sentence to be complete, it must contain a subject and a verb that agrees (in person and number) with the subject. Generally a sentence is considered defective if it lacks these two elements. Writers, however, often use sentence fragments to achieve a rhetorical effect.

EXAMPLE	The mayor wants to knock down this historic house to build a parking lot. **Knock it down?**

Indirect object An indirect object is a noun, pronoun, or word group that sometimes appears in sentences containing direct objects. An indirect object tells *to whom* or *to what* (or *for whom* or *for what*) the action of a transitive verb is done. Indirect objects generally precede direct objects.

EXAMPLE	Marcy handed the **teacher** her test.

Inversion Inversion is the change in the natural word order in a sentence. Inversion is a normal feature of the English language and is a distinguishing feature of a question. (Statement: *We are happy.* Question: *Are we happy?*) Inversion is also a common feature in poetry. It appears somewhat less frequently in prose. Sometimes inversion is used to emphasize a word by removing it from its normal place in the sentence and placing it in an emphatic location.

Loose sentence In a loose sentence, the main clause, which contains the most important information, is placed at the beginning of the sentence, and any subordinate or dependent clauses follow it. The opposite of a loose sentence is a **periodic sentence** (see below).

EXAMPLE	Kiki was furious with herself, since she knew that she was wrong but couldn't admit it. [*Kiki was furious with herself* is the most important part of the sentence; everything that follows the comma elaborates on this main idea.]

Natural Order A simple sentence will normally be arranged in this order: subject, verb, object. Even complex sentences have a predictable, natural order. Simple expository prose, in which the focus is on clearly communicating facts, typically uses natural word order. More rhetorical and expressive styles of prose routinely deviate from natural word order to emphasize one or more elements in a sentence.

Parallel structure Parallel structure, or parallelism, is the use of the same grammatical forms or structures to balance related ideas in a sentence or paragraph.

NONPARALLEL	Robert told me he was interested in hiking and to try out canoeing.
PARALLEL	Robert told me he was interested **in hiking** and **in trying out** canoeing.

Handbook

Periodic sentence In a periodic sentence, the main clause follows one or more initial subordinate or dependent clauses. The opposite of a periodic sentence is a **loose sentence** (see above).

EXAMPLE	Although I know how to change the oil in my car, I find it much more convenient to let professionals change the oil for me. [The second part of the sentence contains the most important information but appears after an introductory subordinate clause.]

Phrase A phrase is a group of related words that does not contain both a verb and its subject and that is used as a single part of speech.

EXAMPLES	Naomi, **my next-door neighbor, has planted** tulips **in her backyard.** [*My next-door neighbor* is an appositive phrase. *Has planted* is a verb phrase. *In her backyard* is a prepositional phrase.]

Polysyndeton is the opposite of **asyndeton** (see above). While asyndeton omits expected conjunctions, polysyndeton includes conjunctions that are not strictly necessary. Beginning each new sentence with *and* is a common form of polysyndeton. Polysyndeton is a common stylistic feature of the King James Bible:

> And the earth was without form, and void; and darkness was upon the face of the deep. And the Spirit of God moved upon the face of the waters.
> —Genesis 1:2

Sentence structure Sentences vary in their degree of complexity. A **simple sentence** contains one independent clause and no subordinate clauses.

EXAMPLE	Anne and I went to the park. [Independent clause and no subordinate clauses.]

When a sentence has two or more independent clauses—normally joined by a comma and a connecting word—it is called a **compound sentence.**

EXAMPLE	Anne and I went to the park, but the park was closed. [Two independent clauses, linked by a comma and *but.*]

When one subordinate clause is added to a simple sentence, it becomes a **complex sentence.**

EXAMPLE	When we finished our work, Anne and I went to the park. [Independent clause and one subordinate clause.]

When a sentence contains two or more independent clauses and at least one subordinate clause, it is a **compound-complex sentence.**

EXAMPLE	When we finished our work, Anne and I went to the park, but the park was closed. [Two independent clauses and one subordinate clause.]

Subject The subject tells whom or what a sentence or clause is about.

EXAMPLES	**Ms. Wilson** is taking a trip to Greece. My **computer** has been causing me trouble all weekend.

Subordination Sometimes one idea in a sentence is more important than another, and the writer wishes to downplay, or subordinate, the less important idea. One of the most common examples of subordination is the subordinate clause. (For more information on **subordinate clauses,** see the entry for **clause** in this handbook.)

Syntax The arrangement or organization of the words, phrases, or clauses in a sentence. *Syntax* is also used simply to mean "word order."

Verb A verb is a word used to express action or a state of being. The verb says something about the subject of a sentence.

| **EXAMPLES** | I **overslept** this morning. |
| | Julia Alvarez **is** my favorite writer. |

Verb phrase A verb phrase consists of a main verb and at least one helping verb.

| **EXAMPLES** | I **am sitting** in a chair. |
| | She **may have been** there. |

Word Banks

Literary elements of tone, style, mood, and character overlap to some degree, and students may find that descriptive words listed for one category are appropriate for describing other literary elements.

Tone Words

Tone refers to a writer's attitude toward the subject, characters, situation, or audience of a work. Refer to this list when you develop a literary analysis to help you pinpoint the fine distinctions of a writer's tone.

accusatory	disdainful	insolent	resentful
admiring	dismayed	intimate	respectful
ambivalent	earnest	irate	restrained
analytical	effusive	ironic	reverent
apathetic	enthusiastic	irreverent	sarcastic
approving	exaggerating	jovial	satirical
bantering	facetious	judgmental	scornful
bemused	factual	judicious	sentimental
benevolent	fanciful	learned	sincere
bitter	fascinated	lyrical	solemn
callous	flippant	matter-of-fact	straightforward
candid	forthright	mocking	strident
clinical	gloomy	moralistic	superficial
conciliatory	grudging	nostalgic	sympathetic
condescending	harsh	objective	taunting
confident	haughty	optimistic	unsympathetic
contemplative	impartial	patronizing	urgent
contemptuous	indignant	pessimistic	whimsical
critical	informal	pretentious	witty
cynical	informative	reflective	
detached	insistent	remorseful	

Style Words

A writer's **style** is his or her distinctive way of expressing ideas—through word choice, detail, organization, point of view, imagery, rhythm, literary techniques, sound devices, sentence structure, punctuation, and prevailing attitude. For example, contrast Hemingway's austere style with Poe's florid one. Use the words below to describe a writer's style and to discuss how that style affects the reader.

abstract	detached	moralistic	scholarly
analytical	disjointed	objective	symbolic
argumentative	expository	obtuse	terse
bombastic	figurative	pedantic	trite
colloquial	homespun	plain	understated
complex	informal	poetic	wry
concrete	instructive	precise	
conversational	interpretive	reasoned	
descriptive	metaphorical	representational	

Mood Words

The **mood** of a work—the overall emotion it creates in readers—is often closely tied to the work's setting. As you analyze setting, consider the mood created by the writer's details, and use words such as those in this list to examine the effects of those details.

bleak	haunting	quizzical	suspenseful
dark	lonely	reproachful	tense
delirious	ominous	satiric	threatening
dismal	peaceful	serene	uplifting
eerie	playful	soothing	whimsical

Character Words

Great writers bring memorable characters to life. When you discuss characters, particularly their motivations and attitudes, use words from this list to make your analysis clear and precise.

absorbed	bitter	detached	naïve
aggressive	bored	devious	noble
aloof	carefree	devoted	pompous
ambitious	churlish	envious	scrupulous
amorous	compassionate	fretful	sincere
anxious	conniving	gregarious	slovenly
apathetic	curious	intelligent	spontaneous
argumentative	deceitful	loquacious	suspicious
arrogant	demure	manipulative	vindictive

Handbook